$10·00

30

Better to Die a Wolf than to Live the Life of the Dog

by Zen Moisey

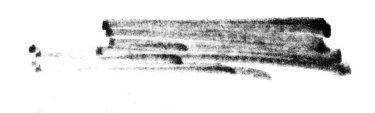

This book is dedicated to my Canadian baba, our relatives and friends in Ukraine and The Heavenly 100. Painting *La Annunciation, 1984* by Marco Tulio Lamoyi, 1.5m x 1.7m on plaster.

Published by Mount Makivka Publishing Ltd.
Sherwood Park, Alberta, Canada
First Edition, first printing 2017
Website www.UkraineWolf.com

Commercial reproduction and distribution, in whole or in part, is prohibited, except with written permission from Zen Moisey. For more information, contact Zen Moisey at Zen@incentre.net

Library and Archives Canada Cataloguing in Publication
Moisey, Zenith Raymond, 1940

Better to Die a Wolf than to Live the Life of a Dog: A Story of Resistance and Hope, by Canadian Zen Moisey / Zenith R. Moisey

KDP ISBN 9781973499381   Canada ISBN 978-1-7750045

Finding the Zenith Moisey ancestral family, History, Memoir, Ukrainian Roots, Investing in Ukraine, Invasions and Heroine Olena (Yarema) Kuz, Some Relatives, Activities with Ukrainian Families, Russia, Tsars, Putin Propaganda, Perestroika, Perebudova, Soviet, Kolhosp, Nationalism, Gulag, Bukovina, Galicia, WW11, Sich Sharpshooters, Ukraine Jews, Religion, Maidan, Ukraine Wolf, todieasawolf, Heavenly Hundred, Poroshenko, Rotary, Carpathian, Diaspora, Europe's largest Country, Ukraine propaganda, Europe's breadbasket, Soviet Union, Sergei Magnitsky, Bill Browder, Philanthropy, Moscow Myth, Ukraine Nationalism, Canadian Ukrainians, Family Reunion, Drilling for Oil in Ukraine, Holodomor, Ukraine Canada, Ukraine Scholarships, Odesa Mafia, Computer IT, Crimea Annexed, Donetsk and Luhansk Russian Invasion,

For ordering information, contact

Mount Makivka Publishing Ltd.
http://UkraineWolf.com
53263 – Range Rd. 225
Sherwood Park, Alberta, T8A 4V1

Prologue

Author Aleksandr Solzhenitsyn in his book *The Gulag Archipelago* writes:

And thus, it is I am writing this book solely from a sense of obligation — because too many stories and recollections have accumulated in my hands and I cannot allow them to perish. I do not expect to see it in print anywhere with my own eyes; and I have little hope that those that manage to drag their bones out of the Archipelago will ever read it; and I do not at all believe that it will explain the truth of our history (Russia) in time for anything to be corrected.

These words of Solzhenitsyn, motivated me to record the encounters and observations I experienced over a quarter century of travelling to Ukraine on thirteen occasions. Ukraine, the country of my ancestors, had, when I began my travels, just emerged from the collapse of the Soviet Union in 1991, after approximately a decade of Perebudova (a renewal like Perestroika in Russia). My travels there have given me a better understanding of the true history of Russia that Solzhenitsyn alluded to, and of Ukraine's place in the modern world. In the post-Perebudova period of the 1990s, Ukraine began an unchangeable shift towards the Western world. In 2017, Ukraine is taking its rightful place as Europe's largest country.

The first part of this book summarizes Ukraine's long and complex history, making the point that Ukraine has its own history, distinct from Russia's, and one that is more in step with Europe than with Russia. I present a brief history of ancient Ukraine, and discuss their peak years of leading Europe, when Kyiv had a population of 100,000 with masonry fortified walls and gold-gilded towers, at a time when Paris had 25,000 folks living within a wooden stockade. After these few hundred years, resource-rich Ukraine was constantly invaded and occupied by foreigners who enslaved the population. Eventually, the horrid conditions found many Ukrainians rebelling against their oppressors. The Bukovina region led these nationalist rebellions near the turn of the twentieth century. From this region came most of the first Ukrainians to emigrate, with huge populations moving to Western Canada, Brazil and Europe. Ukraine and Crimea also saw the forced expulsion of its population, herded to Russia's gulag and later to other Soviet-controlled areas.

The second and third chapters of this book describe our efforts to learn about and connect with the Moisey family in Ukraine, beginning with finding the first Moisey. My wife Doreen and I landed in Odesa in 1994 to investigate potential business opportunities. Escaping a lion's den of mafia, failing to enter Moldavia and then chauffeured by Kim Philby's (the British double-spy agent) personal bodyguard to the Cheremosh River, we found my first long-lost relative in Banyliv, Bukovina. This began a process of reuniting distant strands of the Moisey family from two continents. My Ukrainian eight great-grandparents immigrated to Canada in 1898. They had since then rarely, if ever, communicated with the Moisey (Мойсей) family in Ukraine.

Visiting Ukraine my Canadian parents and some relatives quickly bonded with their long-lost Ukrainian family. Many discussions were held with tough-minded 80 and 90-year-old Moiseys and their relatives. Tears of joy and sadness were shared on many occasions. A large 100-year family reunion was held on the ancestral home-site in Ukraine in 1998. Our

Canadian business was successfully passed to daughter Zena in 1993, allowing us the freedom to immerse ourselves in my ancestral community, where we entered a variety of ventures, ranging from a private school, to philanthropy, and drilling for oil. I have been an active Rotarian since 1968. This means I am one of 1.3 million volunteer members of Rotary International, the worlds' largest international service organization, established in 1905, and today a non-political, non-religious, interracial organization. One needs to be invited to join. As a Rotarian I have been hands-on with many projects to sustain the Ukrainian community.

From Ukraine's archives, we extracted information about some of the earliest family members. Their primary village was Banyliv, Bukovina with a recorded history of 580 years, dating back to before Columbus's journey to America. Records, legends, documented invasions and interviews with the elderly show this mountainous region was a difficult area to survive in. Banyliv is on the right bank of the northerly flowing Cheremosh River in Bukovina (now Chernivtsi Oblast) and almost directly across the river from Yabluniv, from where the first few Ukraine families emigrated to settle in Western Canada in 1891.

Learning more about the people of Ukraine changed my relationship to the Ukrainian Diaspora back home. I was born in Canada in 1940, and for six years lived on a small plot of land adjacent to the homestead of my great-grandparents located at the center of Ukraine's first homesteaders. My family then moved to Canada's northern, boreal-forest at Lac La Biche, a most diverse ethnic community, with Ukrainians being a minority, where everybody was financially poor, but for a youth, adventure was unlimited. Lac La Biche (population 1,200) was primarily inhabited by Metis, Brits, French,

Germans, Syrians, Lebanese, Italians, others and only a few Ukrainians. We knew everybody in town. My father John Roman was catcher for the Lac La Biche Dodgers, an amateur baseball team that played against nearby communities. The furthest team, about seventy kilometers away, was Amber Valley, which had all black players. To go there, we all piled into and a crowded bus (and even onto its roof rack) for an overnight stay in the homes of the players. These were among my happiest years, and these youthful experiences make me feel at ease no matter where I might travel. At age 12 we moved to the big city of Edmonton and did not associate with the Ukraine community, except when duck hunting and attending weekend dances in Andrew, Alberta, where I slept at my loving Baba Moisey's farm. After the first visit to Ukraine, we became involved with many of Edmonton's Ukrainian groups.

Over our quarter century of visits and activities in Ukraine, we met hundreds of Ukrainians, ranging from the homeless to hard-working families, to educators, to business movers and shakers, to mafia and many local government officials. I was like a fly on the wall watching these folks, while discovering an amazing country. We experienced tensions between the old communist guard and pro-western youth. After several visits, I understood how close-knit elderly Moisey siblings could be commies, fascists or nationalists, and yet dearly love each other. All these siblings suffered at the hands of brutal invaders. This book discusses some fascinating and significant individuals. On our twelfth visit, for example, I learned that my third cousin removed is a heroine, from my ancestral village, who was instrumental in removing the last Russian Tsar from Ukraine. Her exploits were published in European and American newspapers. She was recently acknowledged in Ukraine as a patriot for her actions at Mount

Makivka.

But mostly, this book reveals ordinary, close-knit families living in Ukraine, with their different philosophical views, religions and status. It contains hundreds of Ukrainian family surnames that settled in western Canada. If you are of Ukrainian heritage originating from Galicia or Bukovina, you will probably find mention of your family in Ukraine. The world is smaller than most of us envision. You will gain an appreciation of how your distant cousins lived in this last quarter century, in a very exciting time in Ukraine.

Chapter five discusses the Russian myth, perpetuated today by the tyrant Vladimir Putin, who has fostered a surrogate war in Ukraine. In 2014, twenty-one-year old Wasyl Moisey was the fifth person killed among the "heavenly hundred" by a Putin sniper at Maidan's peaceful demonstration. Shortly thereafter, Putin annexed Ukraine's Crimea and in 2017 occupies regions of Donetsk and Luhansk, daily killing Ukrainians. He is fighting a losing battle as Ukraine is a most nationalistic country, with a vast number of active patriots who have countered the Russian threat with Ukrainian propaganda and a growing military. I titled this book after some of the last words uttered by Wasyl, as he lay dying at Maidan. "Better to Die a Wolf than to Live the Life of a Dog" is a phrase well understood by patriotic Ukrainians.

How modern Ukraine strives for its freedom despite Putin is the theme of chapter six. Ukraine's communication systems, its infrastructure, and its ever-so-slow battle against corruption have improved enough by 2017 to allow Ukrainians to travel to the European Union without visas and to almost shed the yoke of the Russian federation. Ukraine has finally escaped the clutches of the Russian bear. Putin's attempts to revive days of old have stalled. Ukraine's social media has countered Putin's lies with truths, and today even kindergarteners defy him. Solzhenitsyn, I am sure, would feel vindicated knowing today's Ukrainians have thwarted tyrant Putin's propagation of the "Moscow Myth."

The glue binding Ukraine is its millennium of culture, vast Diaspora support and quest for freedom. Ukraine's youth embrace freedom and the future, while Russia's future, living under the illusion of freedom is stagnated by ruthless Putin, who clings to the old, failed Soviet system. Russia is trying to control Ukraine again, but will never succeed, as most Ukrainians are patriots, who know it is "Better to Die a Wolf than to Live the Life of a Dog."

The seventh and final chapter describes our emotional last visit to Ukraine in 2016. Overall, this book records our love affair with Ukraine. We have received so much more than what we shared. Opinions are largely mine and may be controversial to some readers. Some names have been changed to protect lives. Please note the extensive Appendixes included for your convenience, should you wish to pursue more details on a topic. We hope others will be motivated to record their Ukrainian experiences.

Our contribution is no different than that of thousands of fine Canadians. We are a light, among thousands of Ukraine Diaspora shining for Ukraine. Contributions to their welfare have occurred and are occurring across Canada and other countries daily, mostly unknown to the public. All profits from this book are forwarded to the Doreen and Zenith Moisey Rotary Endowment for Economic and Community Development in Ukraine.

Zen Moisey,
Edmonton, Alberta, Canada,
November 2017

Contents

CHAPTER 5 • RUSSIAN MYTH

CHAPTER 6 • UKRAINE STRIVES FOR FREEDOM DESPITE PUTIN

CHAPTER 7 • MY LAST VISIT

APPENDIXES

ACKNOWLEDGEMENTS

CHAPTER 1

Ukraine

Post Perebudova
(Perestroika in the Soviet Union), 1991

In 1991, my wife Doreen and I were recovering from a disastrous economic downturn in Alberta, Canada that claimed most of our assets in the early 1980s. We were into our seventh year with a new business (Tanks-A-Lot Ltd.) that I had founded to manufacture concrete wastewater treatment plants such as septic tanks, potable water cisterns, and precast pipe.

After attending a large Edmonton reception for Ukraine's President Kuchma in 1993, my thoughts were consumed with Ukraine, the country of my ancestry. Excitement rippled up my spine when learning about a decade of Perebudova (renewal) in Ukraine that was in the forefront of the breakup of the Soviet Union's flawed system. Ukraine declared Independence in August 1991. Not a shot was fired; the cruel counter-productive system simply collapsed. Immediately, Canada and Poland became the first countries to recognize Ukraine as an independent country.

Being of Ukrainian ancestry I wondered could it now be explored? Would I be successful in finding distant roots? Would having small business experience allow for a business venture or two? My mind and heart were open to allow instincts to lead the way. The sense of adventure was high. My wife Doreen shared the excitement. The die was cast. Ukraine, here we come. But first some research was necessary before going, as I knew very little of my ancestry. We had no contacts in Ukraine as Canadian Moiseys never communicated with their homeland. I began to research Ukraine's history, and I quickly discovered it to be ancient and complicated as it was a major crossroad of civilization.

Ukraine's Long History

Scholars think that humans have occupied the area that is now Ukraine since about 700,000 BCE. By about 40,000 BCE, hunter-gatherer clans inhabited most of the region. Agriculture, domesticated animals, and technologies like pottery and weaving began to appear by around 5000 BCE, soon followed by copper working. Between c. 4000 and c. 2500 BCE, the Trypillian culture flourished, centered around the Dniester River valley, but reaching to the Dnipro as well. The Dniester River basin was at the time, likely the most advanced culture in Europe. Eleven other areas of Ukraine had less advanced cultures. Near Galicia and Bukovina (home to the Moisey family) the Stanove culture existed from the fourteenth to the twelfth centuries BCE.

Because of its long and complicated history, the geographic area of today's Ukraine has gone by many names: Trypillia, Cimmeria, Scythia, Sarmatia, Rus (pronounced as in duce) and Ruthenia (a term sometimes used to describe the lands inhabited by the people of Kievan Rus, and sometimes used to describe Eastern Slavic people like Ukrainians and Belarusians, but not Russians.) Iranian Cimmerians appeared in the area around 1500 BCE. The Scythians displaced them in about 750 BCE. The first millennium BCE also saw the Iron Age in Ukraine, as agriculture, metallurgy, and commerce continued to advance. As early as 700 BCE, Greek city-states had trading colonies in the region. Invading nomadic horsemen intermingled with the Scythians and created an empire that was powerful enough to repel an invasion by Persian King Darius in 513 BCE.

The ancient Greek Herodotus (c.484 - c.425 BCE) is acclaimed to be the "Father of History" because he authored the first book that can be considered a systematic history. In Chapter IV in his "Histories," he included the history of Scythia, ancient Ukraine. Later, the Greek Thucydides (c. 460 – c. 400 BCE) wrote what is acknowledged as the first critical history in his "History of Peloponnesian War," ranking him as the greatest historian in antiquity. Thucydides said of Scythian Ukraine:

The Empire of the Odrysians was a very powerful kingdom, in revenue and general prosperity surpassing all in Europe in population and military resources coming decidedly next to the Scythians, with whom indeed no people in Europe can bear comparison. No group in Asia was equivalent to them. They were not on a level with other peoples in general intelligence and the arts of civilized life.

Around 250 BCE Sarmatians invaded and occupied the region. Like the Scythians, who they had likely assimilated, they traded with the Greek city-state colonies. Several of the more prosperous of these colonies on the Black Sea's north coast formed the Bosporan Kingdom in the 5th century BCE, which lasted until Rome defeated its last king in 63 BCE. In the meantime, Sarmatian offshoots like the Alans and Roxolani engaged in seesaw struggles between themselves and Goths from the north.

In the first millennium of the Common Era (CE), what is now Ukraine saw a series of invaders and occupiers over several centuries. Germanic tribes from the Baltics conquered the Sarmatians in 200 CE. Eastern Germanic Goths fought Rome and seized colonies in the region in the third century. The nomadic Huns overtook the area in the fourth century as most Goths fled west of the Danube, with a few remaining in Crimea. In the fifth century, the Volga Bulgars occupied Ukraine. The Avars did the same in the sixth century, as did the Khazars in the seventh, followed by the Magyars in the ninth.

From this already complex storyline of cultures in the region, a city-state centered on Kyiv began from murky origins in the 9th century, and started to become a regional power. Kyiv's Slavic and Persian roots slowly spread to Europe and lands to the north. The Kievan Rus ruler Volodymyr was baptized in 988 and Christianity flourished in the region. The city of Kyiv became the cultural and political center of Kievan Rus, a loose federation of principalities stretching north to the Baltic Sea and governing most of Eastern Europe from the late ninth to the mid-thirteenth centuries. At the time, Kievan Rus was the largest European state, and one of the wealthiest and most culturally advanced, despite its relatively sparse population.

Through marriage and children, the royalty of Kievan Rus began to intertwine with the royal genealogies of Western Europe. For instance, in 1051, the daughter of Kyiv's powerful King Yaroslav the Wise, the Kyiv-born Princess Anna Yaroslavna, married King Henry the 1st of France. Upon Henry's death, Anna's seven-year-old son Philip became King of France. For the next fourteen years, King Philip the 1st ruled France overseen by Queen Anne, his Ukrainian mother. Anne's three sisters–Elisaveta, Anastasia, and Agatha–also married European royalty, becoming the Queens of Norway, Hungary, and England, respectively. Yaroslav's son Vseveolod the 1st also fathered Eupraxia, who through marriage became Holy Roman Empress of the German Kingdom in 1089. During the next approximately 200 years, there were thirty-eight Ukrainian royal marriages with European rulers. Anna Yaroslavna and her sisters left their indelible mark on Europe, even extending their genes to Britain's current Queen Elizabeth, which she has acknowledged.

Portrait of Queen Anne of France (r. 1051-1071) consort of King Henry I. Lithograph by Delpech, Paris, 19th Century.

Meanwhile, Kievan Rus continued to face invasions from Pechenegs, Turks and Cumans in the tenth, eleventh, and twelfth centuries, respectively. Kievan Rus became fragmented, and began to decline, partly because its main trading partner Constantinople was also in decline. Finally, in the thirteenth century, the Mongol Empire invaded between 1237 and 1240 besieging and destroying several Ukrainian cities including Kyiv, which it turned virtually to rubble in late 1240.

Mongol rule lasted until 1362, when the Grand Duchy of Lithuania absorbed most of present-day Ukraine. In 1569, Poland and Lithuania united under a Polish-Lithuanian Commonwealth. Some parts of Ukraine were still controlled by the Crimean Khanate at this time. In the 1650s, parts of Ukraine fell under the control of an expansionist Russia, and in the late eighteenth century Poland was partitioned, the Crimean Khanate was defeated, and Ukraine became split between the Russian Tsardom and Habsburg Austria.

After the 1917 Russian Revolution, and while WWI still raged, Ukraine descended into a chaotic war for its independence. Post-Soviet Ukrainians refer to this war as the Ukrainian-Soviet War: a war between the Russian Bolsheviks and the Ukrainian People's Republic (an independent state declared in the wake of the Russian Revolution). The UPR was short-lived, overthrown in 1918, but is seen today as a precursor to modern, independent Ukraine. In 1922, the victorious Russian Bolsheviks occupying Ukraine made it a republic within the Soviet Union. Besides a few years of Nazi occupation during WWII, Ukraine remained under Soviet control until the early 1990s.

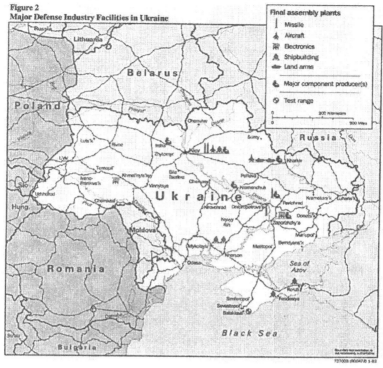

Figure 2
Major Defense Industry Facilities in Ukraine

Final assembly plants
| Missile
⚓ Aircraft
🏭 Electronics
⚓ Shipbuilding
🚂 Land arms

🔧 Major component producer(s)

⊙ Test range

Ukraine Map.

Throughout its long history, Ukraine has sat at the crossroads of important trade routes: a north-South one linking Scandinavia to the Middle East along the Baltic Sea, Dnieper River, and Black Sea; and an east-west route from the Caspian Sea to Central and Western Europe. Ukrainian people have continually played an important role, politically and economically, in Eastern Europe. The many foreign political powers that have occupied Ukraine have given it a rich and diverse legacy, one that can be seen in some of the tensions in the country today, and one that makes it harder to tell a simple story of Ukraine's history. Western, central, and eastern regions of the country have had different experiences over time. Countless invasions have produced a complicated collage of Ukrainians. The common denominator unifying Ukrainian lands and state formations has been, and is today, the Ukrainian people, who are united with a common language, and some unique social, cultural, and religious specificities. Invaders came, but the people prevailed under harsh domination. These invaders, in turn, were replaced by still more powerful invaders. The most recent (2014) invader is the tyrant Vladimir Putin of Russia. His presence is a minor wound compared to what Ukrainians have experienced over the last 1000 years.

Contrasting Ukraine With Russia
Through much of its history, but especially in the Golden Age of Kievan Rus, the region of present-day Ukraine has stacked up well in comparison to Europe, and in contrast with Russia. Statistics suggest that around the year 1,000 CE, Kyiv's population was higher than that of Paris or London. Its masonry and gold-gilded architecture of that time also indicate more wealth and power than probably all European cities outside of the Mediterranean. For at least two hundred years in the late Middle Ages Kyiv was one of the most important economic and political centers in Europe.

Compared to Russia and Moscow, the advanced stage of Kyiv and Ukraine in the late Medieval period is even more striking. European mapmakers in the Middle Ages considered Kievan Rus a part of Europe, and described Muscovy as part of Asia associated with the Mongol's Golden Horde. Several early chronicles mention Ukraine by name. The Hypatian Chronicle does in 1185, for example, describing events in Kyiv, Galicia, and other Ukrainian regions from as far back as 860 CE. Some early chronicles, call the region Krajina (country), or Galich Ukraina.

Moscow was first mentioned in a chronicle in 1147, at which time it was only a small village. In contrast, the city of Kyiv, founded in 482, is one of the oldest cities in Europe. Kyiv's Metropolia region also dates to several centuries before Moscow's similar Patriarchate.

In fact, Moscow only grew to become an important center under Mongol occupation between 1238 and 1480, long after Kievan Rus had for centuries been an impressive political, cultural, and economic center. Even when it comes to the Mongols, Ukraine was ahead of Russia, having shaken off the yoke in 1362. Ukraine stopped being controlled by the Mongols one hundred and seventeen years before Muscovy did. Even after 1480, the Tsar of Russia continued to give tribute to the Crimean Khan (the Golden Horde's successor) until 1700, in the first years of Peter the Great's reign.

Ukraine also adopted important trends in Western Europe earlier than Russia did, establishing its first higher learning institutes at the Ostrozka Collegium in 1576, and first universities at the Kyiv-Mohyla Academy in 1632 (its predecessor started in 1615), and Lviv University in 1661. Russia's first higher education institutions, by contrast, were the Saint Petersburg Academy of Sciences, founded in 1724, and Moscow University established in 1755. Institutes of higher learning appeared in Ukraine nearly a century and a half before Russia. Printed books appeared in Ukraine in the late sixteenth century, several decades before they did in Russia. On April 5, 1710, the newly-elected Ukrainian hetman (a high-ranking military title) Pylyp Orlyk announced a 'Pacts and Constitutions of Rights and Freedoms of the Zaporizhian Host'. This was one of the first state constitutions, setting a standard for the separation of powers in a modern enlightened nation, and coming long before similar constitutions were adopted in the United States in 1787, or France in 1791. Arguably, Russia's first (short-lived) attempt at a similar constitution was the limited State Duma introduced by the autocratic Tsar Nicholas II in 1906.

The twentieth century, which saw the emergence and fall of the Soviet Union, has somewhat united Ukraine and Russia in the popular imagination. It is important to realize though, that Ukraine has had a long and complex history independent of Russia. Some people today are even looking deep into genetic differences between Russians and other Slavs to try to separate once again these distinct groups of people. In 2013, Russian news articles claimed that geneticists at the Russian Academy of Medical Sciences had genetically determined that Russian people are not even Slavs, but more closely related to Finnish people. To understand the distinct differences of Ukraine-Rus and Moscow-Russia, read the 1904 historian Michael Rusedski's *Traditional Scheme of Russian History* and Andrew Gregorovich's *Anna Yaroslavna, Queen of France*. Incidentally, my Mother Nellie (née Palichuk) Moisey attended school with Gregorovich.

What's in a Ukrainian's Genes?
DNA testing has evolved as a measuring tool to link the people of today to their distant ancestors of thousands of years ago. My DNA test results from "Origins" (www.familytreedna.com) are 95 percent European (centered in Ukraine), four percent Turkish and one percent sprinkled between Norwegian, Finnish and Spanish. My genes, like many Ukrainians', have no trace of Russian.

Only a minority of Russians has traces of the Ukrainian and European genes. This is logical as there was no reason for Ukrainians from the breadbasket of Europe to migrate to the frigid latitude equal to that of Canada's southern Northwest Territories. Ukraine is the modern state of Medieval Rus, and as I have noted, the name Ukraine mattered long before the name Moscow did. Ukraine's common language, social, cultural, and religious characteristics today are like those of 1000 years ago. The infusion of Russians on Eastern Ukraine soil occurred mostly during the seventy-year period of Soviet control, and primarily during Stalin's rule. Soviet Russia's dominance, mostly in the 1930s to 1940s, forced millions of Ukrainians into the Siberian Gulag and largely replaced them by importing Russians to Eastern Ukraine.

Many mixed marriages occurred and are still occurring. In 2017, there is a slight visible difference between East and West Ukraine inhabitants because of intermarriages, which occurred with some of my Ukrainian family. Inevitably, they absorbed each other's customs. Some of my Ukrainian relatives living in both Ukraine and Russia have mixed marriages. These Russian spouses are among the nicest folks I know and have wonderful, caring families. I have yet to meet a Russian I dislike. They are great people. Their dictators are another story. Dictators, Tsars, Lenin, Stalin and Putin recklessly pit folks against each other, utilizing heavy doses of propaganda. Their form of governing does not care about the havoc they created and the suffering and loss of innocent life. They are the lowest of humanity, the scum of the Earth.

Recently, self-proclaimed historian Putin has hailed the spiritual importance of Chersonesus–an ancient Greek colony founded about 2,500 years ago outside of present-day Sevastopol in Crimea–for Russia, saying in a 2014 state-of-the-nation address that the Ukrainian territory has a "huge civilizational and sacred meaning" for the Russian Orthodox Church (ROC), just as the Temple Mount in Jerusalem has for Jews and Muslims. In 2015, Putin tightened his control over the ROC Church. As the ultimate head of the ROC, Putin is not challenged from within Russia, as the State imposes hardships for those that do. Many political opponents have paid and continue to pay the ultimate price when questioning the Russian State, which is synonymous with tyrant Putin. It is not wise if one wishes to live. In 2015 Putin began replacing history books in Russian schools to reflect his view of history. It should not be a surprise if he changes the name of the ROC to the Putin Orthodox Church. He fantasizes about becoming a god-like the leader in North Korea does today. Mixing politics with religion worldwide is like mixing oil and water. The two do not readily mix; however, demi-gods believe this does not apply to them. Putin is determined to make Moscow the third Rome for the Orthodox Global Churches. This initiative was pursued by Stalin in the late 1940s, and it failed.

Seeds of Nationalism

Over the past 400 years, when Ukrainian territories were occupied by four foreign powers, some folks became educated to the ways of their oppressors. Rebellion started slowly and became entrenched in the Ukrainian mind, primarily to escape serfdom. The urge toward rebellion is still strong in most Ukrainians, as they cope with the 2014 invasion by Russia's dictator Putin.

For four centuries, big-dog invaders, especially the oppressive Tsars and dictators, fine-tuned Western

Ukraine's mindset into rebellious action. By the nineteenth century, a nationalist movement was taking shape, commencing around the time my great-grandfather Stefan Moisey was born in 1846. The ancestors of many Ukrainian Canadians, including my family from Western Ukraine, have been cited in the historical record as taking nationalistic actions. In 1910, Chernivtsi University seethed with students and a few professors fostering nationalistic ideas and taking rebellious actions. One of these students was Olena (Yarema) Kuz, born in Banyliv, fifty kilometers due west of Chernivtsi University. Olena is my third cousin removed, the niece of my great grandmother Wasylena Moisey (née Kuz). Called Yarema by her friends, she has been recognized for her heroics in helping thwart the last Tsar's invasion of Ukraine in 1915. She is a true heroine of Ukraine.

My thirteen visits, over twenty-four years to Ukraine have answered some questions, but more were raised. From adjacent villages, how could siblings, fathers and relatives be opposing active participants on opposing sides of WWII? Why did relatives choose to be Nationalists, Communists or Fascists? Why were there family conflicts in choosing different Christian Churches? To unravel these questions, it was apparent I had to learn more about Ukraine, especially its history during WWII. Unfamiliar to me, and most in the Western Hemisphere, was Ukraine's history after WWII and during Perebudova (the social and political shifts occurring in the decade before the collapse of the Soviet Union in August 1991).

Equally important were changes noted in Ukraine during my visits from 1994 to 2016. These changes are still occurring now in 2017 and defining modern Ukraine, which is forging stronger ties with Europe. Undoubtedly, Ukraine has swung away from Russian dominance to lean closer to Europe. From its oppressive history, hardened Ukrainians are evolving to be leading members in the European theater. It is the largest country in Europe with incredible resources that will no longer be exploited by foreign powers. Ukrainians vow to never again be serfs or live like dogs.

Finally, because Ukraine is now free, we are receiving their perspective on WWII history as it occurred on Ukrainian soil. Ukraine now presents to the world its true role and sacrifices in WWII, from its point of view, no longer someone else's version of its history. It is not the German, Russian, Hungarian, Romanian, American or British and its allies' perspective, all of which have their own flavor.

One presentation of Ukraine's WWII history occurred in 2015 at Kyiv's Ukrainian Institute of National Remembrance by the Institute's Director, Volodymyr Viatrovych. The presentation helped clarify some the complexities of WWII in Ukraine, particularly in explaining some of my ancestors' behavior. It made clear, many of the family stories and testimonials I heard over the last twenty-four years. It is sad how Ukrainians were maneuvered to kill each other for other nations. Ukraine made incredible sacrifices in WWII. The presentation discussed facts and figures and persons, showing a complex pattern of world confrontation on Ukraine's soil and of Ukrainians on all war fronts of the global conflict. I will return later to Ukraine's version of WWII (see Appendix 2, p. 227), which helped clarify the sights and feelings Doreen and I encountered. For now, I will share my memories of our first visit to Ukraine and our attempts to find my ancestors and living relatives. On our first half dozen visits, we were truly naïve. We did not shy away from any situation and tried to savor the moment. Doreen, a truly great supporting wife, allowed me this freedom.

CHAPTER 2

Finding the first Moisey

Our First Visit to Ukraine

Our first visit occurred in 1994, shortly after the period of Perebudova ended with the fall of the Soviet Union. Doreen and I were greeted by Yaroslav at the Odesa airport. I had met Yaroslav a year earlier at a gathering of Canadian businessmen, where he made presentations on business opportunities in Ukraine. Yaroslav was fluent in both English and Ukrainian and had Ukrainian political connections. He was scheduled to go to Ukraine on business, so arrangements were made for us to meet him in Odesa, to look at some business opportunities and to explore Bukovina to find my relatives.

I had information that my Moisey Ukraine relatives lived in a village along the Cheremosh River. I had no names or other contact information. Yaroslav had relatives living in a village at the Cheremosh River who were willing to help us in searching for my ancestral family. Some of my Canadian relatives had previously traveled to Ukraine. My father and cousin Mary Ann Tymchuk (née Moisey) revealed what they knew of these previous visits.

In the 1970s, my Canadian-Ukrainian relative Anna Navalkowsky (whose mother was a Moisey) and her husband Ludwig toured Moscow and then journeyed to Chernivtsi, Ukraine, to find the Moisey family. Anna is a cousin to my father. Communist restrictions at the time prevented them from leaving Chernivtsi to visit the Cheremosh River area; however, Chernivtsi officials allowed them to have a party for Ukrainian relatives. A few relatives from the Cheremosh River area were contacted by government officials who invited them to attend the Chernivtsi party. Anna said she met a Kateryna Mandruk from Banyliv at the party. Kateryna is a niece to Canadian Mary Ann Tymchuk's grandmother. At a subsequent Moisey hundred-year celebration in Banyliv in 1998, Mary Ann spoke to Mrs. Mandruk, who confirmed she attended the Navalkowsky party in Chernivtsi. Mrs. Mandruk had several photos of the Moiseys in Canada.

Also in the 1970s, Anne and Mike Chorney travelled from Chernivtsi to the Cheremosh River to find relatives. Anne is also a Moisey. Their hired driver drove them to Banyliv where they were intercepted by the military and escorted to Vyzhnytsia for interrogation. They were questioned separately, Anne for two hours and Mike for four. In 2014 I met a Mykola Grygorovych Moisei, who remembered seeing the Chorneys in Vyzhnytsia, but was not allowed to communicate with them.

Doreen and I were interrogated in a similar manner as the Chorney's in the same police building on our sixth visit to Ukraine in late 1996. One evening Valentyn our lawyer mentioned he was told to inform us to report to the police station. The next morning, we walked with Valentyn down the main street to the building where a uniformed policeman stood guard. We climbed the few steps and entered the building and were met by two uniformed officers. Valentyn shook their hand and introduced us. After polite chitchat Valentyn proceeded to explain our presence in Vyzhnytsia. I uttered a few poorly spoken Ukraine words I thought appropriate, which clearly indicated I did not know the language. We were preparing to leave when one officer pointed to a stairway leading to the second level of the building and told us his superior wanted to see us.

18

At the top of the stairway stood a man dressed in crumpled pants and a well-worn green suit jacket. He led us past his desk to a bench located along the wall. He returned to the desk where he casually stubbed his cigarette into a half-filled ashtray of butts. He then sternly looked at us, making us feel uneasy to be in his office. Suddenly he smiled and walked towards us, extending his hand to greet Doreen. She refused to shake his hand, which immediately removed the smile and he abruptly turned to sit at his desk. He then addressed Valentyn to explain our presence in Vyzhnytsia. I assumed he heard all our discussion downstairs from his ideal vantage at the top of the stairs as he questioned only Valentyn. From time to time Valentyn would patiently ask me to clarify some detail the superior requested. After a considerable time of interrogating us, I took one of the clarifying issue occasions to boldly protest that in Kyiv, Lviv and other towns we were not required to report our arrival. I emphasized as best I could with Valentyn's help to explain Ukraine was now an independent country free from the tight control of the Soviet system. I tried to disarm the superior's stern stance and it worked. Taking advantage of the change in mood of the interview, I pressed Valentyn to view the written law the police station had stipulating where visitors must report. The superior then lead us downstairs, spoke to one of the officers and returned up the stairs without further acknowledging us. An officer told Valentyn there was no further business and wished us a pleasant visit. A day later Valentyn received a two-page photocopy of the old Soviet law. It probably was the exact law used to apprehend and interrogate Canadians Mary and Mike Chorney. We later learned the superior was the KGB in charge of the Vyzhnytsia region.

Another member of the Canadian Moisey family preceded us to Ukraine when the Chernobyl nuclear disaster occurred in April 1986. It was my second cousin Dr. Clarence Moisey, a recent graduate in pediatrics from the University of Alberta, who Greenpeace had hired. He mapped the disaster area for radiation contamination and was easily recognized on many televised news reports, as he wore an Indiana Jones hat and carried a Geiger counter. After this project, he stayed in Ukraine for several years, focusing on his profession and working mainly at Kyiv's Hospital Number One. With some of his Alberta university professors, he pioneered several of the first Alberta doctor exchanges that saw Kyiv Hospital Number One upgraded. He became well known in Ukraine and Canada for his efforts, and outspoken opinions. Many people from the Cheremosh area consider him a hero.

The Navalkowsky and Chorney visitors have passed on. I have never met or spoken to Clarence Moisey to obtain information he may have uncovered about any Moisey family in Ukraine. Nastasia, daughter of old Nikolaij Moisey from Banyliv, mentioned she wrote to Clarence at the Kyiv Hospital several times without receiving a response. The Canadian Moisey family has reached out to our Ukrainian relatives whenever an opportunity arose and there have been stories and wonderful reunions that should continue for at least a few generations.

Odesa and Yaroslav

On our first visit, we tightened our seatbelts as we approached the Odesa airport. Cigarettes were doused, while a stewardess removed empty glasses of consumed vodka. As we landed, a rousing clapping of hands echoed throughout the aircraft. We walked down the portable stairway to a waiting, smiling Yaroslav, who whisked us into the back seat of a large black Mercedes. We never left the car at the airport. Near the exit, a non-uniformed official stamped our passports that we extended through the car window. No questions were asked and off we went. We bypassed the lineup at immigration and customs. On this visit, we travelled with only hand luggage and quickly arrived at a dingy apartment building. We walked up one flight of stairs, were let in and told to be ready for supper in an hour. The black-suited chauffeur controlled our movements, including carrying Doreen's hand luggage and handing us the apartment keys.

The one-bedroom apartment was lavishly decorated in bright red colours and prominent Chinese red-lacquered furniture. A red and white polka-dotted teapot with matching cups and dishes sat on the kitchen counter. We quickly showered. Yaroslav arrived and took us to a downtown hotel restaurant.

The streets were eerily deserted, and commercial buildings were unlit; most were boarded up. The hotel exterior and interior were well lit. Two tables had men drinking, smoking and nibbling on snacks. Most acknowledged Yaroslav. I assumed they were security.

The rear restaurant wall and large street windows were decorated with heavy, gaudy, wine-coloured curtains from ceiling to floor. The windows also had fine semi-sheer curtains. The restaurant did its best to present us with typical Odesa food, which was delicious. Gazing out the window revealed the streets were still deserted. I noticed in the far corner more than a hundred bolts of semi-sheer curtains, like those draping the windows. Yaroslav mentioned this was his inventory. He specialized in semi-sheer curtains. We quickly ate and returned to the apartment for much needed sleep.

In the morning, a maid arrived to prepare breakfast. We washed down the caviar, salmon roe and lox with crisp thin bread with orange juice and champagne. We finished with back bacon, eggs and herbal tea. There was something more to Yaroslav than we expected. Our curiosity was intense.

We toured the nicest parts of Odesa (Ukraine's third largest city), an architecturally gorgeous city built by Catherine the Great some two hundred years ago. Sadly, it was neglected by the Soviets for many years and needed repair. Downtown was somewhat busy with young office people. All were slim, and the women generally blondish and beautiful, decked out in short skirts and the latest high-heel styles, demanded a second glance. We encountered no tourists. At the marvelous Opera House, also in need of care, we met a singer Oksana from Canada, who was rehearsing. In the afternoon, driving with Yaroslav, we toured the beach areas. Yaroslav continually pointed to properties he recently acquired with his Odesa friends. There were few cars.

Odesa Opera House.

The following day after breakfast, we toured the Black Sea coast to the north. Most large factories were skeletal ruins and were stripped of everything that could be moved. Not a light bulb or window remained. One large prestressed-precast concrete factory had a large overhead, unused crane with a serial number tag with the date 1990, some four years ago. What was happening? Why would this new piece of equipment, too heavy to move, unless heavy machinery was used, be in an empty building that was gutted of windows, doors, electrical, plumbing and furniture? Everything moveable by manual labor was gone. Who rendered these large factories to skeletons? Was it the various mafia or just the local folks? Nobody seemed to know and avoided giving an opinion.

We stopped at a group of carefully kept small homes, whose gardens were tended by Tartar women. They were shy, friendly and not too communicative. I was enamored by their kaleidoscopic-coloured eyes. In the distance, we could see where Hammer, of Occidental Oil fame, had left huge chemical factories that had disposed of by-products directly into the waterways, causing environmental havoc. Smoke stacks were now idle.

Lion's Den

One evening back in Odesa, Yaroslav and I attended a business meeting in a below-ground wine bodega. The entrance was off an unlit, deserted sidewalk. Inside, the bodega's brick-lined walls gently curved to the low multi-arched ceiling. Recent sand blasting exposed a soft red-orange brick.

The crowded room had a few paintings and a large vinyl-covered table. We were directed to chairs at the end of the table, joining eight men in a dimly lit room filled with cigarette smoke. A middle-aged woman in a dark blue wool hat entered from a side room and sat in the single chair opposite to us. Partly consumed bottles of vodka and ashtrays were on the table. After introductions by Yaroslav, and several shots of vodka, tongues began to loosen.

Author Zen 1994; luxury in a dilapidated Odesa apartment building.

Although I could not speak Ukrainian or Russian, I understood a few words. Yaroslav translated, and I quickly discerned that I was being set up to become involved in a business venture or two. Because of the dim light, it was difficult to study facial expressions. Only two people spoke during the session, Yaroslav and the woman. Yaroslav elaborated on my businesses. The woman questioned if I had access to finances and interest in investing in the Odesa area. Yaroslav responded that money was not a problem for me and that I already had some international business dealings. I felt a bit uncomfortable in the presence of these people, sensing they were shifty opportunists. I was anxious to leave and found an excuse to end the meeting. Yaroslav promised he would stay in contact with them

Early next morning, Yaroslav arrived with a driver. Doreen and I spent a tiring day touring a large chicken operation, a concrete batch plant and an idle precast concrete factory. These were apparently owned by some of the attendees at last night's meeting in the bodega. Yaroslav encouraged us to invest in these entities. I knew the concrete operations (as I owned one in Canada) would be a disaster as the technology and dilapidated equipment required a complete makeover. The chicken operation was well cared for and professionally managed.

Yaroslav reported to the wool-hat woman about our tour. I avoided meeting them again, as we were tired and anxious to prepare for our visit to find the Moisey families in Western Ukraine.

Moldovan Border

In the early morning, with Yaroslav, we waited to board our first-class seats on the train to Chernivtsi, Bukovina, to find the Moisey family. Gypsies with their children were working the crowd on the multitrack platform. Many passengers were boarding trains in both directions. Our train would pass through bandit-controlled territory in Moldova. The first-class semi-compartment seats were divided by a narrow table that folded upward from the train wall. The windows were sealed with screws. The air conditioner had not worked in many a year, even though we paid extra for this luxury. We were excited and popped a bottle of delicious champagne as the train jerked into motion. Most men and the odd young girl boarding were smoking. Train travel was the common mode of cross-country transportation. We were off to find a Moisey in Bukovina (now Chernivtsi Oblast).

Our conversation kept us from viewing the countryside. In short order, we arrived at the Moldovan-border, where we presented our documents to enter. Doreen and I cleared the armed border but Yaroslav did not, as he forgot a document. A quick decision was made not to go on without Yaroslav, so we crossed several tracks to the south to board a freight train to return to Odesa.

A small crowd was assembling for the ride to Odesa. We followed the locals and boarded the ancient diesel freight train with its few passenger cars lined with wooden benches. There were no freight cars attached. Most passengers had sacks of garden produce, quiet fowl with securely corded feet, as well as one tethered pig, presumably for the Odesa market. A few bicycles stood in the center aisle next to their owners.

We were the curiosity of the train. Yaroslav was uncomfortable and apologetic for the surroundings. For us, we were in a familiar element, as we had traveled often to other continents with hand satchels, dressed in blue jeans and T-shirts. We were more at ease here than on the first-class train. We easily exchanged friendly smiles with passengers.

The train reached its maximum speed of 30 km/h, and it was easy to observe the countryside. Both Doreen and I were shocked to see ragged folks and many children with distended stomachs and reddish-streaked hair, a characteristic sign of malnutrition, walking the parallel dirt road. Lack of sufficient food was quite evident, and images of malnourished children were imprinted in our minds. We spotted a few single horse-drawn wagons and bicycles. The

Moldovan border appeared to be a difficult place to exist.

On the train to Moldova, 1994.

A uniformed train conductor at the far end of the car began collecting tickets. We showed him our paid first-class, unused tickets, and he passed onto the next passengers. When he completed his collection, he returned to us and insisted on money for the fare. He became quite brazen. Suddenly, directly behind Doreen, a buxom, blond, middle-aged lady jumped to her feet and walked into the face of the conductor. With a loud voice, for all to hear, she scolded him for being rude to foreign visitors and trying to extort them. The poor guy felt lucky to escape with his life. He disappeared, and we never saw him again.

One does not know Doreen until her Irish is aroused. It can be to defend a position or to show an act of kindness. As the lady took her seat, Doreen immediately turned to the back, put her knees on the bench, and embraced the lady for her braveness. In the same motion, she removed from her purse a pair of Canadian flag earrings and presented them. The lady refused. Doreen persisted and helped until the earrings dangled from her ears. Doreen proceeded to have Yaroslav inform the lady that with her braveness and kindness, Ukraine would be a great country. There were tears.

Yaroslav would frequently ask which business I thought was best to invest in. He also pressed for how much money I and others could bring to Ukraine. I avoided giving an opinion.

Back in Odesa, we insisted Yaroslav find a car with driver to take us to Bukovina. While waiting for his search, we met Yaroslav's girlfriend, the daughter of the police chief. He often insinuated his political contacts and people like the police chief would prevent an investment from going astray. He bragged about a $10,000 donation he made to a group running the affairs in Odesa and area.

We were happy with the search after a brief interview with the driver and viewing the condition of the car. We were picked up the following daybreak. The driver's English was better than my limited Ukrainian, so we had sufficient communication.

If we drove all day we would be lucky to reach Milijev, Bukovina, on the Cheremosh River an approximate 450 kilometers distance on roads skirting the northern Moldovan border. Yaroslav had relatives that would put us up for the night. We knew the Moisey family was from some village along the Cheremosh River at the foothills of the Carpathian Mountains.

We learned that Victor our driver had been the personal bodyguard for Kim Philby, the famous British MI6 and Soviet double agent who had defected to Russia and lived some of his last years in Odesa. Victor was slender and muscular. He had excellent driving skills and was keen for the drive, as it was always his dream to visit the Carpathian Mountains. We convinced him to bring his wife, who had never been outside the city. She would also be good company on his return to Odesa. We would depart Ukraine from Lvov, now spelled Lviv.

Bukovina by Car
We travelled twelve hours, encountering little traffic, mostly green army trucks. Cars were always full and were mostly Russian Ladas and Skodas, of old vintage. We saw the odd Mercedes and no American cars. Strangely, we saw no passenger buses!

Every hour or so, the mostly paved road would converge with up to four other roads. Here was a major guarded checkpoint, manned with many military personnel. Each road had a draw bar. We stopped and were interrogated. One or two armed, uniformed guards peered into the car as Victor hand-cranked down his window. A large compound of stored vehicles was nearby, which I assumed were confiscated. Victor calmly withdrew his wallet and flashed a few documents. He was asked to wait until a superior approached, who, after viewing the documents, smiled, saluted and granted passage. Up went the hand-controlled counter-weight barrier. This occurred at all checkpoints, without any hassle. It felt reassuring to be with Victor.

We made our first stop before noon at an unassuming wooded roadside area. It was good to get out of the car and stretch. As there were no washrooms, we used the bush. The girls used the other side of the road. We had not encountered a gasoline service station or restaurant nearly one third of the way into our journey. The countryside seemed deserted. Farm fields were overgrown with weeds and dominated by a blanket of blood-red poppies, which are considered a weed in Ukraine. Victor opened the trunk. It was packed tighter than the car. More than half the trunk was lined with jerry cans of gasoline and the balance with clothing and food. We refueled from one large jerry can.

Out came a red and white-checkered tablecloth, which Doreen helped spread it on the long grass. A cloth bundle was untied, and we sat on a blanket and feasted on chilled fried chicken, incredible bread, pickles and sweet tarts. We emptied a large bottle of red soda, and we were off again. At a subsequent stop, Doreen was shocked when a block of smoked pork fat was sliced into chunks, and one was handed to her on a thick slice of homemade bread. I remember well my grandfather savoring this snack. Two similar stops were made before we arrived in the dark at Milijev on the Cheremosh River.

It is amazing that the long trip we took from dawn to dusk was void of roadside service stations, bathrooms or restaurants, except for the odd caboose, where outside a hibachi usually burned, fueled by wood or charcoal. Near the caboose were a table or two and a huge container of hot herbata (tea).

It was now dark and several inquiries found Yaroslav's relative in the village of Milijev, where we spent the night. Most neighbors were asleep. We were well greeted and had a few vodkas and a snack of bread and garlic sausage. After an hour of spirited talk we were off to bed. Awaking to a crowing rooster, we ate a large breakfast and went to find a translator who lived nearby. The sky was black with voronas, crows with white head patches that invade the area. Hordes blackened the sky as they descended on every corn patch, ignoring decorative scarecrows.

Several enquiries in Milijev revealed a Moisey might live in Banyliv, a village to the north on the Cheremosh River. At Banyliv after more enquiries, we were told to check a house located four houses to the north of the large Ukrainian Orthodox Church of the Dormition, where an old man lived.

Meeting the First Moisey in Ukraine
Bingo! Elderly Nikolaij was the first Moisey we found. He was eighty years old and walked with a cane in a stooped posture. As we passed through the veranda, entering the kitchen, he removed his hat, revealing jet-black, curly hair with the odd strand of white.

Nikolaij, Doreen, the translator and I gathered by the kitchen pich (a large ceramic, wood-burning stove). Nikolaij and I sat on the edge of his bed located next to the pich. We were engrossed in talk among his strewn documents and photos. He explained how he was related to the Moisey family that moved to America in 1898. His charcoal eyes would penetrate mine from time to time. He repeated several times "a miracle" had just occurred. He went on to say that annually, with an older cousin Ivan Moisey, they prayed for the departed Moisey souls, whose ship they thought had been sunk on the journey to America. It was so good to be near him.

Our meeting was interrupted by a burst of excitement from Olena Paraniuk, Nikolaij's younger daughter, a kindergarten teacher from down the street. Word spread quickly and soon we were joined by the eldest daughter, Nastasia, also a schoolteacher. Tears were shed, herbata made, photos taken, and arrangements were made to sleep at the houses of Nastasia in Vyzhnytsia and Olena in Banyliv. Olena's house is near the left bank of the Korytnytsya Creek, which enters the nearby Cheremosh River. The village is approximately 580 years old, existing before Columbus came to America.

We located and visited more relatives and toured Banyliv, a large three-part village with no commercial area, except for two government stores. Entering a store was akin to entering a large warehouse with counters. A 1920 cash register, a large ledger recording purchases and walls lined with empty shelves could not be missed. One shelf held three jars of preserves and the one below had six loaves of appetizing bread. There were no customers and four clerks. The government store was on the main gravelled street entering the village from the north and directly across the street from old Nikolaij Moisey's house.

Several enquiries on Banyliv's population drew shrugs. Some guessed it was 4,000. Most houses were on approximately one-third-acre lots, each with a water well, outdoor toilet, and a small barn with a pig, a cow, or both. Chickens were everywhere, busily scratching in the fenced yards. All yards had apple, cherry or pear trees. Olena's area had rows of houses forming a rectangle around an approximately ten-acre parcel, where each house had an unmarked garden plot. On the southeast edge of Banyliv, across the rail tracks towards and against the ancient Cheremosh River bank were many approximately one-to-ten-acre plots, each with zero to four houses laid out in a haphazard order. These sparsely fenced parcels were connected by footpaths and winding, rutted grass roads. Some house groupings were occupied by related family members. Three of the large plots were owned by the Moisey families. Michaelo, Ivan and Frozena (née Moisey) Andryuk were separated by about two kilometers.

Awaking early at Nikolaij's daughter Olena Paraniuk's house, Doreen helped prepare breakfast. I was in the barn hand-cranking a silage chopper into which her husband fed corn stocks to make them more palatable for the cow. After breakfast, and with directions from Olena, we set off to Frozena's house, walking the few kilometers. It was a beautiful, slightly sunny, crisp morning.

Here we were on the same dirt, grass-lined road trod countless times by Moisey blood. Doreen allowed my rambling speculation on the things that might have happened here. We held hands and noticed smoke from household chimneys, chickens scratching in yards and women busy with chores. It was easy to spot a water well as they either had a hand pump-jack or pulley with bucket and rope. A cow with milk-laden utters was occasionally led by a man to a stall attached to the rear of the house.

About a kilometer from our destination, we spotted a bicycle. As it drew nearer, a tall, babushka-clad, blue-eyed lady in high rubber boots, with a big smile, dismounted. She laid her bicycle on the road edge and rushed to us. She had already heard we were in the village.

Arms outstretched, we embraced rosy-faced Frozena. She was panting heavily from pedaling her balloon-tired, vintage bike and the excitement of our meeting. Looking into each other's eyes and expressing our mutual happiness, we walked to her home. Frozena left the bicycle on the roadside. Soon we were sipping hot herbata, periodically holding hands and shedding tears of happiness.

Frozena explained her husband Elai was accused by the Banyliv Kolhosp (a collective farm instituted by the Soviets), a short distance to the east, of stealing some pork. He was jailed nearby, became very ill and was returned home. Elai, unable to walk or stand, was dumped over the picket fence. Frozena dragged him into the house, where he died shortly thereafter on February 16, 1984. He was fifty-eight years old.

Frozena's home with a detached summer house, shed and barn with large garden was laced with flowers and fruit trees. Immediately to the southeast and to the west, Frozena told us this land was part of the original Moisey home site. This is where her (and my) forefathers lived. Further to the east and just above the ancient Cheremosh river slope (100 meters east of Frozena's house) the Moisey forefathers also owned what she estimated to be more than fifteen acres.

Now in 2017, the properties to the southeast are subdivided into small residential lots with newly constructed homes.

Frozena or other Moiseys derived no financial benefit from these early Moisey properties. In 2017, her remaining one-acre plot is neatly fenced, and adjoining to the southeast is a beautiful, newly constructed chapel with room for about four people. It is loaded with icons and other religious paraphernalia. It is well used and usually has one to twenty candles burning.

Later in the day, we walked the few kilometers from Frozena's to a kindergarten, not far from the high school to again visit Olena, who was one of the kindergarten teachers. Her older sister Nastasia was the headmistress. The school was clean, bright and well organized. Nastasia earned twenty dollars per month and Olena three dollars.

After visiting with the children, we walked to Olena's house, crossing on the Korytnytsya Creek's small bridge. The road had drainage ditches on both sides, and its center was grassed. We walked on the potholed road as there were no sidewalks. Crossing an intersecting road, we stepped over a rusted, ten-inch natural gas pipeline. Cars and steel-rimmed wagons rode over this exposed, pressurized pipe. Houses were heated by wood in a pich as gas was for other purposes. Wooden electric power poles were strapped with heavy wire to short, protruding concrete posts. Power was typically functional for half-day periods. The town infrastructure was cruder than the infrastructure in Alberta small towns and villages had been in the 1930s.

Late in the afternoon, we walked several blocks through a neighborhood with Olena's sister. Women were busy with yard work. We met a man in his fifties walking towards us wearing an alpine hat, carrying a shoulder bag. As the discussion progressed, he reached into his satchel and gifted Doreen with three champagne bottles. One bottle was popped, and we sipped bubbly made from fermented barley. My immediate thought was that one needed to be drunk to keep sipping. I offered to pay, but he was greatly insulted. An elderly lady watching her tethered cow smiled at this encounter. It was explained that bartering was typical in the village, especially among people who knew each other.

After more visiting we prepared to return to Canada. Victor our guide from Odesa drove us to Lviv, a seven-hour drive over a deeply rutted highway. Victor and his wife from Odesa were great company for the long distances we travelled. We were never to communicate with them again.

After touring Lviv for a day, we boarded a plane for Canada, via Frankfurt. On the return home we reviewed our conversations with Frozena and her two Moisey sisters, Maria Shandro and Paraska Vatrich and how they all suffered from the brutal Soviet system.

Paraska's husband, Michaelo Vatrich, was active in one of many nationalistic resistance groups. I enjoyed Michaelo's descriptions of skirmishes and hiding out in the heavily forested Carpathian hills. He bragged of caches of armaments he and friends (some of them mercenaries) had, some still buried nearby. Michaelo was a man of action with intestinal fortitude. He told me the location of a cache.

Maria suffered in the early 1930s; on several occasions, Soviet soldiers came and removed all Maria's chickens and farm animals. They then proceeded into the house and took her food. In addition, they bayoneted her large decorated pillows and removed loaves of bread she had hidden. She begged for a bit to be left for the children, but to no avail. Maria, Paraska and Frozena, along with neighbors, experienced similar inhuman treatment.

Of the three sisters, only Frozena and Paraska are alive in 2017 and live in their homes in Banyliv and Ispas, respectively. Maria, a high-spirited woman with a perpetually outgoing personality, died on April 27, 1997. A lack of penicillin and proper medical care killed Maria. My angel wife Doreen, a registered nurse from the Edmonton General Hospital, always packed our luggage with medications. I remember Doreen treating Maria's hemorrhoids as they huddled near Maria's pich. Maria often warmed her hemorrhoids bending to the pich as close as she dared.

In Ukraine, my extended Moisey family had many divisions because of their political philosophies. Choices were made by uncontrollable circumstances forcing them to make immediate decisions to survive. Some became ardent Soviet Communists, Fascists allied with Germany, or diehard Ukraine Nationalists. Many fathers disowned their children because of choices their children made, especially if the children sided with the Soviets. Frozena, a tall, attractive woman, was acknowledged as an efficient agriculture field worker in the 1950s, when the area was under Soviet control. She and some neighbors took pride in this honor and today are incredible gardeners. Frozena gravitated to the Soviet ruling power for economic survival, even though she lost her husband under their rule. Her sister Paraska, a very strong-minded person, was a Nationalist, primarily influenced by her active Nationalist husband, Michaelo. He was imprisoned for fifteen years in the Siberian gulag. His cell was without heat, and he became ill after five years and was released. He paid for his patriotism with time spent in the Soviet prison and subsequent health issues. Maria Shandro (née Moisey) also assisted Michaelo and many Nationalist fighters. She was active, assisting in hiding the hunted Nationalists.

Tanasi Moisey (Мойсей), 1882 - 19??, born on oldest known homesite where Frozena lives. He had three wives, all predeceasing him.

From Frozena's house, a few kilometers north, downstream of the Cheremosh River and along the railroad track, is Nikolaij Moisey's lot, by the church, facing the main Banyliv street. I learned that the street is referred to as the ancient Turkish Way. The house is large with a few sheds filled with his well-worn blacksmith tools, forge, inventory of dry oak, metal sheets and steel flat bars. In an attached lean-to stood a partially completed horse-drawn wagon under construction. The rear shed was for farm animals. Nikolaij hand-hewed oak into spokes, hubs and sections of the

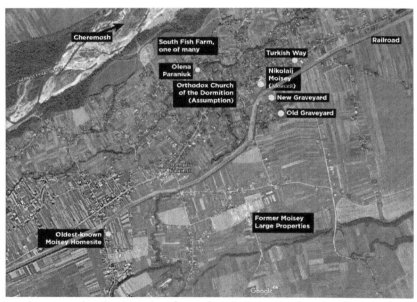

perimeter wheels. He also forged and shaped a band of steel to bind the wheel pieces securely and serve as the portion that rolled over rocky roads. He skillfully manufactured each component of the wagon, selling it for the equivalent of around two hundred Canadian dollars. I would love to have a completed, painted wagon on our Canadian farm.

Banyliv 2017.

Nikolaij, severely bent from age and mostly from beatings by Bolsheviks, was his own man. There was nothing politically correct in his statements. He hated the Bolsheviks, several times pointing out their stupidity. It is amazing he survived abuses experienced on his property from Bolsheviks, Germans and Romanians (who were the puppets left in control after the German blitzkrieg). His daughter Olena presented me with twelve pages of hand-written information about her father's past (see Appendix 13, page 297).

On August 7, 1932, Stalin decreed the death penalty for anyone taking a few kernels of grain from a field. Before the arrival of the Bolsheviks and their flawed Communist system, Ukraine was the breadbasket of Europe and its own region. In 1931 and 1932, Stalin was busy sending trainload after trainload of wheat to keep Moscow from starving. More trainloads of grain were sent to China to show the successes of Russian communism. Mao murdered 75,000,000 in his march to communism, and Stalin killed 10,000,000. Stalin's decree was never rescinded. Many remote Kolhosps continued to harshly punish members for minor offensives during and after Perebudova until the early 1990s.

Lurking Family Shadows
Back in Edmonton after our first visit, we quickly fell into the daily routine of making a living, while memories of Ukraine flashed through both our minds. Doreen and I decided to do something for the Ukrainian families we had met. One day there was a message on the phone that Yaroslav (from the Odesa lion's den meeting) called! I sensed he was looking for money and ignored his phone call.

Visions of the first visit persisted. Images of malnourished children entered my dreams. Abandoned, empty warehouses and factories lacking windows, doors, surrounded with uncut grass and shrubbery, reminded me of ghost towns seen in movies. Thousands of square kilometers of farmland sprouting weeds and poppies lay idle. People hurriedly walked roadways, and one never saw a single passenger bus. Either the folks could not afford to pay, or for some strange reason, the communist system did not make buses available.

A hint of family members, politically divided from the brutality of war and many stories of hardship would occasionally dampen our eyes with tears. We soon began to ask ourselves what could we do to give my distant Ukrainian family a helping hand up?

Canadian-Ukrainian cultural groups are among the strongest globally, but we had minimal connection with them. After a few inquiries we found the Edmonton office of Meest, a commercial shipping facility delivering services from Canada to Eastern Europe. We provided Meest with a list of bulk food items we thought would provide relief to the relatives we had met, items such as large sacks of sugar and flour, spices, cooking oil, hams and canned goods. These items were purchased in Ukraine and delivered to specific families for distribution to their close families.

Our Canadian business was struggling to expand from a past recession. I paid myself low wages, while Doreen worked as a registered nurse. We avoided bank debt as the past recession almost claimed all our assets, including the house. Doreen said we must do something so we borrowed $10,000 to purchase food to be distributed to my distant family.

We received thanks from surprised family members for the

goods. Packages were sent to the eldest in a family group. We reasoned they would know best on how to divide the food among their siblings and other family members. We had given temporary relief for the coming winter, easing our concerns.

Subsequent visits to Ukraine revealed a lot about how the food was distributed among the family groups. We learned who was caring, who cheated with the distribution among their own family. This knowledge helped us in choosing family members for ventures we later initiated in Ukraine. Buying the food prevented us from stepping on the many business landmines experienced by most foreign business ventures in Ukraine as it struggled to move on from its communist past.

On the 1996 visit to Ukraine with Dad, Doreen and I slept a few days at Olena Paraniuk's (old Nikolaij's daughter) home, where we observed her son Roman approaching his teen years. He had an incredible talent for art and sculpting; winning a few national awards. The arts are his total focus. He presented us with some of his work, and I purchased the remainder, which we keep in our Canadian Ukraine room.

On the visit in 2014, I viewed Roman's specialty of metal sculpturing. He walked me through his welding and blacksmith shop with three-year-old son Daniel tagging behind. I noticed a few well-worn tools, which I assumed came from his grandfather's shop. Roman's wife, Oksana, who was born in remote northeast Russia and studied art in St. Petersburg, sat on a swing with seven-year-old daughter

Bohdana.

3 meter metallic Angelic face on Mount Makivka commemorating heroine Olena (Yarema) Kuz from Banyliv, by artist Roman Paraniuk.

With translator Oksana Chorney and business-minded Tatyana Krasniuk, I quickly understood the difficulties Roman was encountering in his attempts to promote his sculptures. Roman was very distraught and in tears as he had just received news that he had lost a friend in Putin's invasion in Eastern Ukraine. After much discussion, he agreed to create a sculpture to represent peace between Western Ukraine and Ukrainians trapped in the Donbas battle zone, where war was fomented by Putin's infiltrators.

Roman would design the sculpture. He asked for a few days to present us with a sketch after consulting his artistic friends. We accepted his design without changes.

On an early visit, Frozena invited me to her church in Banyliv, and I readily accepted. Her son Tanasi drove us to the church, a red-brick shell under construction still lacking glass in the window cavities. We went in while son Tanasi settled into his car for a snooze. The churchyard had carefully stacked bricks, waiting to be mortared into a future position. There were few parishioners in attendance as we knelt on plastic sheeting, on a yet-to-be-constructed floor. The church, a Russian Orthodox Church (ROC) controlled from Moscow, is of immense importance to Frozena, a very religious person.

Two metre metallic artwork by Roman Paraniuk from Banyliv.

Not too far away, on Banyliv's main street is the old Ukrainian Orthodox Church of the Dormition (Assumption), attended by some of her siblings. To many family members, especially the younger generation, there was little importance as to which church they attended or were married in. Recently, Frozena learned the Russian Orthodox Church is a department of the Russian government. She was shocked to know some of the priests were Russian sympathizers, providing political information and sending her church donations to support Putin. It took several of her children and grandchildren to convince her about the activities of the ROC. There are examples of how the Russians over the years absconded with funds or desecrated thousands of Ukrainian churches. Most of these stolen Ukrainian church assets are still under the control of Russia, through the ROC. Most villages simply accepted this theft, preferring not to rock the boat. After Perebudova, villagers began to construct new churches according to their religion. One example is the new church in Ispas, twenty minutes south of Banyliv, which Doreen and I supported with a donation. The church elders placed our contribution in their acknowledgement book on page 100.

Ispas Ukrainian Orthodox Church, Kyiv Patriarch.

Our 1996 Visit with Dad and a Family Reunion
My father John Roman Moisey, Doreen, and I travelled to Ukraine to find more Moisey family stories, to firm up details for our Lingcomp school that we were developing, and to hold a large family reunion.

46

Dad's command of the Ukrainian language was perfect according to old-timers. He was liked, and the older folks opened their hearts to him. The elderly were happy to hear Ukrainian words such as Tak, Tak (yes), instead of Russian Da, Da. They were happy Russia did not destroy the Ukrainian language. The Soviets were brutal with their oppression of Ukrainian culture. Dad brought a supply of Ukrainian flags (the colour of a blue sky with gold wheat field), which were immediately hoisted to rooftops and up long poles.

Each day, dad spent hours with old Nikolaij. They bonded instantly and enjoyed each other's company. Nikolaij was born in 1914, and my dad a year later in Canada. Watching them spend a few weeks together was an incredible union to observe. Dad also bonded with Michelo Vatrich (married to Paraska Moisey, Frozena's sister) and Ivan Moisey, who was several years older than old Nikolaij.

Zen and dad 1996, sign at the south entrance to our ancestral village of

Banyliv.

These three old-timers despised the Bolsheviks and Nazis. They pestered these regimes whenever possible, and were punished when apprehended. Nikolaij told many stories about himself and his family. He was an ardent Nationalist, resisting the Bolsheviks, the Germans and their occupying Romanian puppets. Later he was conscripted by the Soviets and was on the front lines of vicious battles to stop the Germans at the outskirts of Moscow. Many of his friends were killed, deported to Siberia, or imprisoned. Many others suffered, including Nikolaij.

Dad and Nikolaij's meeting, 1996.

His evasive actions were described to me by his cousin Maria (née Moisey) Shandro, who every few days helped him to survive. She was his only contact who knew his whereabouts. Maria explained she would bring water and food to his various underground hideouts. One type of hideout consisted of a shallow hole in an open field, with a few branches covered by earth, and camouflaged with surrounding vegetation. She described an occasion when his stench was noticeable from several meters away. When captured, the Bolsheviks beat him with gun butts, smashing his fingers, breaking his shoulder and damaging his back.

Maria Shandro (nee Moisey { Моисеĭ}) 19?? – 1997, oldest daughter of Tanasi's third wife, talking with my father John Roman.

At one time, he escaped to nearby Romania, assuming the name Moisiuk. I saw his Romanian identification document. In Romania, he continued his blacksmith trade. Back in Banyliv, he was sent to the Russian front, where he repaired tanks and gunnery during battles. He would hold his ears as he described deafening explosions of large guns that shook the earth. Long afterward, he had dreams of these events. Nikolaij often mentioned his hatred of the Bolsheviks. He called them stupid little men. Maria could not believe the inhuman treatment Nikolaij received, and the brutality she endured from the Soviets, Germans and Romanians.

My father was excited about a large family reunion he and Nikolaij were planning. They arranged for it to be held at old Nikolaij Moisey's Banyliv house, north of the church on Main Street (Turkish Way). Families normally met at weddings and funerals, so a reunion was an oddity, but welcomed. A day was selected a week before we were to depart for Canada. Dad succeeded in inviting some fathers and their children who previously refused to meet each other. Some were divided philosophically because of WWII and the Soviet system. These members had not spoken to each other for a long time. Dad managed to overcome this divide by convincing them that blood was thicker than water and their political views. Many shed tears of long-held guilt. Dad had a distinct way of bringing people together.

Ukrainian women are community organizers and doers, and they instructed Dad to oversee the purchase of a pig. They would handle other details. The Kosiv weekly bazaar across the Cheremosh River had livestock for sale.

The Kosiv bazaar is the largest in the area, where every product imaginable is available. Trucks with rugs from Turkey, special meats from Poland, wine from Romania, used clothing from America and smuggled cars from Hungary stretched as far as the eye could see. The mass of moving humanity stirred slowly, raising clouds of dust. Galicians and Bukovinians with sacks of products, including tobacco, livestock, home preserves, woodcarvings, traditional needlework and clothing pleased the senses. Merchandise was delivered by foot, wagon, bicycles and machinas (cars and trucks).

Enroute to the Kosiv Bazaar to acquire a pig for a large family reunion 1996. Lady is transporting two sacks of potatoes uphill by bicycle.

Dad and Ivan, our escort, haggled for a live pig, which the vendor led a long distance to Ivan's car. A long discussion between Dad, Ivan and the vendor centered on how to transport the pig in the small car, a Citroën. They tied the pig to prevent it from kicking and escaping. The vendor quickly produced some twine from his back pocket and he and Ivan tied the hog. Four of us struggled to lift the pig into the back compartment of the Citroën hatchback.

Dad and I loading the pig into a vintage Citroën to the amusement of the crowd.

We all hopped in, and Ivan set the car in motion. Doreen yelled that the pig was loose and was pushing the cover behind her seat. We jumped out, opened the hatchback to once again secure the pig. It jumped out and hobbled down the road with Dad and I in chase. With a mighty dive, I tackled the beast, smothering its body. The squealing pig twisted and gashed a gaping hole in my jeans, but I held on. Dad then took charge and hog-tied the beast so that it was almost motionless. The Citroën drove up and in went the pig, mud, poop and all. Five of us piled in with our purchases, and off again we went, slowly maneuvering with the heavy, squealing load down the dusty road.

The day before the family reunion, dad butchered the pig and left it with the women at Nikolaij's house, where a flurry of activity was taking place. Nikolaij's home and yard received the best cleaning it had seen in decades. In Nikolaij's workshop, pyrohies and holobtsi were made, while appropriate songs were sung, which made for its own party. One song, which seemed to go on for an hour was about making pyrohies. Women took turns describing a short humorous scene and then all joined in with the pyrohy chorus

All was ready the next early afternoon, and sixty-plus guests arrived, each man with a bottle or two of homemade spirits. There was a nice mix of children and elderly folks. Dad was in his element with the elderly, telling story after story and answering questions about Canada. Many walked up to ten kilometers to attend. Eventually, as undone domestic chores entered people's minds, the party ended. Dad cajoled those with cars to make several trips to drive home those living the farthest away. A large Moisey love-in across the vast ocean had occurred.

Dad and Nikolai the 3rd

Old Nikolaij was the keeper of the Moisey graves across the railroad tracks from his house. His parents, grandparents and other elderly family members occupy the extreme northeast corner of the cemetery. These graves are well marked with steel-pipe crosses, welded by Nikolaij. His wife Wasylena's (née Maksymiuk) grave is marked with a snow-white, concrete headstone, containing an encased photo of her and the date of her passing in 1980. Nikolaij never remarried.

Yabluniv Internat resident school for homeless students. Andre had a severe cold, 1996.

Nikolaij's son Nikolai the 2nd has one child, Nikolai the 3rd. We learned that Nikolai the 2nd married Luba, who had two boys from a previous marriage. Alcohol soon destroyed the union. Nikolai the 2nd was intoxicated on all our visits. Luba with the three boys lived across the Cheremosh River in Stari Kuty. Nikolai the 3rd, about twelve years old, was in an Ivano-Frankivsk State institution called an Internat. This Oblast (province) has approximately eleven Internat schools for parentless children. Nikolai the 3rd's Internat School, which has both male and female children, is in Yabluniv, across the Cheremosh River, west of Banyliv. Yabluniv is the town from where the first Ukrainians migrated to settle in Canada in 1891. After discussing the boy with old Nikolaij, my father's eyes met mine. We instantly knew we had to travel to Yabluniv to find the twelve-year-old.

We arrived early morning at the Yabluniv Internat

School. The air was damp with a chilling wind. Three pre-teen boys were crossing the street to enter the school grounds. Two young girls leaving the schoolyard hand in hand greeted the boys, exchanging a few giggles. We noticed the girls' destination was an empty lot lined with outdoor toilets against an unpainted picket fence. A few students loitered near the toilets. Frozena's son Tanasi, our faithful, jovial driver, engaged the boys in some laughter. All three were huddled in adult winter clothing, and one had a runny nose, which he wiped with his overcoat sleeve. We learned they lived at the school and had no parents. They loved their teachers. Tanasi extracted the location of the school director's office. We enjoyed the encounter with the boys, as they munched on candy we offered.

Dad, Tanasi and I walked to the open office door and introduced ourselves to the director, who was curious and amiable. She summoned hot water and poured large cups of herbata (tea from local herbs, berries and orange peel). Midway through our second cup of herbata, in came a few teachers, and we learned of Nikolai the 3rd's circumstances. The teachers, and especially the director, were filled with empathy for the boy and said they would care for him at the school for up to another year. They did not want him to go back to Stari Kuty as they were aware of bad influences there that were detrimental to the young boy.

The director arranged for the boy to join all of us gathered in her office. He was treated as an adult and was told who we were. Dad and I wanted to spend a few minutes with him in private, and this wish was granted. The boy, dad, and I found a bench under a tree, where we embraced this beautiful child. He shed tears from time to time, and dad and I choked-up as we learned about his difficult childhood.

Nikolai shivered in the cool air, and I removed my multi-coloured jacket, covering his boney shoulders. He sat between dad and me. We learned that he dearly loved his mother, Luba, and that he knew the Internat was good for him. The boy did not want to talk of his father.

Yabluniv Internat School teachers with resident student Nickolai 3rd Moĭceŭ with my gifted Guatemala coat of many colours standing in front of me and the school director, 1996.

We returned to the director's office, where the teachers were assembled, and with young Nikolai 3rd, we sipped steaming herbata. Tanasi was snoozing in the car. As we said goodbye, this beautiful child started to remove the jacket, which I quickly returned to his shoulders. It looked so good on him, and he shyly thanked me for the gift.

We were now alone with the director and told her that we wanted to work to contribute to her good work. Dad gave her two US hundred-dollar bills, one for her and the other for what she thought appropriate for the boy (teachers in 1996 earned $40 to $80 per month). I told her I was a Rotarian and what we Rotarians do. I knew a few Rotarians at the Ivano-Frankivsk Club and said I would explore further if they would be interested in partnering with a Canadian Rotary Club to help the school.

At a meeting with the Rotary Club of Ivano-Frankivsk, the club agreed to manage a Rotary World Community Service Project for the Internat school. The project, if accepted by the school, would see them obtaining a forty-foot long, by eight-foot wide, by nine-foot four-inch-high ocean container of materials they desired.

The school director faxed the Ivano-Frankivsk Rotary Club a wish list of what items would make the school a better place. The Ivano-Frankivsk Club and I approached Caritas (a Catholic Charity) in Ivano-Frankivsk and received assurance from the bishop that he would arrange for import papers to receive the container in Ukraine. The club would then unload the container and transport the wish list items from Ivano-Frankivsk to the Yabluniv Internat school. I would find a partnering Rotary Club in Canada to fill the container and pay the shipping costs to Ukraine.

From the Yabluniv Internat school, we drove south to Stari Kuty to find the boy's mother, Luba. The house was in a disorganized cluster of small houses, accessible by a grass-lined footpath. We parked in a lot next to a large house with signage explaining that this was where Ivano Franko spent a good part of his early life. The house was well kept.

We located Luba's house, where we met one of her sons, who set off to find Luba. We were in a hurry and after a half hour decided to leave without meeting her. As we drove from the parking area, we saw Luba and her son running toward us. Dad and I left the car and walked a bit for privacy with Luba, explaining what happened with our meeting with her son in Yabluniv.

Apple time, south of Yabluniv.

Luba informed us of her difficulty earning money. Her best money source was collecting boxes of apples and other produce from neighbors and taking the train to Moscow to sell them on the street. She knew Valentyn and Maria Krasniuk, as Maria also journeyed by train to sell woodcarvings on the streets of Moscow. Dad gave Luba $100. He advised her that Maria (Frozena's daughter) and Valentyn would be the best way to keep in contact and that we liked her boy. Luba, a petite, struggling mother, was appreciative of the minutes we spent with her, and she shed tears. I choked up several times as we hugged.

Luba said he was a good boy and had to remove him from very bad influences in town. She said he slept in her bed, where he felt secure. He did not acquire the street smarts of his older half-brothers and their friends and was relieved the Internat school accepted him.

Edmonton Rotarians quickly filled the Internat school wish-list of materials and stored them at their Rotary Humanitarian Aid Warehouse, where subsequently the goods were loaded in a container. Tanasi, Frozena's son from Ukraine, was in Canada and at the warehouse to help load the container. A year later in 1997, the container was unloaded by Ivano-Frankivsk Rotarians, and their report was encouraging; a few hundred children would have some material security before they were turned out on difficult streets.

Later on another visit, Rotarian Laetitia de Witt from the Vegreville, Alberta Rotary Club, her Ukrainian-speaking friend and I visited the Ivano-Frankivsk Club and the Yabluniv Internat school. The visit to the school was unannounced. Climbing the stairs to the main hall brought tears to my eyes. Everything was freshly painted with great care. Poster-sized student drawings covered all the walls. Corridors had working light bulbs. Word spread quickly. We disrupted classes by playing ping-pong on one of several tables sent from Canada. The hallways were warm and dry. Children dressed immaculately in T-shirts and jeans swarmed us when they realized who we were. I warmly embraced dozens of children and the school director. We both shed tears as we hugged.

Classes were suspended. Herbata, Coca-Cola and orange soda were poured. Laetitia and her friend were a great hit with the teachers, and they engaged in animated discussion after the excited children got to their ping-pong games and an unexpected chance to play outside.

We were taken to the dorms. The walls were brightly coloured, displaying children's drawings. There were real curtains on windows, and every bed was perfectly made. Gone was the heavy, damp bedding that must have been 50 years old. Each bed had a small rug on the well-worn linoleum floor.

After much excitement, I wondered where young Nikolai 3rd was. Nobody knew his whereabouts. I later learned from Maria and Valentyn that the boy and his Mom had been in contact with them. They assisted Luba a bit and had last heard the boy was working on a large pig farm and his employer was happy with him. I look forward to hopefully meeting him again, the grandson of old Nikolaij, the first Moisey we met in Ukraine.

The Trust Factor

Yaroslav had been pestering me for a considerable time to invest in his many opportunities. Many times, I declined. One day, Yaroslav phoned, announcing he was in Edmonton with his wife and baby. He invited me to be the child's godfather at an Edmonton Orthodox Church service. Doreen and I met them at the church. His wife was a beautiful person and seemed much younger than Yaroslav. I became godfather, and Yaroslav's sister became godmother.

I next heard from Yaroslav when he phoned from Odesa. He sounded desperate and pleaded for money for a sure deal. I refused, and he rudely hung up. A few weeks later, I received a threatening hand-written letter demanding money. Once again, I felt the ominous dark cloud of the

Odesa bodega lion's den. I ignored the letter and never heard from him again. In Ukraine, some months later, I heard he received a bullet to his head.

I was still looking for some businesses in the Ukraine to invest in. I pressed dad to name someone I could trust, as I had become a bit paranoid after the Odesa experience with Yaroslav and the way that some of the food packages had failed to be fairly distributed earlier.

I continued to ask dad whom to trust, as I wanted to become more involved with the Lingcomp private school. Without hesitation or qualification, he selected Valentyn Krasniuk, who was very quiet at all our previous gatherings. In the morning, I gave money to Valentyn to buy Mila's apartment and prepare it for a school. Slowly pieces were falling into place with good people.

We purchased additional desks, tables, computers, etc., for the school and had them installed. Within the next two years, we maxed out at over two hundred enrolled students, everybody prepaying for their lessons. Many students were teachers from more than thirty nearby high schools.

It became apparent the Vyzhnytsia area needed an Internet system. A fifty-kilometer line from Chernivtsi was installed. We donated a computer to be the server. Within a year the community had eight customers online. This was accomplished with assistance from Ivan Paliy from Chernivtsi, a technical wiz for the national telephone company. Ivan is married to Olga, the likable daughter of Lucian Moisey from Ispas, a half-brother to Frozena.

Our first visit to Banyliv had brought us to find our first Moisey, to open a larger community of relatives and to begin some philanthropic opportunities to improve people's lives. But we were not yet done exploring, or being shaped by, Ukraine and its people. Subsequent visits saw us expand our search for my ancestral roots and along the way my understanding of, and connection with, Ukraine.

CHAPTER 3

Ancestral Roots

Origins of the Moisey (Мойсей) Family

Tracing Ukrainian family roots is difficult. It is complicated because invaders have often occupied Ukraine. There have been many invasions and on more than one occasion, they have even occurred simultaneously. Many archival records, especially those from churches, were destroyed.

There is a legendary Egyptian connection between the Moisey name and the biblical Moses. Moses in Egypt is known as Moshe. Many Ukrainians consider Moisey to mean the biblical Moses. The root "Moi" is also said to come from Moldavia in the 16th century. There are various names known to be related or that may be connected to these roots. These include: Moisey, Moysey, Mojsej, Majsej, Mojsaj, Moisie, Moiseiek, Moisei, Moys, Moyse, Moss, Moyes, Moyses, Moisa, Moisan, Mosha and Moisii. Throughout this book, I tend to use my personal spelling of the name for simplicity's sake, even though sometimes I may be referring to someone whose name may be spelled differently.

There were Moiseys in medieval England in the thirteenth century. The 1199 Yorkshire Pipe Roll records have an Elyas Moyses appearing in 1210 and a Moyses appeared in the Norfolk Roll in 1230. A 1414 "Rent-roll" listing land donations to the Battle Abbey in East Sussex, England, lists Jeffrey Fitz Moyse and William Fitz Moyse releasing rent for their lands. In another place and time, the Sept. 1 1678 records of St. Michael's Parish in Barbados, in the Caribbean, lists a Susanna Moysey.

In Ukraine the family name is Мойсей in the Cyrillic alphabet. Мойсей was changed involuntarily to Moysey, Moisie and Mojsej during Austrian and Polish occupations. There were also other volunteered changes during Romanian and other occupations. These spellings exist today, and some can be traced in archives, school enrolments and other documents, a confusing situation to say the least.

My great grandparents Wasylena and Stefan Moisey, pioneer farmers

in Western Canada, 1898.

Records of the Moisey name in Ukraine and region date back to the early 1700s. The Moisey name is not common, but it is found in many countries. A few of my Canadian and Ukrainian relatives have researched the Moisey genealogy. Most Moiseys are found in Western Ukraine. The Cheremosh river valley, which includes Banyliv, has a concentration of Moiseys. Of those I met living in Bukovina, and other parts of Ukraine with the name Moisey and versions thereof, most trace their ancestry to this area.

In nineteenth century Ukraine, the Chernivtsi 1840

Marriage Archive records Wasyl Moysey's birth in 1794 in Banyliv. Wasyl is the grandfather of my great-grandfather, Stefan. Wasyl's marriage registration is also in the Chernivtsi archives. He was married in a village a few kilometers south of Chernivtsi, near the Romanian border. The archive contains his age, dates for three pre-marriage notifications; his wife's name; his village; and notes that he was a foot soldier stationed near the Romanian border. Marriages were recorded in the wife's village. They had a son Tanasi Moysey (1821-April 19, 1881), who married Irene (Gregory) Andryuk.

My father John Roman Moisey, 1996 at the corner of Banyliv's second school on the west side of the Turkish Way, where his father attended when he was ten years old in 1897. The oak tree is estimated to be 100 years old. Banyliv's first school opened in 1856 with Moisey enrolment. It no longer exists and was located nearby, about a block east of the Turkish Way.

School registers are another good way to find ancestral records. When Banyliv school opened in 1856, one of the first five schools to open in Bukovina (now Chernivtsi Oblast), the first day of school registered the following Moyseys: my great-grandfather Stefan (at the time aged nine), Ivan (aged twelve) and Tanasi (aged eleven). The occupying Austrians opened these five Bukovina schools, after more than one hundred years of rebellion, and demands for social change from the Ukrainian locals. A major rebellion had occurred just a few years before, in 1848, when Stefan was only two years old. In the first year at the Banyliv school thirty-two boys and one girl (all between the ages of six and twelve) enrolled from a total of 558 children in the village. A half century later, the academic year of 1906-07 had a much better 412 out of 629 school-age children enrolled.

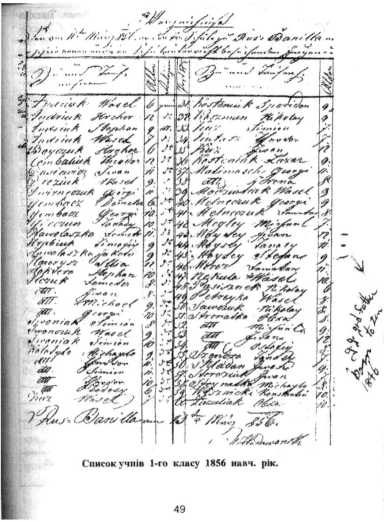

Список учнів 1-го класу 1856 навч. рік.

49

First Banyliv School Registry. Only four other Bukovina Schools were allowed to open for the first time ever by occupying Austrians. My greatgrandfather Stefan and his two brothers are near the middle of the right column.

There are also a few different spellings of Moisey in Canadian records, often due to Canadian officials forcing name changes to fit English spelling conventions. Since there were no instructions on how to make those changes, one person often even ended up with more than one way to spell their name. For example, Stefan Moisey's son Oleksa came to Halifax, Canada, on the S.S. Bulgaria in April 1898 and is recorded as both Moysey and Majsej. When Stefan and his remaining family arrived in New York, on the S.S. Pretoria in August 1898, they were listed as Moysey and Mojsej. Again, this is confusing to say the least, but do not get too hung up on the spelling of names.

Homestead-related documents of the "Canadian Dominion Land Office" list several of Stefan Moisey's sons with different spellings of the last name, at times on the same document. Most interesting to me is one document containing the names Stefan, Oleksa, and my grandfather Gregory. The father and sons have different spellings of their last name.

Other of Oleksa's homestead documents also have different spellings. Oleksa's homestead document from the "Dominion Land Office" in Edmonton, stamped with the received date Dec. 23, 1902, and stamped received in Ottawa on Jan. 2, 1903, shows his name as Alexander Moisey. This document (No. 59915 748020) also noted that he was single, that he entered the homestead site on Jan. 25, 1899, and that he began residency there in February 1899. When absent from the homestead, he stated, he was a laborer at a Blairmore, Alberta, coal mine. Another homestead document (No. 1367602) on Form No. 46 for this same land parcel located on SW1/4-32-57-15W4 shows his name as Alex Morse, aged twenty-five.

While talking about Ukrainian names in Canada, it is worth noting that more than a few Western Canadian towns and villages take their names from Ukrainian place names. Here are just some of them: Bukowina, Chernowci, Sniatyn, Kysylew, Skowiatyn, Sachava, Wostok, Luzan, Ispas, Zawale, Czahar, Lwiw, Molodia, Krakow, Huwen, Zhoda, Kaluz, and Paraskevia. I attended grade one at South Bukowina School, beginning in 1946.

In Canada, the family struggled to find an anglicized spelling using the English alphabet. To accept Moysey, the spelling insisted on by their Austrian oppressor, was not acceptable; the family in Canada chose Moisey. Ukrainian Canadians like my Moisey ancestors spelled their names in ways that resisted the foreign powers that occupied their homeland. Over the centuries of occupation in Ukraine's turbulent past, multiple occupiers had imposed their systems of how they thought Ukraine should be and how family names should be recorded. This imposition failed. Incredibly, Ukraine has on multiple occasions reversed these changes, retaining only the values its people desired. Their culture, music, art, close family ties, values, customs, agrarian skills, work ethic, religion and language remained solid.

This resilience reminds me how when I first visited Ukraine, immediately after Perebudova, ninety percent of homes had already removed photos and memorabilia of Lenin. Out came religious icons draped with the finest embroidered shawls (rushnyky). Only a few diehard communists desired to retain their white plaster busts of Lenin, which they displayed throughout their homes. Since 1991, Ukraine twice changed its currency from the Russian ruble, finally settling on the hryvna, which was used in the region in the eleventh century. Soviet desecration of Ukrainian traditional arts, customs, literature, history and language began to end. The bazaars and shops are now filled with sophisticated traditional works of art. The imposed Russian language is slowly disappearing, and pride in the Ukrainian language is escalating.

Today, the country is awash with the blue and yellow colours of the Ukrainian flag. This is understandable because throughout Ukraine's history brutal oppression by foreign invaders slowly but surely created pockets of resistance throughout the country. Russian Tsars and dictators, Poles, Germans, Romanians, Austrians Hungarians, and Putin today have pushed Ukrainian nationalism to a fever pitch. Ukraine's blue and yellow flag is proudly displayed everywhere. Wherever one looks there is a sea of blue and yellow. Bus stops, homes, fences, churches and even bridges are painted in these colours. On one of our first visits, we presented Nikolaij Moisey with a large flag, which he immediately raised and flew at his home. No other Ukraine flags were visible in Banyliv at that time.

New publications of Ukrainian poetry and history are abundantly available. In my ancestral village of Banyliv, Степан Кузъ (Stefan Kuz) has published a book of poetry titled *Не Ділить Україну (Ukraine Do Not Believe)*. His second book will soon be printed. He and his wife both work to self-finance these publications. The current mayor, Nicolai Andryuk, in 2013 published *Банилову, 580*, a book on 580 years of Banyliv history. He self-financed and printed it locally. Another version is soon to be published. Another example comes from the home of my Baba Moisey's parents Kalyna and Semon Worobetz (Оробець) whose village of Zaluce (Залуччя) on the north-east outskirts of Chernivitsi published a quality hardcover village history book in 2004. Rapidly, a local publishing industry has evolved in small towns throughout Ukraine. Today, hundreds of villages have recorded their history. It is easier now for Ukraine's Diaspora to locate their motherland families and village histories. Publishing the truth is part of an unstoppable wave of national pride, which greatly annoys the tyrant Putin.

Living the Life of a Dog
In the 2014 Maidan Winter Rebellion, Wasyl Moisey, twenty-one years old, was the fifth protester to be killed by a roof sniper, backed and trained by Putin's Russia. If you view the documentary "Maidan Winter Fire," you will witness Wasyl dying, as his friends, on two occasions call out his name for assistance. This book's title is derived from a creed Wasyl reportedly declared: "Better to Die a Wolf than to Live the Life of a Dog." I feel the same way, as do a few Moiseys I met in Ukraine. As I hear more news from Ukraine, I occasionally find myself with moist eyes. On these occasions, I sense a dormant trait kicking in to adopt Wasyl's motto. I believe more Diaspora Ukrainians, on learning of Putin's despicable actions, will stand up and be counted to support Ukraine. My wife Doreen does not have Ukrainian blood, but is a fierce warrior for Ukraine. She is current with daily death tolls and happenings in Ukraine and is active on the Internet supporting Ukraine.

Throughout the year 1838, another Wasyl Moisey (my great-great-great grandfather) with his wife Anna and their son Tanasi, aged seventeen, along with many trusted relatives, slept uneasily. They had torched their landlord's barns, homes and wagons. People raided food bins. They took some coin. The uprising is known as the Bukovina Great Revolt. Twenty years earlier, Wasyl, at the age of twenty-four, had been involved in a minor Bukovina Revolt. On the Cheremosh River bordering Galicia, Banyliv was an easy escape route for them, as they knew how and where to cross the river, especially at higher water levels.

Living as serfs and serving in the landlords' armies, eventually led many Ukrainians to rebellion. Mass rebellion commenced in Galicia and Bukovina in the early 1800s, with some killing and sabotaging of landlords' assets. This led to, and included, a major uprising in 1848 in Western Ukraine, where thousands of landlords were killed. The mainly Polish landlords were now replaced by Austrians, with promises of reform to serfdom. The year 1848 was a key year, when most serfs in Western Ukraine started to believe there was hope to escape living the life of a dog. A wolf was free to roam and do as it wished, while dogs were chained and fed dinner scraps. A half century later, many from Banyliv believed it was "Better to Die a Wolf than to Live the Life of a Dog," as the expected serf reform had not arrived, to most of the population.

In 1849, the Austrian Empire slowly granted concessions to appease Ukrainians, most of who were living in serfdom. Repression was like slavery in America. Most serfs and slaves were bonded to the landlord and usually remained an asset when land was sold. Slaves consisted mostly of gypsies and Tartars. Very few were freemen. My ancestors from Western Ukraine's Bukovina were predominately Ruthenian, also known as Rusyans (nothing whatsoever to do with the name Russia). My mother's ancestors (Palichuk), who came from across the Cheremosh near Kosiv, Galicia were Hutzels. Palichuks are found there today.

Bukovinian rebellious actions resulted in the Austrians granting minor social concessions such as opening the first five schools ever in 1856; one was in Banyliv, where the three Moysey boys were enrolled. On my twelfth visit to Banyliv, I watched as a large new house was constructed on the very same spot that the school once stood, and I visualized the three boys attending. For a long time, a sizable percentage of Moiseys have chosen education as their vocation. This is true in Ukraine and Canada.

In the late nineteenth century, the Moiseys participated as forced labor building a rail line that passed through Banyliv on its way to Vyzhnytsia. These were bountiful times for the landlords, as they illegally micro-managed the harsh Austrian laws originating from distant Vienna. Rebellion was no longer an option in Western Ukraine as troops could rapidly arrive by rail in substantial numbers to put down any disobedient act.

A bit of rebellion runs in most Moiseys, on the Canadian side of the family too. I vividly remember my father John Roman describing how he defied a schoolmaster who had issued harsh physical punishment for a minor act of disobedience. One day after school, Dad waited under the small Whitford Lake creek bridge with a sharp stick. As the teacher's buggy crossed, Dad poked the spear through a crack between the planks directly into the horse's belly. The startled horse ejected the teacher from the buggy and raced off into the distance. This rebellious trait seems prevalent in the Moisey genetic code, as Moiseys in Ukraine and Canada are known to engage in similar rebellious acts.

In my youth, I heard of a Moisey in Ukraine in the 1890s who was hunted by the Austrian army. Recently, I mentioned this to my second cousin Mary Ann Tymchuk (née Moisey). She responded that it was her grandfather Nikolai Moisey from Shandro, Alberta. Nicolai is the oldest son of Stefan, our great-grandfather. Mary Ann described what her grandmother, Nikolai's wife, told Mary Ann on more than one occasion.

Mary Ann's just-married grandmother was leaving Ukraine for America with the Wasylena and Stefan Moisey family. Reaching Hamburg, Germany, they planned to board the S.S. Bulgaria in the spring of 1898 for Halifax, Canada. They knew the Austrian army was hunting for Nikolai and always watched for police and military. In the lineup for boarding, son Olexsa led and crossed the line to the safe loading area. The remaining family noticed the presence of the Austrian army police, so they left the lineup. If they gambled and followed Olexsa to the safe boarding zone, the German authorities would have prevented the Austrians from apprehending Nikolai.

After the close encounter, the family probably waited in Hamburg, as the return home was 1,500 kilometers, and there was the ever-present Austrian army on the lookout for Nikolai. Lying low in Hamburg would save money and allow for contacts to find another passage to Canada. What a wonderful experience for the children to witness many cultures and learn a little of the German and English languages, which subsequently proved to be of value, especially for Gregory (my grandfather aged eleven) and his sister Mary. They returned a few months later in July and boarded the S.S. Pretoria, departing for New York, then on to Edmonton by train.

My great-grandmother Wasylena Moisey's (née Kuz) grandsons, John Roman (my father), his older brother Steve, and their mother (my loving Baba) have spoken of Wasylena often. Wasylena was petite but demanding. She disliked my father and Baba. She favored Steve, who looked more like her son Gregory. They lived in the same small, primitive Canadian house, where many tense moments occurred. My Baba told me her husband Gregory was Wasylena's favorite. Wasylena was always present and ruled like a military officer. She ordered Baba Paraska to do all the house and yard chores. Stern Wasylena never dirtied her fingers. Baba often told me she disliked Wasylena, because she treated Baba like a servant, not even permitting her to eat until everyone else had finished their meals.

Nobody smoked in Wasylena's house. After Wasylena's funeral in 1923, Baba said the household was peaceful. Baba, mother of ten, did not ease up on the rule against smoking in the house, except when the weather was bitterly cold, and then she allowed the boys to blow their smoke into an open stove damper while they rested on the linoleum covered floor, removing the smoke from within the house better than modern-day building exhaust systems.

Thirteen visits to Ukraine have me believing Ukraine is a more matriarchal society than Canada. My interpreter Ohla said most women know the man is the head and the woman is the neck. The head must follow where the neck turns. Maybe hundreds of years of men being away from homes while enlisted in armies helped created this matriarchal society. Men were often away in adjacent Carpathian forests for extended periods of time to hunt wild animals to supplement the meager food obtained in serfdom. Hence, Western Ukraine was forced to have women as head of families. Today, after a quarter century of visiting Ukraine, Doreen and I agree Ukraine women seem to exceed North American women as head of the household.

Statistics in the Internet Encyclopedia of Ukraine show that, in 1897, there were 1,008 women for every 1,000 men at the age of twenty. The imbalance increased to 1,090 women in 1926 and 1,040 women in the early 1990s. In contrast, Diaspora Ukrainian men in the West exceeded the number of women. Wars in Europe and emigration from Europe contributed to these numbers.

My Great-grand relatives

Doreen and I attended several weddings on our visits to Banyliv in the 1990s. We have hours of videos of these extensive ceremonies. A wedding lasted three to four days. Older folks told us marriage proceedings now were the same as when they were children. Many guests we observed walked up to sixteen kilometers to the festivities. A surprise pagan dance is often incorporated, usually after guests have consumed copious quantities of home-brewed vodka. Guests wore traditional costumes; men danced with men to a live band. We danced on a tented, wood-planked floor. All were dressed in winter clothing, many with fur hats to stave off the cold. The drunkest I have been in decades (and without a hangover) was at one of these enjoyable weddings. There was a constant supply of homebrew and food over the four days.

It was a bitter chilly night, after a wild Ispas wedding, when Doreen and I first slept at the Moisey ancestral site. We had arrived late with trusted driver Tanasi, Frozena's son. Everybody knew we were from Canada. Doreen swears she danced at least twice with every man, and some women.

Her petite feet were stepped on several times during the wild dancing, and by the end of the evening her feet were bruised. I remember that night I had the strangest thoughts and slept little. The pagan dancing and excellent homebrew contributed to a night we both will never forget, which ended with us tucked under the thick quilt. We did not know it at the time, but later archival research revealed that my earliest ancestor Wasyl Moisey, born in 1794, also slept here.

We awoke late morning, and after a hardy breakfast, Frozena applied an herbal remedy to Doreen's bruised foot. Slowly we limped a few kilometers in bitter cold towards central Banyliv to visit other relatives. Doreen looked cute wrapped in Frozena's babushka. Most wooden-fenced yards were busy with women attending daily chores. All busy yard inhabitants were friendly and many had previously met us. The sound of a chicken announcing to the world that it had laid an egg, and the clang of a metal pail as it contacted the rock lined water well was very pronounced in the still bitter-cold air. These sounds created an orchestra to the crunching of our boots on the crisp snow.

It was a perhaps similarly chilly morning on October 13, 1868, when twenty-five-year-old Ignati Tanasi Moisey, born in Banyliv, nervously waited at a small village church for his bride Anna Wirtsty (a widow), aged thirty-four. The wedding was taking place in a small village near the Gerza army base, just south of Chernivtsi (and today a portion of south Chernivtsi, the capitol of Bukovina). The Gerza barracks guarded the contentious Romanian-Austrian border. Ignati was stationed as an infantry foot soldier at Gerza, while Anna (born in Korytne, a village close to Banyliv) lived near the base. Archives register that Ignati and Anna appeared at the church on three occasions, to record their intention to marry. To attend the wedding, Ignati's parents, Irene and Tanasi Moisey, and Anna's parents walked from Banyliv, fifty kilometers away. The one-way journey from Banyliv to Graza was a two-day walk. Ignati's younger brother Stefan (my great-grandfather) was serving in the Austrian army, stationed at another location, and could not attend.

For an unknown reason, Ignati's marriage to Anna ended some years later, and he remarried. On January 21, 1879, Ignati married thirty-three-year-old Wasylena Ilchuk. They lived with Ignati's parents on the home site, where Frozena (née Moisey) Andryuk lives today. Frozena is the great-granddaughter of Irene and Tanasi. All this information is based on marriage records from an 1860-1899, Banyliv archive in Chernivtsi. Those archives record Banyliv as the birth and death place for Ignati and Wasylena. His parents (Irene and Tanasi) and grandparents Anna and Wasyl are also buried in Banyliv. Anna and Wasyl are the earliest Moisey ancestors found in archives to date.

Ignati's brother, Stefan (my great-grandfather) was also conscripted into the Austrian Army. He served at least two times in the army. The first time, he was registered on Verlust-liste Nr. 871 and was shown as Stefan Mojsej. He married Wasylena Kuz October 25, 1870, when he was approximately twenty-four years old. Stefan is also registered in now digitalized documents at the National Library of the Czech Republic as "Mojsej Stefan, Infantry, k. k. LIR. Nr. 30, 6. Camp, Galizien, Zubrze, 1874; kriegsgef, Moskau, Rubland." By that year, Stefan had one-year-old Nickolaj Moisey, who in 1898 immigrated to Canada with the family. The Czech National Library also registers Stefan in the infantry, IR Nr. 24, at camp Ispas in

1875.

Many more Mojsej, Moysey, Moise, Moisse, and Moisze males are listed in army records. Lack of fathers and older sons at home obviously contributed to food shortages and the subsequent onset of diseases, leading to high infant death rates. Wasylena and Ignati had nine children, five of whom died before the age of five. Great-grandfather Stefan's three-year-old daughter Irena died of scarlet fever in 1879 in Banyliv. Times were harsh and difficult, as emancipation from serfdom promised by the Austrians never quite occurred in a way that gave true freedom. Two generations of high death rates, despite the support of close-knit Banyliv families, occurred. So sad. See Appendix 6A and 6B, pages 252-255 Family Tree.

Zen's Ancestral Village Банилову (Banyliv)
Still, the people of Ukraine, and of Banyliv, have persevered, survived, and worked hard to make their lives better. Nikola Andryuk's 2013 book *Banyliv 580 Years Old* is a valuable account of the Moisey's ancestral village.

Nikola Andryuk's book includes a photo of Doreen and Zen.

It shows some of the progress that has been made there. The italicized section over the next several pages is digitally translated from his book.

Banyliv is first mentioned in 1433 in literature by O. Dobroho, a Moldavian governor. There are several versions of this name. First, the name of the village comes from the Moldovan money "baths," which were collected by the Turks' outpost. Second, it may come from the Turkish word "ban," which means "governor" in the Ukrainian language. The archival documents mention that the village existed during the Shypynskoyi land control of the 14th century. This is some 100 years before Columbus came to America.

On the border of two states, Banyliv has long been a center of struggle between the Polish kings and Moldovan governors. In

1538, Bukovina was under the domination of the Sultan of Turkey. Banyliv to this day has a "Turkish" Way (Main Street) because of it being a "Turkish" guard post. In 1775, Banyliv fell under the Habsburg Empire. In 1886, Banyliv Ruska opened a post office. In the 1890s, it had a railway station adjacent to the original Moisey homesite, with rails extending from Vienna to Vyzhnytsia along the right bank of the Cheremosh River.

During WWI, Banyliv was the scene of fighting between the Austrian and Russian armies.

During WWII, on April 8, 1944, Soviet troops entered Ruthenian Banyliv. Three hundred residents fought the Nazis. Fifty-three were killed and missing. For Military Merit, five villagers were awarded the Order of the Red Banner, the 3rd Order of Glory III; fourteen villagers were awarded the medal "For Valor." Many others were awarded various other medals.

In 1950, the Banyliv state farm (Kolhosp) was established. A medical clinic also opened. In 1952, the Melnivka Creek hydro plant began to function.

Banylivskoyi, the structure of the Village Council, governed two settlements, Banyliv and Berezhnytsya, with 4,555 hectares and 999.9 hectares, respectively.

Educational institutions:

Two secondary schools: Banylivska secondary school degrees and secondary school Bereznytska UC-II levels. In south Banyliv the preschool educational institution operates, which is designed for 63 children. Open Music School.

Health care and social assistance: In the village, the council operates a medical clinic and family medicine practice (south Banyliv), which has an ambulance and health posts in south Berezhnytsya that is fully equipped with medical staff and if necessary offers aid to all segments of the population. The village has two stable dental offices. There are three pharmacies.

Culture, sport and tourism: There is a library in each village. The People's House has the national folk group "Banylivska toloka," led by Mazuryaka VM, participating in all events held in the village, district, and region and beyond.

In the Banyliv People's House, there is a museum of history. The first room of the museum covers the history of the village of stone "yanoho age" to the end of the 19th century. The second room of the museum covers the period of the early 20th century to 1940. The fourth small room is an interior room from the late 19th and early 20th centuries.

In the village located near the school gym, there is a beautiful stadium with a bituminous running track, football field, volleyball court and basketball court.

There are four registered religious communities. They are 1. Assumption of the Blessed Virgin Mary, Ukrainian Patriarchate. 2. St. Nicholas Church Moscow Patriarchate. 3. Prayer House ASD. 4. Michael Church of the Moscow Patriarchate. The village has an Orthodox, Jewish and Polish cemetery.

Another interesting account of Banyliv comes from Irina Belova. Her writing about Banyliv especially shows the progress made there since the fall of the Soviet Union. She also explains how Nikola Andryuk is much more than just an author and historian, and plays an important role in Banyliv. The following is from Irina Belova:

On October 14, 2014, in the village Banyliv erected a monument to Olena Kuz, a member of Sich, a Ukrainian military group, who demonstrated unprecedented courage during the hostilities of 1914-1918. The idea for a bust came from Kuz's niece Helena, who, along with George Menzak and other donors, brought it alive and turned her from someone relegated to oblivion into a recognized heroine. The monument is located on school property, and therefore is a notable example of invincible spirit and heroism to the younger generation.

The unveiling event was attended by Deputy Head of District Administration Claudia Nazarenko, Manager of the District Council George Ivonyak, Head of Education District Administration Mikhail Andrych, Chairman of the District Committee of Union of Education Yaroslav Badger, Chairman of the district branch of the All-Ukrainian Association "Enlightenment" Dmitry Nykyforyak, Head of Banyliv Village council Nikola Andryuk, teachers, parents, students and villagers.

Father Elijah blessed the bust and read a holy prayer for peace and tranquility in the country. Addressing the audience, Claudia Nazarenko noted Banyliv's role in history and that the community honors significant figures who created that history. "Undoubtedly, Olena Kuz is an example of female heroism. And that is the example of such historical figures we must educate the younger generation about, so that they grow up real patriots, nationally conscious citizens of Ukraine," she said. The Banyliv school students' folklore ensemble "Banylivska Toloka" performed and welcomed the participants to the historical event honoring the village warrior. Finally, Nikola Andryuk thanked the sponsors and all the participants and said that gradually all the heroes whose names were erased from history in Soviet times would be returned from oblivion and honored.

In the Chernivtsi region, trout fed the entire village of Banyliv. Banyliv has one the biggest fisheries in Ukraine. Many Bukovinians know Banyliv village thanks to the famous trout farm. The owner, Levon Terteryan, for 13 years has controlled the breeding of fish. He is now growing trout and sturgeon, and anyone can purchase directly from the farm. For example, a kilo of trout goes for $60 US, sturgeon $100 US. And 90 *percent of the fish taken from the village are shipped alive. This is a very powerful economy. More than half of the trout in the Ukrainian market are taken from here. The owner cultivates trout in the purest water, using the latest technology, according to village head Nikola Andryuk. People from many countries visit the site. Next to the pools with trout and sturgeon is a special seating area where visitors can try to catch fish. To see so many trout together is amazing.*

Learning so much about my earliest Ukrainian ancestors, only motivated me more to try to do something to help improve the lives of people in Ukraine. Doing so continued to strengthen our connection to, and appreciation of, Ukraine, and to enlarge the network of people we know there. We even got to meet Nikola Andryuk, and (at his urging) to help pay for the monument to Olena Kuz that Irina Belova describes above. The next chapter describes some of the philanthropic activities Doreen and I have done as we became increasingly "invested" in Ukraine.

CHAPTER 4

Investing in Ukraine

Scholarships

In September 2014, the Krasniuk family and I were invited to a Banyliv school ceremony honoring my great-grandparents Wasylena and Stefan Moisey. The school also expressed gratitude to the Krasniuk family and me for creating and providing an award of $300 to a graduating girl and boy annually at the Banyliv high school since 2005. Details of award winners are at *www.moiseyscholarship.org/wswinners2005.html*. Ivano-Frankivsk and Chernivtsi Oblasts have also received this award, with the total number of award winners now approaching one hundred students. This most friendly reception was attended by school-teachers, directors, oblast educational representatives, and local and regional government representatives. A special treat were performances by early-grade students with their dance and song. They invited me to dance. What fun it was.

Dancers, 2014, Banyliv School reception for the Krasniuks and Zen for funding the Wasylena and Stefan Moisey Annual Scholarships.

Dancers and guests, 2014, Banyliv School reception for the Krasniuks and Zen for funding the Wasylena and Stefan Moisey Annual Scholarships.

Dedicated teachers with Zen at the Banyliv School, 2014.

Immediately after the festivities, Mayor Andryuk invited Tatyana, translator Oksana and me to his office in an adjacent school building. The mayor showed us stacks of old photos and records, and gave us a quick tour of the museum. Oksana was a student at our Lingcomp English School and later graduated from the University of Chernivtsi with five years of English as her major. She was a gem in keeping me informed regarding the reception and meeting with the Mayor. During this visit, Mayor Andryuk, also the town's unofficial historian, tapped me for $300 to buy cement and materials to erect a bronze bust of heroine Olena (Yarema) Kuz. It was at this meeting that I first learned she was a Ukraine heroine.

A teacher holding the high school student trophy. Forty-seven $300 student awards were presented in 2007 by the Doreen and Zenith Moisey Canada Scholarship in the Ivano-Frankivsk, Lviv and Chernivtsi regions. Each also received a trophy and diploma.

In addition to organizing a new Lingcomp School (described in the next section), we provided existing public schools with new student scholarships. One group of scholarships remains at the Banyliv School, in honor of my Canadian great-grandparents, Wasylena and Stefan Moisey.

Doreen and I had funded the scholarship to honor Wasylena and Stefan, born in Banyliv, Bukovina, who had migrated to western Canada in 1898 with their six children. Banyliv School scholarship winners have their names engraved on a wood trophy, which includes a carved picture of Wasylena and Stefan. Scholarships worth $300 have been granted annually since 2005. Each year a Banyliv girl and boy are selected, based on the best exam scores. If there are several candidates with the same score, then the winner will be determined by a jury of five teachers, including the school principal. Winners must enter a higher educational institution. The dedicated management of the Banyliv Scholarship awards is conducted by Valentyn, Maria and their daughter Tatyana Krusniuk from Vyzhnytsia. They also provide money for the awards. The Banyliv teaching staff and their director, Mrs. Nykoforik, select the winning students.

Scholarships and trophies are administered by lawyer Valentyn Krasniuk. The Lingcomp School project was successful because of him.

We provided a second group of scholarships through the "Doreen and Zenith Moisey Canada Scholarship Fund" we have at the Edmonton Community Foundation (ECF).

Money from the ECF was then channeled through the "Canada Ukraine Foundation" (CUF) for additional student scholarships. A Scholarship Report by the Lviv Office of the CUF for the 2006-7 school year noted that forty-seven graduates from Ivano-Frankivsk, Lviv and Chernivtsi had won grants from our fund. At awards ceremonies throughout those regions in May and June 2007, competing schools won honored caps, and winning students received certificates and scholarships worth $300 Canadian. The CUF also multiplied the number of grant winners, and gave more scholarships to students in the Physics and Mathematics Lyceum at Lviv University who had won the All Ukrainian Olympiads. The CUF has now closed its Lviv office. In 2015, CUF was planning to open a Kyiv office as Canadian Prime Minister Steven Harper's government provided $1.5 million for this purpose. It is my dream for Ukraine to form its own regional and city "Ukraine Charitable Foundations." This is easy to accomplish, if based on the Canadian model of the "Edmonton Community Foundation," which can be viewed at: *www.ecfoundation.org/*

One of Wasylena and Stefan's children was my grandfather Gregory, who until the age of 11 also attended the Banyliv School, before leaving for Canada. In Canada, Gregory became a teacher, Canada's first Ukrainian Justice of the Peace, and a Reeve of Alberta's Wostok District, all while raising his family on a farm. Many Canadian Moiseys established the "Jean & Gregory Moisey Scholarship" at the high school in Andrew, Alberta. The Scholarship is managed by the Edmonton Community Foundation (ECF) and has been awarded annually since the 1990s.

Banyliv School scholarship winners can be viewed at *www.moiseyscholarship.org/wswinners.html*. This website is managed by Nick Bilak from Chernivtsi. A list of CUF scholarship winners and awards events can be found in Appendix 4, on page 247. If you are of Ukrainian heritage from Alberta or Bukovina (now Chernivtsi Oblast), you are likely to find your family name listed there.

Lingcomp (Our Private School)

Increasing the literacy rate in developing countries is one of the most effective ways to advance the standard of living in a community. In Ukraine, we discovered an exceptionally high literacy rate with 70 percent having post-high school education. Ukraine's literacy rate ranks fourth in Europe and exceeds the United States. High literacy, to our surprise, did not translate to a good standard of living. Ukraine's standard of living was less than many developing countries we had visited. We encountered many relatives with adverse medical conditions, some who died prematurely, for lack of common medicines. Doreen, a registered nurse, was especially perplexed.

Schoolteachers, at times, were not being paid for months, and when they were paid, in parts of Bukovina, it was with vodka from the state-owned distillery. A teacher would receive bottles of vodka at retail price value and then go to the street to sell them at below wholesale prices to earn their salary. Times right after Perebudova in 1991 were difficult for most government employees, especially teachers. We noticed many women left Ukraine to work abroad and send money home. The collapse of the Soviet Union destroyed whatever so-called productive means that remained. Women worked for lower than minimal wages in countries they travelled to illegally. Meanwhile, Ukraine, the largest country in Europe, has the fourth most educated population, with a literacy rate of 99.7 percent. Europe's most powerful software engineering forces are in Ukraine. E-commerce is growing at an astounding rate of twenty percent per year.

Between 1994 and 1996, Doreen and I visited Ukraine another five times and solidified more family and non-family connections. Ukraine was progressing two to three steps forward and one back. Everyone was happy, except old die-hard commies, slowly being pushed out of their position of privilege. During these visits, we packed large suitcases with used eyeglasses and computers, believing this would help the Cheremosh River valley keep up with big-city education. Carpathian rural schools were not treated on an equal basis to Kyiv schools. Ukraine lacked funds, and when funds were available, the big cities advanced while rural areas were neglected.

We decided to put our efforts into establishing a private school called Lingcomp (Linguistics and Computers) to assist students in the English language and the latest in computer technology. A Canada/Ukraine Joint Venture founded by me in 1994, Lingcomp was a pioneer in Ukraine, training at times more than two hundred students to be proficient with computers and English from its private school in Vyzhnytsia, Chernivtsi Oblast. After a decade, every surrounding community had competing private schools. Lingcomp has organized over thirty high schools in the Vyzhnytsia Region of Bukovina. A few Edmonton Rotary Clubs provided the first-ever computers, printers and Internet connections to the schools. Participating schools collected $100 from parents to initiate the process. One teacher sold his horse to help raise the required $100 for his high school to participate. In the early 1990s, Kyiv's successes with vast sums of money injected into its school for computer training paled in comparison to the successes of the private Lingcomp school.

Some of my Ukraine relatives, Ivan Vatrich from Ispas and Valentyn Krasniuk from Vyzhnytsia, quickly found Nick Bilak and Taras Masaruk. The four of them firmed up a plan to create a Computer and English School, and became part of Lingcomp's backbone. Nick had just completed five years of university in computer engineering. Our Lingcomp private school ordered computer components from China, and Nick Bilak and his group assembled them. Taras had was a school principal who spoke impeccable English. He previously achieved national recognition for his progressive teaching. Taras won a competition that allowed him to visit Canada and the U.S., and he had studied Saskatchewan's educational systems.

Author Zen and the incredible Taras Mazaruk (Lingcomp English School Director) 1996.

The first computer classes began in Valentyn's house and Taras's school office. Students paid for each class they attended on computers or English. Students' fees of fifty cents per lesson helped pay the instructors. The instructors received the largest percentage of fees collected. We paid for all necessary materials such as computers, printers, software, textbooks, headphones, tape recorders, etc. Doreen and I provided capital for necessary items, including the purchase of classroom space. This was a way to give a helping hand up. The more we got involved the more we grew to like the loving folks of Ukraine.

We soon found Olena, from Vyzhnytsia, a bright young graduate with five years' computer training and excellent English, to teach from her home. Olena worked for the government for $50 per month, and we paid her $25 for afterhours teaching. Her husband sold liquor. They just had a baby. Olena was working herself ragged.

It became apparent a permanent facility was needed for worthwhile progress to be made. A main concern was to find a permanent, well-located building to serve as a private school. Ivan, Valentyn and I visited the mayor of Vyzhnytsia, who showed us several government buildings that could be purchased after a lengthy process involving Chernivtsi government officials. We concluded we would be going in circles and wasting energy trying to secure an unused government building.

Valentyn knew where there was an apartment for sale, owned by a single mother named Mila who had been given the apartment by the Soviets. We were told that it was at one time a Polish prince's palace, a grand old building that was now divided into five apartments. Located on 78 Ukrainian Street, Vyzhnytsia, near the town's central square, it stands on the edge of the business district and across the street from a few high-rise apartment buildings.

Three of five aparments (pink) purchased and renovated for the private English and Computer Lingcomp School in Vyzhzytsia.

At sixty years of age, Mila was burdened with health problems, and she wanted to live near her sister in Chernivtsi. She had a thirty-year-old daughter bent on going to New York, where her friends were working in bars. The apartment required extensive repair, but was ideal for the Computer and English School. We agreed to purchase the apartment for $8,500 US. Mila gifted us with a ruby glass, hand-painted decanter and six matching glasses, which when we use them bring fond memories. They are decorated with hand-painted white flowers. She said it was made in Romania and inherited by her grandmother.

First classroom purchased was Mila's apartment. Mila's gift of ruby glassware to Doreen, which was inherited from Mila's Moldovian.

Sign commemmorating school, still proudly displayed in 2017.

To create the school, we needed a capable lawyer, and we were in luck. Frozena's daughter Maria Andryuk had married Valentyn Krasniuk, a recent graduate with a law degree. Maria had been born on the same property as my great-grandfather Stefan. Valentyn, a careful academic who avoided bending rules, agreed to help us form a legal entity, which was crucial for the formation of Lingcomp. This was not an easy task as post-Soviet rule had no sound and proven process to form a legal entity, like we have in the Western world. Valentyn consulted his legal contacts, and we decided to form and register "Lingcomp Canada/Ukraine Joint Venture". Quickly, Valentyn prepared documents with help from colleges, which the legal representative of Vyzhnytsia region subsequently approved. Valentyn prepaid for the services and left money for others in the complicated process. Near the end of 1994, we received the legal entity "Lingcomp Ukraine/Canada Joint Venture." Lingcomp was the first joint venture between Ukrainian and Canadian entities to be established in the region. The Linguistics and Computer school functioned at 78 Ukraine Street in Vyzhnytsia for a bit more than a decade. A sign to commemorate the school was proudly erected at that address, and one can still view it today.

The one-apartment school was immediately filled with students, leading us to purchase two adjacent apartments from Orletsky for $10,500 and Klym for $11,500 respectively. (See Appendix 3, page 245 for details). We now had three adjacent apartments of the five. The apartments were held in Valentyn's name for several years and later transferred to my name.

Ceiling of Mila's apartment redecorated for the school classroom. Note stenciled wall work unique to this region and common in the 1800s.

Within months, a complete restoration, inside and outside, was completed to what the families believed the building looked like some two hundred years earlier. The inside walls were an uneven plaster, which the family repaired and hand painted with an old stencil system completely foreign to me. For generations, older homes and some churches along the Cheremosh River between Banyliv and Vyzhnytsia have incorporated the system. Family members selected by Maria Krasniuk, Valentyn's wife, the daughter of Frozena, completed all the work.

On all our first visits, we brought computers and accessories. Once in Kyiv, customs questioned us for carrying three computers and printers. After informing customs about Lingcomp, they wished us the best of luck and we proceeded without paying taxes. Once officials were told of our activities, they never harassed us, even when we were bringing items and copious amounts of U.S. dollars into the country.

Tatyana modelling her creative skills in 2014. Sales are as far away as Costa Rica, USA and Canada. Ukraine and Canada signed a free trade agreement in 2017 that should facilitate more sales to Canada.

In May 2000, my brilliant friend, David Salues from Miami, travelled to Ukraine with me. He easily assimilated into the Moisey family. He often explored on his own, not knowing a word of Ukrainian but managing to communicate with the aid of a translator. David was impressed with the sensitivity and artistic flair of young Tatyana Krasniuk. When he left, he gave Tatyana his camera. David, a five-year graduate from computer engineering and the owner of a few Miami Beach stores, always had the latest and best of equipment. David and I travelled with Ivan and Boris Vatrich to the Polish border, where David departed to tour neighboring countries. I continued with the brothers to Warsaw to meet Doreen and a few of our Edmonton Rotarian friends who were part of a Polish team organizing a "Rotary Projects Fair."

Boris's twelve-passenger van moved at maximum speed when it was not maneuvering around potholes. Ivan and Boris knew each pothole, as they crossed the border approximately twice a week with products and passengers. Within forty kilometers of the Polish border, trucks tended to bunch together in long lines. Ivan was constantly in the passing lane dodging oncoming traffic. Seldom did we encounter a passenger bus, and this was nine years post-Perebudova. The last ten kilometers before the border were crowded with trucks, stopping and starting, and moving at a snail's pace. Our van kept to the passing lane with many an oncoming vehicle dropping its wheel onto the road shoulder. This maneuvering continued to the front truck at the border gate. A quick squeeze to the right had us positioned to meet the border guard.

The guard smiled and greeted Ivan as if he was a best friend. He took some documents to the kiosk, where they were quickly processed and returned. Again, I noticed Ivan slip a roll of money to the guard. On a previous year's crossing, when Boris picked me up at the Warsaw airport, the truck traffic did not face a lineup as the Poles had an efficient border-crossing infrastructure. I also noted Boris greasing the guard's palm. Within the next two kilometers, Boris was waved down by Ukrainian so-called 'town police', whom he paid more money while exchanging friendly chitchat. These three stops were in view of each other.

Ivan said some policemen owned the biggest of houses. I told the brothers that bribes did not exist in Canada. They rolled their eyes at my naiveté about doing business. I never paid a bribe, even at the Thai-Malaysian train-crossing border, where Doreen and I were once detained. Many a bribe was requested, but we never gave in. My Miami Beach friend David, raised in Bolivia, was amused at my lecturing, as he understood this form of private taxation. A few years later, after several foiled Ukrainian government attempts to curb bribery at borders, one of the brothers was caught and could not escape, even with doubling down on his bribery offer. He was fined several more times the annual salary of a well-paid Ukraine employee.

At a Warsaw hotel, we were met by Doreen and two good Rotarian friends, Eunice Maris and Betty Screpnek. They arrived the day before, as we were to participate in a Rotary International Projects Fair in Kielce. These three energetic gals had no trouble in touring Warsaw, buying their favorite Glenfiddich scotch and unwinding after their trans-Atlantic flight. Immediately in one of the rooms, after drinks flowed and much laughter, we discussed a potential business initiative the Vatrich boys and I had previously explored. Betty spoke excellent Ukrainian, and with her proven business record, she quickly translated the issues. She winked at the boys without me seeing the wink and told them I was a nice guy and would gift them the container of paintbrush hair. I immediately interrupted and strenuously objected with a "no" "no". The boys broke out in uncontrollable laughter. Eunice, a successful entrepreneur, added clarification where needed. Basically, I would travel to China with the brothers and fund the purchase of a container of paintbrush pig hair for the brothers' paintbrush factory. They had large sales, within and outside Ukraine. An agreement was made, subject to the brothers' confirming details of the China visit. Drinks and laughter continued, and the boys left to attend to business.

Entrepreneurs 54-year-old Ivan Vatrich and 76-year-old author Zen Moisey; obviously related.

A few weeks later, Ivan Vatrich informed us that he did not need funding for the container of pig hair. Apparently, bypassing their friendly Polish supplier could potentially jeopardize some of the brothers' international sales. The brothers' sales were partially facilitated by the Polish supplier. Ivan is an astute businessman, like many I met in

Ukraine. His elderly mother, Paraska, (née Moisey, sister to Frozena), in my presence told the brothers to be careful of the Russian bear. She said the bear never gives up trying to control Ukraine. The brothers, with their Mercedes cars, hotel, bars and other businesses, almost rudely laughed off the threat. In 2017, we now see Russia's brutal aggression in Ukraine. The brothers continue to succeed, but they maintain a much lower profile. They must be heeding their mother's warning.

The next day after the brothers departed, Eunice, Betty, Doreen and I spent leisurely hours in central Warsaw. The area was a promenade, newly constructed after the bombing destruction of WWII. It was re-constructed from photos and salvaged documents. It was an uneasy feeling, visualizing the inhabitants as they were bombed. Snapping back to the warm sunny day under an umbrella, sipping from a frosted beer mug and watching the pedestrian parade created an incredible contrast of emotions. How lucky we were to be Canadian. We split up to go window shopping. Doreen fancied a flowered traditional Polish tea set, and some amber-studded, crystal liqueur glasses. Later, I explored a pawnshop looking for handmade glass beads.

On our travels, we always keep an eye open for the kind of beads my great-grandparents Wasylena and Stefan Moisey brought to Canada from Ukraine. The beads were handed down from past generations from either Wasylena or Stefan's family. A legend, often repeated by Wasylena Moisey to her grandchildren, told of a Moisey male youth taken to serve as a Turkish slave. The Turks also took many women. The boy, tall and strong, served in the Sultan's palace in a faraway land. He worked in the stables caring for the Sultan's horses. Many years later, after gaining favor with the Sultan for his skill as a horseman, he escaped with the finest horses and the beads. For many years he was hunted but would escape capture by crossing the Cheremosh River and living in the mountains.

These beads were handed down through the family, usually from female to female. In 2015, my uncle Arnold Moisey gifted one bead to Doreen. The remaining beads are with a few of my father's siblings. One bead was gifted back to Ukraine by my aunt Angie Brower. As a boy, sleeping with my grandmother Paraska, I noticed an ashtray of loose beads on her dresser. A Warsaw shop had a complete necklace of similar looking beads, which we purchased, that had belonged to a ninety-year-old Ukrainian woman.

One of the beads brought to Canada from Ukraine by Wasylena and Stefan in 1898. It is the only item of theirs know to exist.

As I explained in Chapter One, my DNA has a trace of Turkish ancestry. My four percent Middle Eastern genes probably were inherited in the era of the bead story. On visits to Ukraine, I met Turkish tourists who said they were comfortable in homes of elderly Ukrainians. They commented on the shrillness in traditional Ukrainian folk songs, somewhat like their own, the large wall and floor decorative rugs of Turkish design, and the down-to-earth welcome they received in the homes.

Rotary International

Rotary is an important part of my life. I joined the Rotary Club of Edmonton West in 1968. Rotary was founded in 1905 and is the oldest and largest NGO, operating in more than two hundred countries and regions, with 35,800 Rotary Clubs in more than five hundred defined geographical districts. Rotary Clubs, Districts and Rotary International elect a new president, executive and board of directors annually. Rotary does not get involved in political, religious or racial issues.

Each club strives to serve in the following five Avenues of Service: **1. Community Service**: provides benefits to its local community. **2. International Service**: works with a Club/s in another country or region to provide benefits, usually to a less-developed area. **3. Vocational Service**: usually occurs within the club's area. **4. Club Service**: involves weekly meetings to enhance fellowship to members and family. **5. Generational Service**: by nurturing youth, Rotarians help provide the skills young people need to succeed as future community leaders. Rotary is also based on a simple 4-Way Test: "The 4-Way Test of the things we think, say or do: Is it the **truth**? Is it **fair** to all concerned? Will it build **goodwill** and **better friendships**? Will it be **beneficial** to all concerned?"

My passion was and is International Service, and I so far have experience in more than one hundred self-sustaining projects; primarily in Central America. Rotary had two clubs (in Kyiv and Lviv) when I first arrived in Ukraine. Lviv's Rotary Club, had previously been disbanded by the Soviets in 1939. Thirty-eight Ukraine Rotary Clubs sprang to action by 2000 after the fall of the Soviet Union in 1991. Today there are more than 1.2 million active Rotarians worldwide. Today, there are forty-six Clubs in Rotary District 2330, which includes Belarus and Poland. To date, some Edmonton clubs have completed fourteen Ukraine International Projects.

I am especially proud of three projects done in partnerships with the Rotary Club of Ivano-Frankivsk, which was chartered in 1995. Rotarians Volodymyr Humennyk, Rostyslav Hul and Ihor Komar, along with Club secretary Natalia Ifonska, were the key contacts working with the Rotary Club of Edmonton West. The first project supplied eleven computers and accessories to the Ivano-Frankivsk School of Business. In the second project, we shipped a forty-foot container of clothing, bedding, sports equipment and school supplies to the Ukraine Internat School for homeless children. I visited the school, located in Yabluniv, before and after the container shipment. The first visit tugged at my emotions, bringing tears. The school operated without heat, and dreadful outdoor toilets were located across the street.

Ivano-Frankivsk Rotary Club members. The indespensible Natalia Ifonska stands between me and the Bishop. Great active Rotarians.

Rotary was essential for our Lingcomp, supplying

modern computers, modems and printers to thirty-five of the thirty-seven high schools in the Vyzhnytsia School District of Chernivtsi Oblast. Eddie Southern, representing the Government of Alberta, Canada, was present when the thirty-five school principals, many teachers and local mayors traveled from their towns to receive the equipment. A celebration was held in Vyzhnytsia, where the Rotary Club of Ivano-Frankivsk was well applauded. Rotary and Lingcomp's work in the Vyzhnytsia School Region, helped propel the region forward toward computer and English language skills, more than in the big cities of Ukraine. Hundreds of students are now working abroad because of these skills.

Rotary Project Fairs originated in Central America more than twenty years ago, with American and Canadian Rotarians meeting annually in rotating Central American countries to partner in Central America Community Projects called "Uniendo America." More than a thousand projects have been partnered. Doreen and I have been fortunate to attend eleven of these productive annual gatherings.

The first Rotary International "Projects Fair" for post-Soviet Union countries was held in Kielce, Poland, from May 5-7, 2000, and brought together Rotary participants from Belarus, Ukraine, Poland, Norway and Western Canada. Four clubs from Russia planning to attend did not appear. In 2017, dictator Putin banned Rotary Clubs in Russia; however, many Rotarians there remain active and some attend Rotary International's annual conferences. It is impossible to kill the idea of Rotary and its good works.

The Kielce Fair displayed community projects from Belarus, Ukraine and Polish Clubs that were seeking financial or material support, and partnered them with European and Western Canadian Rotary Clubs. The three-day event was extended to four days, and it was roll-up your sleeves, meet eye-to-eye, from morning to late night to make sustainable community projects a reality. Lasting friendships were forged. After two years, seventeen projects were partnered. Western Canadian Rotarians Eunice Maris, Betty Screpnek, Doreen Moisey and an angel from Poland, Rotarian Halina Stepien organized the Kielce Fair. Betty said, and I agree, that we "worked our butts off" to facilitate Rotary-partnered projects, touching and improving the lives of thousands.

Dr. Larysa Bondarenko from the Kherson, Ukraine Rotary Club traveled the longest distance (by train for two days) to attend. As the director of the city's abandoned-children's shelter accommodating 900 children, Larysa put her heart and soul into the hope of finding outside assistance. She gave up hope of receiving financial help from Kherson City and Oblast. The Soviet system had created havoc in her world. Only the rundown buildings, unpaid staff and volunteers with caring hearts provided for the children, mostly aged three to fifteen. Desperate folks dropped off boxes of babies on Larisa's doorstep. Many times, she said, "Rotary is the only hope for Ukraine."

Larysa's project was partnered with Norwegian and German Rotary Clubs. On the last night, before Larysa was to board her train, Doreen learned Larysa did not have money for a place to sleep. I slept on the couch while they shared the bed. We maintained contact with Larysa for a few years, and suddenly it ceased. She was physically rundown and in need of rest. Larisa is a true Mother Teresa. I feel blessed to have met her.

Philanthropy for Ukraine

Through my travels and philanthropic work, I slowly gained empathy for the hardships faced by my distant and current Ukraine families, from invading Tsars, dictators and today's mafia, led by tyrant Putin. Most in Ukraine and many of its Diaspora (twenty million resettled around the world) detest tyrant Putin, while respecting the good Russian people. Most of my life I was ignorant of the atrocities committed in Ukraine, and now in 2017, my disdain for Putin's repression in Crimea and bloody attacks in Eastern Ukraine are equal to that of most Ukrainians I have met worldwide. Instant digital communications constantly expose these inhumane atrocities.

Still, Ukraine and its people are resilient. Amazing results are propelling Ukraine toward becoming a star on the European stage, despite the bitter war with Putin. The youth of post-Perebudova have tasted democracy and Western lifestyles. Nothing will deny them achieving their dreams, not even old commies, now confined to their beds, if not their graves. Dinosaur Putin cannot win, and the youth know this. The Russian Federation pours money into spreading false information to gain Russians' support to maintain and expand Putin's clique of bandits who strive for self-enrichment. Many unhappy folks in the Russian Federation visualize Putin joining fellow dictator Gadhafi in a similar death. These two tyrants are among the most hated in the late 1900s and early 2000s.

Ukraine has again distinguished itself as a global food basket and is now the world's number one exporter of sunflower oil and number two in grain. Fields that were idle and weed-infested under the Soviet system are now productive. On our first visit in 1994, on two occasions, we witnessed a wife guiding a one-bottom plough, while her husband in front pulled like a horse to till a small plot in a vast weed-filled field. We watched in one inclined field where a couple carried the plough back to the top of the incline to ease their work by ploughing only downhill. Flashes of this type of back-breaking work that generations of my ancestors endured in both the Soviet and earlier foreign-controlled times keep appearing in my dreams.

On the legislative slate, in one year, beginning in December 2014, Ukraine adopted and drafted new laws that developed reform strategies in more than forty areas of national interest. All this occurred while tyrant Putin waged war on Ukraine soil. The Canadian government is at the forefront in assisting Ukraine. On any given day, there are more than 1,000 volunteer Canadians giving their time to advance Ukraine. Each of these Canadians has a story to tell, and hopefully, many of them will record their stories. The global Diaspora of Ukrainian people have greatly helped Ukraine to be resilient and bounce back from its hardships. The Ukrainian World Congress (UWC) for fifty years has advocated for Ukraine and keeps Ukraine on the international agenda. The UWC has national chapters, with the Ukrainian Canadian Congress being among the strongest of Ukraine's supporters.

Ukraine in 2017 is ready and ripe for philanthropy. Its social and legal infrastructures have advanced incredibly since post Perebudova to allow caring citizens to have their own Ukraine Charitable Foundation (UCF). Though they do not have one yet, a UCF would benefit its donors beyond any Ukrainian's wildest dreams. The UCF could possibly be based on a model I have known since its inception: the Edmonton Community Foundation (ECF), which is the fourth largest such foundation in Canada. There are a few examples of Ukraine already receiving benefits from Charitable Foundations like the ECF. The Rotary Foundation (TRF) and the ECF enabled the Yabluniv Internat School to upgrade, a Kherson orphanage to save lives and more than a hundred Ukrainian students to receive $300 scholarship grants. These are just a few examples; they and others have exposed Ukraine to the possibility of having its own Ukraine Charitable Foundations.

A UCF is simple to create. It requires Ukrainian donors and their funds to be secured, invested, and that a portion of the earnings must be distributed to those they deem in need. The balance of annual earnings is retained to increase the value of the fund. The fund grows forever, and its capital is never spent. This is how TRF and ECF operate. This proven knowledge is available for Ukraine. The secret to launching Ukraine's own UCF is to protect the donors' money. We all know a pot of honey attracts flies. The pot of Ukrainian money must be protected from flies. This is possible as proven by hundreds of existing foundations in other countries. Unfortunately, in 2017 Ukraine lacks sufficient laws and other infrastructure to protect a UCF's funds. Slowly but surely Ukraine is advancing this infrastructure to where it will one day be able to join the world of global foundations.

There exist various foundations in Ukraine, but none modeled on the ECF, which allows a multitude of persons and corporations to donate, protect and direct fund earnings to permitted beneficiaries of the donors' choosing. In my city of Edmonton, at the time Perebudova was occurring, the Edmonton Poole family donated $15,000,000, creating the ECF. In 2015, ECF granted $21,200,000 from earnings. In

2016, ECF was valued at $500,000,000. The Poole family was joined by thousands of Edmonton donors, including Doreen and me, to build this huge, successful foundation. This is the model Ukraine is ready to follow, but its legal and fiscal laws require substantial improvement for individual average Ukrainians to donate and to become true philanthropists.

Many worldly people understand the importance of philanthropy. Winston Churchill, once said, "We live to get; we make a life by what we give." My loving Baba Moisey, before she died, gave away the farm and a house she owned. She had no investments, living only from her large garden and a modest Canadian pension. She lived frugally and managed to save $9,000, which she gave away a year before she died to those she deemed most in need. All her life, she was a giver of love and excess material goods. Baba Moisey knew how to live and was loved by everyone.

Unfortunately, at this moment, time will not wait for good Ukrainians with a surplus of assets to give on a perpetual basis, as its laws will take another decade or so to protect their money. I earlier stated that "Ukraine in 2017 is ready for philanthropy" but the truth is that, at this time, any donation of money would quickly be contaminated or consumed by flies, just as would a pot of honey.

Fortunately, today any Ukrainian without the luxury of time can pass some of their assets in a philanthropic manner via existing proven foundations, as for example, "The Rotary Foundation (TRF)" with a more than one-hundred-year record of successful experiences. Please let me suggest how this can be done. Bill Gates spoke to 40,000 of us Rotarians at the Rotary International Conference in June 2017 in

Atlanta. After the Conference, I googled information on Bill and read his list of 169 names of wealthy people willing to make a pledge of one billion dollars to charity. To my surprise appeared the name of Viktor Pinchuk.

I met Viktor when he visited Edmonton with Ukraine's President Kuchma to address more than three hundred Canadians. They were seeking support for Ukraine and successfully found some support from dozens I knew in the room. Today, many more have joined in supporting Ukraine. I want to suggest to Viktor to form "The Pinchuk/Kuchma Rotary Endowment for Economic and Community Development in Ukraine" which would provide funds in perpetuity, leaving a worthy legacy to benefit his family, neighbors and Ukrainians. This is a simple way to honor Viktor's pledge to Bill Gates.

Doreen and I struggled over how we could follow in the footsteps of Baba Moisey, but on a sustainable basis. We were convinced that a charitable foundation was fundamental as we witnessed the useful work powered by them. For fifty years now, Doreen and I have been involved in more than one hundred hands-on community projects in Ukraine, Central America and other countries. We have gained much pleasure from this volunteer work and have been rewarded with international lifelong friends. We even have an adopted Guatemalan godchild (Amelia Coroy Chiz), who is like a daughter to us, who now has her own family, and a Malawi Minister of Justice (Samuel Tembenu) calling me Dad. We witnessed how small, uplifting gestures can be of immense help for folks to help themselves, and to live a better life. I am convinced foundations are essential for this to occur.

In late 2016, shortly after returning from Ukraine, our Rotarian friend Betty Screpnek invited Doreen and me to meet Rotarian Carolyn Ferguson. We told her of our failed effort to establish a fund for the needy in my ancestral homeland. We emphasized the fund must be secure and effective. Carolyn explained that this was possible. Before taking a second sip of dark rum and coke, I looked into Doreen's eyes and without a word between us, I saw that she accepted Carolyn's proposal. Carolyn explained that the Rotary Foundation's "Arch Klumpf Society" (AKS) has a special focus area, where one can donate to a country of choice. Incredibly, our donations' earnings would in perpetuity be designated to the country of our choice, Ukraine.

A donation to AKS is secured by the Rotary Foundation, as such donations have been for the last 100 years. Rotarians in Ukraine use the earnings of the endowment annually to benefit their community. Our donation of $250,000 US to AKS formed "The Doreen and Zen Moisey Rotary Endowment for Economic and Community Development in Ukraine." All profits from the sale of this book will be added to this fund. This means that Rotary Clubs in the Rotary District that have Ukraine Clubs will receive annual financial earnings in perpetuity.

Rotarians in approximately two hundred countries volunteer to make their community a better place to live. They commenced doing this in 1905, more than a century ago, and know their cities' and villagers' needs, and how to fulfill these needs. Like us, you can donate safely to aid a country of your choice, by contacting a Rotarian living close to you and explaining how Doreen and I used AKS. The contact information below will also be of assistance:

Carolyn Ferguson, Senior Major Gifts Officer, Zone 24
e-mail: Carolyn Ferguson Carolyn.Ferguson@rotary.org
You can also contact the author at Zen@incentre.net

Drilling for Oil in Ukraine
The best man at our wedding, engineering classmate Steve Benediktson, introduced me to Eddie Southern. Eddie and Steve planned to drill for oil in Ukraine. Both owned successful oil companies in Western Canada and Colombia. I invested in their Ukrainian company called Kroes Oil (Kroes is Steve's wife's maiden name). Eddie, with Darrel Zakreski, pioneered bringing Canada's oil industry know-how to the Lelyaki, Chernihiv Oblast oil field, via their investment in the Kashstan Petroleum Ukrainian-Joint Venture Company shortly after Perebudova. In 1994, Zhoda purchased UK-Ran Oil International Inc. On Jan 8, 2002,

Kroes Energy Inc. acquired Zhoda 2001 Corporation, which held a forty-five percent interest in Kashtan Petroleum. Zhoda's partner in Khastan was UkrNafta JSC, the Ukraine State Company. They spudded the first well on Jan 19, 2001, and hit oil on February 16 that year. Eddie claimed this was the first Canada-Ukraine Joint Venture, which I challenged, as Doreen and I had created Lingcomp, a Ukraine-Canada joint venture company in 1994 in Western Ukraine.

Doreen and I became good friends with Eddie. He was appointed the Alberta Consular to Ukraine. We spent a lot of time with Eddie in Kyiv and Vyzhnytsia, as well as during a visit to the Eastern Ukraine drilling site. Eddie and Doreen are active, devout Catholics and became close friends. We both liked Eddie's positive attitude, especially for Rotary projects in Ukraine, where we incorporated his skills and contacts to ensure Rotary community projects did not go awry.

Sketch of Eddie's Ukraine drill site that Doreen and I visited.

During Easter of 1996, Eddie organized a train tour to Crimea. A party of sixty, mostly Canadian oil-business folks, travelled from Kyiv to Yalta. Kroes Energy Inc. was well represented. Steve Benediktson and his wife Adriana were present. The group departed from Kyiv on former President Mikhail Gorbachev's private train, which was well appointed and cared for. They left on a Thursday and returned on Monday. Adriana enjoyed the tour, but commented that the standard of living in the countryside, particularly the housing, equipment, and general care of farmland and roadways, was primitive. People encountered were friendly and polite. She did not notice any malnourished children.

On June 8, 2004, after a few hours' drive from Kyiv, Doreen, Eddie, our chauffeur Victor and I arrived at the Lelyaki oil site, where a rig was noisily drilling within meters of anticipated pay dirt. We were presented with new, unpackaged hard hats and safety glasses, the first time ever such safety items had been used in the Lelyaki field by visitors and workmen. Doreen was the first woman ever allowed on the drill deck.

The drill rig's main structural members were made of heavy oak timbers, like the American and Eastern Canadian oil fields of the early 1900s. The tools, chains, and service equipment were well worn. Five on-site housing trailers shaped like loaves of bread had tiny windows and protruding wood stove chimneys. Eddie pointed with pride to the new well blowout preventer below the work deck. Eddie introduced the first workable blowout preventers used in the Lelyaki field. Many a life has been saved using blowout preventers. The Lelyaki field has been producing oil since the 1960s. Poorly managed, the field had previously suffered from water flooding, requiring experienced geological supervision to correct, which Eddie brought from Canada.

After scrambling by the crew, the large diesel engine with a faulty muffler was shut down. New boots, hard hats and safety glasses were adjusted. One of the crew helped Doreen with her hard hat. I noticed none of the workers wore steel-toed boots. We scrambled up the expanded-metal stairs to reach the muddy drill deck. A driller on each side of Doreen held an arm to guide her so she would not slip on the muddy area. The friendly crew were excited to show us assorted items on and around the deck. The now-silent diesel engine revealed that all its gauges were broken, except for one.

After a hot coffee with fresh cream, we drove to the regional oil office, where we sat at a bright, linoleum-covered worktable, loaded with typical Ukrainian food, large bottles of Coke, soda water and plenty of vodka. A dozen men, most dressed in suits, took chairs, and many a toast was made and song sung after lengthy introductions. We were presented with a hard-covered book on Bukovina, my ancestral Ukraine Oblast. It was presented with great fanfare and more toasts. I staggered up to receive the book signed by most present, including Chairman of the Board Ivan Kozar of Naftogaz, which is a joint stock company affiliated with Chernivtsigaz. The several hours of feasting came to an end as the sun set.

Kroes Oil had a forty-nine percent interest with the Ukrainian government-controlled Naftogaz Company. Eventually, interference by the Russian government-owned Gazprom Oil Company squeezed and removed Kroes Oil from Ukraine. We all lost money on this venture. Kroes had introduced the technology of multi-well pump jacks from a single platform. The oil was pumped from the platform to a pipe, with a meter to record production. Eddie showed us a concealed, valve T-section in the pipe before the meter. The unmetered oil belonged to the mafia and was transported by rail to refineries. Eddie considered the diverted oil as a tax and kept drilling.

We stayed with Eddie for a week in his comfortable Kyiv apartment, which was a leisurely walk from the rail transit system. The apartment window looked over a large khastan (chestnut) tree, under which elderly neighbors sat on park benches. Our week's tour of Kyiv, a city of four million, was enjoyable. Kyiv is a very cosmopolitan city. The former main headquarters of the Soviet Union in the central square was now crowned with a MacDonald's and other common Western signage.

When it was time to leave, Eddie drove us to the train station, where we departed for Poland. At the border near midnight, the rail car wheels were changed to fit the Poles' rail track dimensions. This was accomplished by women using heavy crowbars, winches and a turntable. It was a noisy process, but entertaining.

Money Extraction Schemes (Bribes)
Over the years, Doreen and I have encountered bribery schemes. When our Ukrainian Lingcomp School attendance peaked at 205 students, I received a message to come quickly from Canada, as there were problems: government officials were closing our school.

No students were at the school when I arrived. The fire inspector with some of his officials had visited the school. They claimed unspecified infractions with the fire code and instructed the teachers to immediately send students home and close the school. I received a message to contact the fire official, pay a fee and comply before the school could be reopened.

Word spread quickly of the school closing. Our students were children of priests, schoolteachers, government officials, business owners and other hardworking folks. Valentyn asked me what we should do. The decision was to inform everybody that the school would remain closed, as demanded by the fire official. I refused to meet the fire inspector. Immediately, community leaders brought pressure, contacted the fire inspector, and the school was reopened. No fee (bribe) was paid.

In 1998 we had also encountered a bribery scheme at the Lviv airport. Seven Canadian Moiseys and four from Romania went to Ukraine to celebrate the Moisey 100th anniversary of Wasylena, Stefan and their children leaving Ukraine. It was the first visit for my mother and a few others. I was at the back of the line at the immigration kiosk. Everybody cleared, and it was my turn. When asked to pay $15 for health emergency insurance, I declined.

An interpreter was found. He apparently was a representative from the insurance company. Again, I refused to pay, explaining I had international travel insurance and buying additional insurance was clearly not necessary. He introduced me to the chief immigration officer. I refused the chief's suggestion to pay. He was an excellent public relations person. By this time, everybody cleared customs, including my family members, who paid for the insurance. I was the center of attention, and everybody understood I was challenging a rip-off scheme.

My mother spoke up, scolding me to pay, as they were tired. My relative Valentyn (a young lawyer) was at the airport to meet us, and I yelled at him to come and help with the dispute. The chief of immigration agreed to our request to call the Canadian Consulate; unfortunately, the Lviv airport phones were not functioning. No other phones were nearby, so the chief agreed to let me go with his escort and Valentyn to find a phone outside the airport terminal, leaving our group to wait for my return. Finding a restaurant phone, Valentyn first called the insurance company, and nobody answered. We could not reach anybody at the Kyiv Canadian Consulate, so we returned to the airport about a half hour later. Doreen was anxiously waiting, and the airport control did not know whether we would be sent back to Warsaw, as threatened.

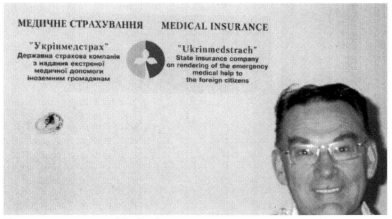

Airport non-existent Medical insurance.

My party was irate when I told them to go on without me, and that I would return to Warsaw. We informed the chief that no one answered when you called the so-called "medical emergency" phone number. The airport passengers cleared, and staff wanted to go home. Everyone was tired, including the chief. Eventually, I was cleared, without a clearance form. I then placed $15 in the hand of one of the cleaning ladies and asked her to share it with the other cleaners. On our return to Canada, Doreen wrote a letter to Ukraine Tourism explaining the issue. She received a nice reply, and on our next visit, we noticed the insurance sign and forms had gone. Later, we heard this was a scheme between someone in Canada and the Ukraine airport control officials.

My mother's relative's home north of Yabluniv, where she lived by herself, 1998. A strong minded, self-reliant loveing woman to all.

We experienced yet another money extraction scheme in Kyiv as Doreen and I leisurely strolled the area of St. Sophia. We were startled as two men in their thirties, very near to us, erupted in an argument after we saw one of them pick up a wad of American money. The man with the money attempted to put it in his pocket, but was prevented by the other. This man then spoke to us in English, stating "the money fell from our pocket". In Ukrainian he then continued arguing with the man to return the money to us. We said it

122

was not our money. The man insisted he saw it fall from my pocket and to check to be sure. As I reached to check my pocket, Doreen yelled "scam, do not show them your money". Doreen was correct as she knew the scheme from an article she had previously read. If we had shown our money they were in an excellent position to simply grab it. We also witnessed, what we were later told were gypsy children causing distractions at a church, and at the crowded Kyiv railroad station begging and apparently attempting to pick people's pockets.

Fewer Ukraine politicians are partaking in bribes in 2017 compared to before Maidan in 2014. The folks spoke, many giving their lives to clean up political corruption. The same cannot be said for Russia, where corruption runs rampant. I, as most folks, wonder how Putin earned forty to two hundred billion (estimated by *Forbes Magazine*) on his government pay cheque.

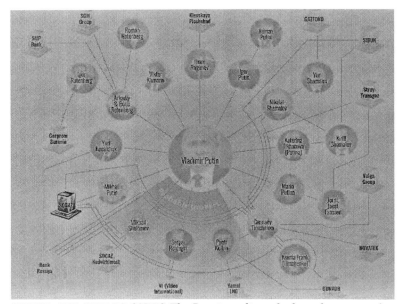

PUTIN AND THE PROXIES The Russian oligarchs have been tamed since Vladimir Putin's arrival to the presidency. The longtime leader has struck a mutually beneficial bargain: Leave the politics to me, chip in when I need you to -- and you can keep, and even grow, your wealth is reported by OCCRP and its long-time partner Novaya Gazeta when they went digging to find out more -- and pieced together the assets of some of President Putin's friends, family, and inner circle. The Novaya Gazeta and OCCRP investigation looked into the wealth surrounding Russian President Vladimir Putin; October 24 2017. The Organized Crime and Corruption Reporting Project (OCCRP) is a global network of investigative journalists; who are an investigative reporting platform formed by 40 non-profit investigative centers, scores of journalists and several major regional news organizations around the globe. Their network is spread across Europe, Africa, Asia and Latin America and teamed up in 2006 to do transnational investigative reporting and promote technology-based approaches to exposing organized crime and corruption worldwide. For additional investigative reporting view https://www.occrp.org/en/putinandtheproxies/

Putin Slips Yanukovych $3 Billion

A $3 billion Eurobond issued by Russia to Ukraine entered the pocket of Ukraine's President Viktor Yanukovych in December 2013 and was due for repayment on December

20, 2015. The Atlantic Council Senior Fellow A. Aslund writes:

"Ukraine has no reason to pay [Russia]. In February 2014, the Kremlin launched military aggression against Ukraine, first annexing Crimea and later pursuing military subversion in southern and eastern Ukraine. For more than a year, Russian-commanded troops with a mixture of volunteers and regular Russian soldiers have occupied three percent of Ukraine's easternmost territories. Moscow's war has caused major damage to Ukraine. [...] Ukraine has no reason to pay such an aggressor; in fact, Russia ought to pay reparations to Ukraine. Putin negotiated this deal personally with former President Yanukovych to provide him with a lifeline. It was never meant to benefit the Ukrainian nation.

The only reason for Ukraine to pay is that it could run the risk of not receiving further funding from the IMF, which is vital for Ukraine's financial sustenance. The IMF has an old practice of not lending to a country in arrears to a sovereign, but that practice should not be applied in this case. [...] The IMF is about to change its practice of not lending into arrears. This is easily done. The IMF Executive Board can decide to change this policy with a simple board majority. The IMF has lent to Afghanistan, Georgia, and Iraq in the midst of war, and Russia has no veto right, holding only 2.39 percent of the votes in the IMF. When the IMF has lent to Georgia and Ukraine, the other members of its Executive Board have overruled Russia. [...] Russia's intransigence has convinced a board majority that the rules must change fast. After that, Russia's argument that the IMF should not pay Ukraine loses validity.

The full article is available at:
www.atlanticcouncil.org/blogs/new-atlanticist/ukraine-must-not-pay-russia

CHAPTER 5

Russian Myth

Great Russia and Russian Myth

Russia has falsified many historical events including the story of its origin, and today advances a false history to bully its neighbors. It is a house of cards built on a faulty foundation that will collapse again from within, just as happened during Perestroika in the 1980s and early 1990s. Ukraine is one neighbouring country, among others, that works to expose these historical falsifications.

The following italicized section has been taken from the prominent Ukrainian historian Yaroslav Dashkevych's essay How Moscow Hijacked the History of Kievan Rus first published in 2011 and then on the Internet by the Euromaidan Press in 2014.

In creating their nation, Ukrainians need to examine and analyze their own history, based on truth, verified facts and historical events. For centuries under the rule of conquerors, Ukrainians were basically deprived of the opportunity to influence the formation of national awareness and the development of their history, with the result that Ukraine's history was composed predominantly to the advantage of their conquerors. Especially troublesome is the question of the pretensions and demands of Moscow, and later Russia, concerning the historical legacy of Kievan Rus.

In his historical work "The Land of Moksel or Moskovia" (Olena Teliha Publishing House, Kyiv 2008, 2009, 3 vol.) Volodymyr Bilinsky presents historical sources (predominantly Russian) that testify to the total misrepresentation of the history of the Russian Empire, which was geared to create a historical mythology about Moscow and Kievan Rus sharing common historical roots, and that Moscow possesses "succession rights" to Kievan Rus.

Moscow's outright fraud that appropriated the past of the Great Kyiv kingdom and its people dealt a severe blow to the Ukrainian ethos. Our obligation now is to utilize hard facts to uncover the lies and amorality of Moskovian mythology.

Let's examine these problems.

The tsars of Moscow and, later, Russia understood that without an imposing past it was impossible to create a great nation and empire. Therefore, it was necessary to glorify their historical roots and even to hijack the history of other nations. So, starting with Ivan the Terrible (1533-1584), the tsars of Moscow applied all their efforts to appropriate the history of Kievan Rus and its glorious past, and to create an official mythology for the Russian Empire.

This might have been less consequential if their mythology had not affected the central concerns of Ukraine and if it had not aimed at the utter destruction of Ukraine: its history, language and culture. Over time, it became clear that Russian Imperial chauvinists did and continue to do everything possible to realize this aim.

Over hundreds of years, and especially starting with the early sixteenth century, they brainwashed and continue to brainwash everyone, saying that the origins of the Russian nation and people are the Great Kievan kingdom. They assert that Kievan Rus was the cradle of three sibling nations — Russians, Ukrainians and Belarusians — and that because the Russians are "older brothers," they have the right to the legacy of Kievan Rus. To this day, Russian historians and officials make use of this woeful lie, which is repeated by the 'fifth column' of communists and almost all Party of Regions deputies in [the Ukrainian] Parliament.

The 9th century ethno-linguistic map of Eastern Europe

debunks the myth of "Three Brotherly Nations" — in the place of modern Moscow, non-Slavic tribes resided, while the territory of Ukraine and Belarus were inhabited by Slavic (Slavonic) peoples.

Here are the facts:

At the time of the Kievan Empire, there was no mention of a Moscow nation. It is well known that Moscow was created in 1277 as a subservient vassal region or 'ulus' to the Golden Horde, established by the Khan Mengu-Timur. By that time, Kievan Rus had existed for more than 300 years.

There are no indications of any connection of Kievan Rus with the Finnish ethnic groups in the land of 'Moksel' or later of the Moscow principality with the Principality of Kievan Rus up until the sixteenth century. At the time when Kievan Rus had officially accepted Christianity, the Finn tribes in 'Moksel' lived in a semi-primitive state.

How can anyone speak of 'an older brother' when that 'older brother' did not first appear until centuries after Rus-Ukrainians? He has no moral right to call himself an 'older brother,' nor to dictate how people are to live, nor to force his culture, language, and worldviews. It is clear that until the end of the fifteenth century, there was no Russian nation, there was no older brother 'Great Russian,' nor were there any Russian people. Instead, there was the land of Suzdal: the land of Moksel, later the Moscow princedom, which entered the role of the Golden Horde, the nation of Genghis Khan. From the end of the thirteenth to the beginning of the eighteenth century, the people in this land were called Moskovites. And Moscow historians are silent about this question of their national origins.

Moskovites, 'Great Russians' – who are they?

During the ninth to the twelfth centuries, the large area of Tula, Ryazan, and today's Moscow region— all this was inhabited by the people called 'Moksel,' including the tribes of Muromians, Merya, Vepsians, Mokshas, Chudes, Maris and others. These tribes eventually became the foundation of the nation who now call themselves 'Great Russians.'

In 1137, the sixth son of the Kievan prince Volodymyr Monomakh, Yurii Dolgorukii (who had been left without a princedom in the Kievan empire) arrived in this land.

Yurii Dolgorukii began the rule of the 'Riurykovyches' in 'Moksel', becoming prince of Suzdal. To him and a local Finnish woman was born a son Andrei, called 'Bogoliubskii.' Born and raised in the forest wilderness among the half-savage Finnish tribes, prince Andrei cut all ties with his father's entourage and with their old Kievan customs.

In 1169, Andrei Bogoliubskii sacked and destroyed Kyiv. He destroyed all the churches and religious artifacts, something unheard of in those times. Andrei was a barbarian who did not feel any familial ties with Kyiv, the holy city of Slavs.

Within a brief time (50-80 years), every Finnish tribe was imposed with a prince of the Riurykovyches, whose mother was either a woman of Mer, Murom or Kokshan... Thus, appeared the 'Moksel' princedoms: Vladimir, Ryazan, Tver, and others. At this time, some missionaries appeared in the land of Moksel to spread Christianity. It is impossible to consider a mass 'migration' of Slavs from the Dnipro river region, as Russian historians insist. Why should the Slavs leave behind their fertile Dnipro lands and relocate more than a thousand kilometers through impassable undergrowth and swamps into an unknown semi-savage land?

Under the influence of Christianity, the land of 'Moksel' started to form their language, which in time became Russian.

Up until the twelfth century, only Finn tribes lived in the land of 'Moksel.' The archaeological findings of O.S. Uvarova *(Merya And Their Everyday Life from Kurgan Excavations, 1872 – p. 215)* support this. Out of 7,729 excavated kurgans, not a single Slavic burial was discovered.

And the anthropological investigations of human skulls by A.P. Bohdanov and F.K. Vovk support the differentiated characteristics of the Finnish and Slavic ethnoses.

In 1237, the Tatar-Mongols entered the lands of Suzdal. All who bowed, kissed the boots of the Khan and accepted subservience remained alive and unharmed; all others who did not submit were destroyed.

The princes of Vladimir, Yurii and Yaroslav Vsevolodovich accepted subservience to Khan Batey. In this manner, the land of 'Moksel' entered the ranks of the Golden Horde Empire of Genghis Khan, and its fighting forces were combined with the army of the Empire. The commander of the Moksel division within Batey's army was Yurii Vsevolodovich, the prince of the city of Vladimir. In 1238, Finnish tribe divisions were formed and marched together under Batey in his invasions of Europe in 1240-1242. This is direct evidence of the establishment of the rule of the Khan in the lands of Rostov-Suzdal.

While Yurii Vsevolodovich was away taking part in Batey's European invasion, his younger brother Yaroslav Vsevolodovich was placed at the head of the Vladimir princedom. Yaroslav left his eight-year-old son Alexander Yaroslavich as hostage with the Khan.

Living with the Horde of Batey from 1238 to 1252, Alexander, only much later named "Nevsky," adopted all the customs and organizational ideas of the Golden Horde. He became a blood brother of Sartak, the son of the Khan, married the Khan's daughter, and eventually became a loyal vassal of the Golden Horde and prince of Vladimir from 1252 to 1263. He never took part in any significant battles — all the 'victories' of

Alexander Nevsky are transparent lies. Prince Alexander simply could never have taken part in the battles on the Neva in 1240 and on Chud or Peipus Lake in 1242 (fantasized in Eisenstein's film) because he was still a child.

It is important to mention that the ruling powers of the local princes of Rostov-Suzdal were minimal. Khan Batey installed his own administrators in all the "ulus" princedoms: on top was the Great Baskak, and under him were the regional administrative baskaks. These were full-fledged rulers from the Golden Horde, who followed the laws of the Genghis Khans. Russian historians are lying when they state that the princes of Suzdal, and later Moscow, were independent from the Golden Horde. The Khan's covenant named the primary rulers of the princedoms his baskak, or 'daruha,' while the local princes were relegated to second and even third- place importance.

The big lie was introduced: that Moscow was founded in 1147 by Yuri Dolgoruky. This is a myth with no supportive evidence. Moscow was established as a settlement in 1272. That same year, the Golden Horde conducted their third census of the populations in their domain. Both in the first census (1237-1238) and in the second census (1254-1259), there is no mention of any Moscow at all.

Moscow appeared as a princedom in 1277 at the decree of the Tatar-Mongol Khan Mengu-Timur, and it was an ordinary 'ulus' (subdivision) of the Golden Horde. The first Moscow prince was Danila (1277-1303), younger son of Alexander so-called "Nevsky." The Riurykovych dynasty of Moscow princes starts from him. In 1319 Khan Uzbek (as stated in the aforementioned work by Bilinsky) named his brother Kulkhan the virtual Prince of Moscow, and in 1328 the Great Prince of Moscow. Khan Uzbek (named in Russian history as Kalita), after he converted to Islam, destroyed almost all the Riurykovych princes. In 1319-1328, the Riurykovych dynasty was replaced by the Genghis dynasty in the Moscow 'ulus' of the Golden Horde. Only in 1598 this Genghis dynasty in Moscow, which began with Prince Ivan Kalita (Kulkhan), was finally broken. Thus, for over 270 years, Moscow was ruled solely by khans of the Genghis dynasty.

Still, the new dynasty of the Romanovs (Kobyla) promised to follow former traditions and solemnly swore allegiance to the age-old dynasty of Genghis.

In 1613 the Moscow Orthodox Church became the stabilizing force to safeguard the sustainment of Tatar-Mongol government in Moscow, offering masses for the Khan, and issuing anathemas on anyone who opposed this servitude.

Based on these facts, it becomes clear that Moscow is the direct inheritor of the Golden Horde Empire of Genghis and that actually the Tatar-Mongols were the 'godfathers' of Moscow statehood. The Moscow princedom (and tsardom from 1547) up until the sixteenth century had no ties or relationships with the princedoms of the lands of Kievan Rus.

Great Russians

The tribe of Great Russians, or the Russian people as known today, appeared around the fifteenth to seventeenth centuries from among the Finn tribes: Muroma, Mer, Ves and others. This was when their history started. There is no history of Great Russians on Kievan lands!

The history of Great Russians starts with the 'Beyond the Forests Land' in Moscow, which was never Kievan Rus. The Tatar-Mongols who entered these lands were a big element in the formulation of 'Great Russians.' The Great Russian psychology absorbed many characteristics — the Tatar-Mongol instincts of a conqueror and despot, with the aim: world domination.

Thus, by the sixteenth century was established the type of a conqueror who was horrible in his lack of education, rage and cruelty. These people had no use for European culture and literacy. All such things like morality, honesty, shame, justice, human dignity and historical awareness were absolutely foreign to them. A significant amount of Tatar-Mongols entered the makeup of Great Russians from the thirteenth to sixteenth centuries, and they accounted for the genealogy of over 25% of Russian nobility. Here are some names of Tatar/Turkic origin that brought fame to the Russian Empire: Arakcheev, Bunin, Chaadayev, Derzhavin, Karamzin, Kuprin, Plekhanov, Saltykov-Shchedrin, Tiutchev, Turgenev, Sheremetiev, and many others.

To appropriate the history of Kyiv lands and to immortalize this theft, the Great Russians had to squash the Ukrainian people, drive them into slavery, deprive them of their true name, exterminate them via famine, etc.

Ukrainians had emerged as a nation in the 11th to 12th centuries, and probably, even earlier. Later they were labeled 'Little Russians' when Russians began to brainwash the world with their 'version' of history. For the smallest deviation from this official version, people were tortured, killed, and sent off to the GULAG. The Soviet period was especially brutal and vicious. During that time, Ukraine lost over 25 million of her sons and daughters, who perished in wars for Russian interests, and during collectivization, tortures, and forced relocations.

This is the way the 'older brother' forced the 'younger brother,' the 'Little Russian,' to live in the savage 'embraces of love.'

Creation of the Historical Myth of the Russian State

Back in the times of the princedom of Vasyli III (1505–1533) Moscow gave birth to the idea of its greatness, articulated by the representative of Moscow orthodoxy, the monk Filofey: "Two Romes fell, a third still stands, and there will never be a fourth."

From there, they created the idea of an all-powerful and 'God-chosen' Moscow – the 'third – and final Rome'. These ideas spread and were confirmed throughout Moskovia. And how much blood was spilt by the princes of Moscow, and later the tsars, over this fantasy-myth!

During the reign of Ivan IV (the Terrible), they grasped not only after the inheritance of Kievan Rus, but now also the Byzantine Empire. Thus, according to accounts, the "Monomakh's Cap" was believed to have been given the Kievan prince Volodymyr Monomakh by his granddad, the basileus Constantine IX.

This was considered the symbol of the transfer of power from Byzantium to Kievan Rus. In addition, Yuri Dolgorukii, the sixth son of Volodymyr Monomakh, was the first prince of Suzdal, so the appearance of this cap in Moscow was a 'proof' of the legacy legitimacy of the Moscow rulers not only to the Kyiv Great Throne, but now also to the inheritance of the former Byzantine Empire. Furthermore, Moscow fabricated a deceptive last will of Volodymyr Monomakh about handing over 'legacy rights' to his son Yuri Dolgorukii, the conqueror of the so-called 'Beyond the Forests Land.' This was all fiction. In reality, "Monomakh's Cap" was a gold 'Bukhara tubeteika,' which Khan Uzbek presented to Ivan Kalyta (1319-1340), who maintained this cap in order to further his fame. (Логвин Ю. Кобила, Калита і тюбетейка «Мономаха» // Час. – Київ, 1997, 27 березня).

Ivan IV (the Terrible) in 1547 was anointed in the cathedral with the title of 'Moscow Tsar' as the 'inheritor' of the Greek and Roman emperors. Of the 39 signatures who affirmed this document sent from Constantinople, 35 were forgeries. Thus, Ivan the Terrible became the 'inheritor of the Byzantine emperors.' Thus, the lie was made official.

Peter I began the massive falsification of his people's history. In 1701 he issued a decree to eliminate from all subjugated peoples all their recorded national historical artifacts: ancient chronicles, chronographs, old archives, church documents, etc. This was especially directed at Ukraine-Rus.

In 1716, Peter I 'changed the copy' of the so-called Königsberg Chronicles to now show the 'joining' of the old chronicles of the Kievan with the Moscow princedoms. The aim was to lay a foundation for the unity of Slavic and Finnish lands. However, both the false 'copy' and the original were sealed.

Peter's falsification became the basis for further falsifications – the composition of the so-called 'General Rus Chronicles Collections' which purported to establish Moscow's rights to the legacy of Kievan Rus. Based on these falsifications, on October 22, 1721, Moscow proclaimed itself the Russian Empire, and all Moskovites were now to be – Russians. In this manner, they stole from the legitimate inheritors of Kievan Rus, the Ukrainians, [the] historical name of Rus.

Peter imported from Europe many specialists, including professional historians, who were assigned the rewriting and falsification of the history of the Russian state.

In addition, every foreigner who entered government work, swore an oath not to reveal state secrets and to never betray the Moscow state. The question remains, what government secrets regarding the 'formation of Russian history' of ancient times could there be? In any civilized European country, after 30-50 years all archives are opened. The Russian Empire is very afraid about the truth in its past. Deathly afraid!

Following Peter I, who transformed Moscow into the Russian state, the Moscow elite began to consider the necessity of creating a comprehensive history of their own country. Empress Catherine II (1762-1796) intensively took on this task.

She could not admit the idea that common Tatar-Mongol elements existed in the dynasty of the Tsars. Catherine was an intelligent and educated European woman and once she had examined the archival sources, she called attention to the fact that all the history of her country was based on oral traditions ('byliny') and had no factual support.

Therefore, on December 4, 1783, Catherine II issued a decree, creating a 'Commission for the Collection and Organization of the Ancient Russian History' under the leadership and oversight of Count A. P. Shuvalov, with a staff of 10 historians. The principal task before this commission was to 'find' new chronicles, rewrite others, and create new collections of archives and other similar falsifications. The aim was to lay the foundations for the 'legitimacy' of Moscow's hijacking of the historical legacy of Kievan Rus and to create an official historical myth about the origins of the Russian state. This commission labored for ten years. In 1792, 'Catherine's History' saw the light of day. The commission worked in the following manner:

– The gathering of all written documents (archives, chronicles, etc.). This effort had partly begun under Peter I. This collection of materials was conducted not only within the Empire, but also from other countries like Poland, Turkey etc.

– The analysis, falsification, rewritings or destruction of historical materials. Thus, they rewrote the chronicles: 'The Tale of Ihor's Campaign', 'Tale of Bygone Years', 'Lavrentiivsky Chronicles', and many others. Many chronicles were rewritten several times, and the originals were either

locked up or destroyed. Thus, were also locked up: the 'History of the Scythians' by A. I. Lyzlov (published in 1776 and 1787), and the 'Russian History from Ancient Times' by V. M. Tatishchev (published in 1747). In his 'Scythian History' Lyzlov showed that the inhabitants of Moscow were a separate people, who had nothing in common with Kievan Rus, Lithuania, Poland, etc.

– The writing of new 'Rus Chronicles Collections' which were now being composed in the eighteenth century, but purported to be from the eleventh to the fourteenth centuries. These collections all propagated the 'General Rus' idea. This was in reference to the times when Kievan lands were inhabited by Slavic tribes (the Polans, the Drevlians, the Severians, and others) who were Christians, while the 'Beyond the Forests Land' was populated by Finn tribes (the Muromians, the Merya, the Vepsians, the Mokshas, and others) who lived a semi-primitive existence, and these tribes had nothing historical in common up to the sixteenth century.

– The new composition of thousands of various collections to establish the 'unity' of Kievan Rus with the Finn tribes. All these chronicles and collections, according to author Bilinsky, exist only in the form of copies, not one original. Not one! All this points to the almost unbelievable in scope and shameless, massive plundering and falsification of the creation of the history of the Russian state.

It is impossible to live a lie forever!

It is time for Ukrainian historians to write the actual true history of Ukraine, which would not be based on the lies of the 'Catherine's Chronicles', the falsifications and newly written in the eighteenth century 'General Russian Chronicle Collections', but rather based on historical reality, established in documents, especially those preserved in countries like Poland, Turkey, Greece, Iran and others. People deserve to know the truth.

Ukraine Declares Independence 1917

The website of Ukraine's Ministry of Foreign Affairs contains the following description of Ukraine during World War I.

For the first time in the twentieth century, Ukraine declared independence declared independence during the First World War. In 1917, the Ukrainian Central Rada was formed in Kyiv, who played the role of a transitional government and declared the creation of the Ukrainian National Republic (UNR).

After the declaration of four fundamental constitutional decrees – Universals – the UNR, as an independent state, instigated diplomatic contacts with England and France along with Germany and their allies.

The Ukrainian revolution began earlier than other countries of this region: in Lithuania, Estonia, Czechoslovakia, Poland, Latvia and the Balkans.

In December 1917, after the Kharkiv puppet government was formed and the Bolsheviks proclaimed a "Soviet Ukraine", the Russian Bolsheviks unleashed war against Ukraine.

The fight against the Bolsheviks continued until 1921. This war and other conflicts exhausted Ukraine and it lost its independence.

The worst of times then began for one of the great European nations. The mass deportations, the Holodomor and the Great Terror claimed millions of lives during this "peaceful" interwar period.

The website can be viewed at: mfa.gov.ua/en/news-feeds/foreign-offices-news/56936-ukrajina-u-drugij-svitovij-vijni (Also, for more information about Ukraine during WWI, see Appendix 9, page 264).

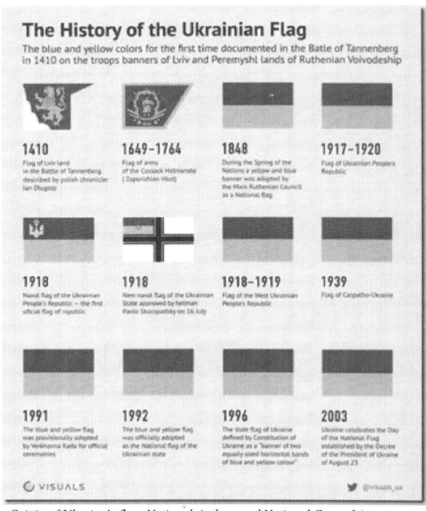

Origin of Ukraine's flag. National Anthem and National Coat of Arms.

1915 Ukraine Heroine Olena (Yarema) Kuz, my great grandmother's niece from Banyliv, my third cousin.

Mount Makivka and my Heroine Third Cousin

One example of many sparks of independence occurred in my ancestral village of Banyliv in 1913, when my great-grandmother's niece Olena (Yarema) Kuz, aged nineteen, was faced with a tragic dilemma. Her father Tanase was falsely accused of collaborating with the Russians and placed in the notorious internment camp of Taleroff in southeast Austria, where eventually he was tried, found innocent, released, but soon died of typhus. Yarema, one of six siblings, left the University of Chernivtsi as a graduate of teaching. She was active in the sweeping nationalism at universities in Western Ukraine and was motivated to avenge the death of her loving father. She then volunteered to enroll with the Ukraine Sich Riflemen Sharp Shooters, Calvary division, after taking sharpshooter training in Vienna. She was in many battles against the invading Russian tsar during 1914 to 1916, where she became a heroine at the Carpathian Mountain, Mount Makivka.

Before WWl, 250,000 Ukrainian volunteers and conscripts were recruited into the Austrian army, who were the occupiers in Western Ukraine. The Ukrainians detested the Russians, who were also present, more than they did the Austrians. Under pressure, the Austrians allowed one group of 2,500 Ukrainians to function independently of the Austrian army commanders. This was a first. This independent Ukrainian division immediately attacked the strongholds of the invading Russian tsar. The Austrian army of 250,000 Ukrainians fought under Austrian command.

The Austrians did not trust the large force of Ukrainians to be as independent as the 2,500 Ukraine Sich Riflemen, thirty of whom were women. One of these women was my third cousin, Olena (Yarema) Kuz. She, with eight Sich Riflemen at night removed the last of the tsar's machine gun nests from the top of famous Mount Makivka. The Mount Makivka battle was the first major battle to push the Russian tsar's army east.

I first learned about heroine Olena (Yarema) Kuz in September 2014, when a bronze bust of her was ready for installation at the Banyliv high school. I was being honored, along with the Krasniuks, for our contributions to many community projects.

When Doreen and I first went to Ukraine, we never saw a Ukraine flag, except for ones we packed from Canada. No sign of nationalism showed its face publicly; however, most Bukovina homes had shed the Lenin busts, photos and other Soviet memorabilia. People were afraid to speak out as the local commie leaders still had some powers.

In September 2014, a few months after the height of Russia's surprise annexation of Ukraine's Crimea and killings in Eastern Ukraine, the country awoke from its slumber. At the Banyliv school reception, I experienced an incredible hyper-wave of nationalism, which was evident throughout Ukraine. My translator's six-year-old son asked his mom to buy him a gun, so he could kill Putin. At the school ceremony, a grade-one student also declared to the audience that he would kill Putin. Clearly, Putin's aggressive acts in Ukraine were felt by the children, creating a new generation of Ukrainian nationalists.

Putin caught Ukraine sleeping in 2014 when he annexed Crimea and committed other criminal bloody acts in Donbas. This was the required fuel to flare Ukrainian nationalism to a fever pitch. The bridges, flagpoles, buildings and many vehicles now match the colour of their beloved flag. Flags are flying everywhere.

After the school reception, my translator Oksana, Tatyana and I were led by Mayor Andryuk to his office, located next to the school, to learn more about the bronze bust of the heroine, which would be erected once funds were acquired. Tatyana and I gave the mayor money to purchase the necessary cement, aggregate and rebar to construct the base for the bust. I could not control my curiosity and began gathering information about Yarema from publications, family members and neighbors.

In 2016, translator Ohla Sokivka, Tatyana and I hiked to the top of Mount Makivka. I carefully studied the mountain and visualized how Yarema would have led a surprise attack on this strategic fortification. Following is my re-creation of events at Mount Makivka:

Six p.m., April 27, 1915: Yarema stamped out her cigarette and with her eight companions carefully inspected their heavy backpacks for the last time. Grenades wrapped in cloth, a loaf of bread, cheese and sausage were packed to prevent shifting of the backpack on the steep slope. Water canisters were full and placed into a side pocket of each backpack.

From nearby tree branches the holstered revolver belts, fully loaded, were strapped to the youngsters' powerful bodies. All were in their teens or early twenties. As darkness set in, the nine companions draped hemp climbing rope over their shoulders and picked up their sturdy walking stick; waving a slight goodbye to the remaining Sich Riflemen of the Korsaka division, they set off for the base of Mount Makivka, approximately three kilometers distance to directly below the Russian machine gun emplacements. They skirted the forested edge of a few small hayfields. Olena (Yarema) Kuz and her carefully selected group darkened their army attire and faces, as well as shedding the army boots for the comfort and quietness of traditional Banyliv soft, forest-footwear.

The troop, led by Yarema, moved silently while all of Ukraine slept. The climb would take two nights. On the first night, the moon slowly began its ascent at six p.m. and near midnight it partially bleached a section of the Milky Way and prominent stars that could be plucked from the heavens.

Tall, mature pine trees on steep slopes provided perfect shadowing to move upslope. Not a word was whispered, and the occasional hand signal was given. On the forested slope, Yarema was in her element, having been raised near her grandmother Kuz's home on the wilderness at the northwest edge of Banyliv, a short walk from the Cheremosh River and its flooded backwaters.

At twilight on the first leg of the climb, the sweating, exhausted group concealed their tired bodies sheltered by a rock outcrop, quickly falling asleep. They were aroused by traces of afternoon sunrays, flickering over their faces. All remained in their sleeping area, shifting occasionally to be more comfortable, while munching food from their backpacks. They took a sip of water, and most dozed off to sleep again, as they knew the most important short climb was approaching to reach the occupied strategic summit, which Yarema had previously scouted a bit higher up from the rock outcrop.

The second night under moonlight they carefully climbed the un-scouted area to the area that was well marked from previous gunfire at the strategic pass. The moon would set at four a.m., and all were positioned within meters of the machine gun emplacements. The first grenade was tossed into a gun nest, and within seconds eight other explosions erupted. Less than a minute later, dozens of grenades exploded, and the occasional revolver shot rang out echoing into the forest. Pandemonium broke out on the site with gunfire and shouting.

Yarema and her men hastily scrambled downslope as daybreak was on the horizon. They quickly reached their secured ropes to rapidly pass steep areas to arrive at base camp in the late morning. They destroyed sufficient machine gun nests, which quickly saw the Russians fleeing Mount Makivka with the Ukrainian Independent Sich Riflemen, Korsika division, leading the pursuit. The Austrian-led army occupying Mount Malika's northwest and central peaks quickly joined in. This occurred between April 29 and May 4 in 1915, which began the removal of the last Russian Tsar from Ukraine.

Yarema later received a wound while pursuing the fleeing Russians to their eastern front line. Accompanied with a fellow soldier, on horseback, they rode to her Banyliv grandmother's house, where she recuperated for a month and then returned to push the Russian line farther east. She then learned from a woman that a top Russian general was hiding in a neighboring house, where with a pistol, singlehandedly, she captured him. This event was subsequently published in many newspapers.

In August 1915, intrepid Yarema's luck ran out. At the Golden Lipo battle at the Golden Oak River mouth, located within Tlumach, Ivano-Frankivsk region, splinter grenades hit Olena's left side and broke her ribs. She fell from her horse and lay unconscious for eight hours, was moved to Budapest for surgery, and in autumn, she was transferred to the Queen Elizabeth Hospital in Vienna for Sich Riflemen of the Makivka battle. She then recuperated in the famous villa of Mrs. Spat after being treated by Dr. Kaiser Kervats, the Emperor's physician, who was interested in the fate of the brave Bukovinka.

The reporter for the regional news weekly "Union of Liberation of Ukraine" later wrote in 1915 on the fate of Yarema Kuz, stating she daily corresponded with her "Kobylyanskaya" sister. The injured Yarema's dream was to return to fight as soon as possible.

Olena (Yarema) Kuz's sister Wasylena often corresponded with her, and then they moved together, and lived together in Vienna. Family descendants said they stayed in Vienna, and Yarema was employed giving French lessons.

First two images are of Countess Olena Kuz, whom Austria twice awarded medals for bravery. The brave Bukovinka, from a simple family, to be called Countess; such a great honour. The third image is Zen's great grandmother Wasylena, who is also the aunt of Countess Olena (Yarema) Kuz.

Vladimir Staruk photographed Olena (Yarema) Kuz, and submitted his photo to the American Press Association, which then appeared in several newspapers on January 24, 1916. Vladimir Staruk reported in 1917, "Olena demobilized in 1917 and lived with her sister Wasylena in Vienna, where she died; when she died is not known."

I and many Kuz relatives' curiosities about Yarema's final adventures are still piqued and can only be satisfied by viewing her gravestone, if one exists.

Upon relating this mystery to Luba Moisey from the village of Stari Kuty near the left upper bank of the Cheremosh River, I was told Yarema returned to Ukraine and lived incognito under the noses of the Bolsheviks near Ivano-Frankivsk. Luba said this was common knowledge to many in Stari Kuty. Pressing Luba for more details, she responded, "Zen, we in our wayward, backward village were on the moon selling our wares to the astronauts when they landed." Luba is an industrious, adventurous mother who provided for her parents and children by procuring and reselling products in all capitals of the Soviet Union and beyond. She is an exceedingly street-smart woman, surviving tough times with alcoholic husband Nikolai Moisey, while raising three children. What finally happened to Yarema, Luba did not know.

In September 2016, I interviewed Maria Tanasiyivna (née Kuz) Luchka, who lives in Banyliv, a few hundred meters east of where Yarema was raised. Maria described how Olena, recuperating in Vienna, worked as a teacher of French. The family always knew her cousin was a heroine, but in Soviet times, to say this was impossible. The family knew that the daughter of Tanase Kuz (my great-grandmother was his older sister) was a courageous woman, who went to the Sich Riflemen to honor her father. Maria's grandmother Wasylena Kuz, said that during the war, Olena (Yarema) Kuz came to her house. Her grandma had said that Yarema came riding from across the Cheremosh River, accompanied by her soldiers. She was wounded in the arm. Maria believes this was the first wound from fighting in the Carpathians. She lived with Maria's grandmother for a month, until the wound healed. Maria's grandmother cooked her food. Olena was carrying a map, which she often looked at. This is all Maria knew of her.

The interview with Maria Luchka took place in the back seat of Tanasi's car, as Maria's husband was ill and she did not want us to become inflicted. Ohla in the front seat translated from a local newspaper article Maria wrote about Yarema. There was a slight drizzle as we sat and talked. It was at this moment that I learned that my great-grandmother Wasylena was the older sister of the heroine's father, Tanase. This was later confirmed from the Chernivtsi archives.

Maria's home is at the north edge of Banyliv, near the Cheremosh River. She pointed in the direction of the river to a large, two-storey, uninhabited building. This building is on the exact location of an old house where heroine Olena (Yarema) Kuz, wounded for the first time, was nursed by her grandmother. Yarema lived in exciting nationalistic times that saw the adoption of today's Ukrainian flag, national anthem and symbol. In Appendix 9, page 265, there are more documented accounts about Yarema.

After the pleasant meeting, Maria opened an umbrella and returned to her house. Tanasi, translator Ohla and I drove to the vacated building, where we were immediately charged by two German shepherds from a nearby fish farm. We quickly jumped back into the car, calling it a day, and departed for Valentyn's home. On my thirteenth visit in September 2016, Valentyn introduced me to Ohla Sokivka, an excellent translator, who lives across the Cheremosh River and was not familiar with any of my Ukrainian relatives and friends. Ohla was quick at grasping and handling many sensitive issues that I wanted to better understand to try to make this book accurate, while not offending too many acquaintances.

Ohla, a young university graduate in English, earns a living by providing private English lessons. She quickly bonded with Valentyn's daughter, Tatyana. The two girls, jovial Tanasi and I spent long days as we travelled to meet my objectives. One such day was a visit to Mount Makivka, where Olena (Yarema) Kuz became a Ukrainian heroine.

Tanasi and I, as usual over the years, were the guests of Maria (his sister) and Valentyn at Vyzhenka, three kilometers from Vyzhnytsia, adjacent to a tributary of the Cheremosh River. We had private upstairs rooms in their scenic Carpathian home. Breakfast was usually shared with Maria and Valentyn, where we reviewed the exploits of the previous day and made plans for the coming days.

The breakfast table is next to a large window, clearly revealing the rising sun over the heavily walnut and pine-forested mountain. The adjacent yard to the south is where Valentyn's mother lives, and each morning she moved the tethered goat to a fresh grazing area and tended the elevated rabbit pens as chickens busily clucked near her house. Dew-covered grass succumbed to the sun's rays producing rising whiffs of steam. Their grass was cut and piled in three huge, rocket-shaped stacks with a tall center stake protruding skyward, which sheds rain and snow while occupying a small footprint in the yard.

One day, a bit before daybreak, Maria and I were finishing a breakfast of potato pancakes, eggs, cheese, coffee and cherry compote as Tanasi drove up the steep incline to the house with Tatyana, who lives at the Lingcomp School, three kilometers away. Within minutes, with my shoulder bag packed with snacks and four empty two-litre pop bottles, we drove to a nearby metal pipe flowing with cool spring water. After filling the bottles and taking a sip from cupped hands, we were off to pick up translator Ohla for our journey to Mount Makivka.

Within a few kilometers, we crossed the large bridge over the mighty Cheremosh River and drove near Stari Kuty's one-time home of Ivano Franko towards Kosiv. We passed the large field on the right side of the road where the weekly Kosiv bazaar is held, and the memory of my deceased father flashed through my mind. That was where we tackled the pig for a family reunion in 2006. I murmured to myself, "I love you Dad."

As we entered Kosiv, Tanasi phoned Ohla. We met her on a main street, a few blocks from her mom's home, which she shared with her sister. Her mom lives in America. Ohla joined Tatyana in the back seat. After a half hour, I dozed off into dreamland. This gave the girls their first chance to talk uninterrupted. From time to time, I was aroused by a bump in the road. The tempo of their chatter increased, and they frequently burst into laughter. They were bonding and today are friends.

We did not have definite information on the shortest route to Mount Makivka. Enquiring from time to time, even when near the mountain, we were met with shrugged shoulders. The road map and smart phone were of minimal value. After a few wrong turns, the protruding mountain was in view. The dilemma was which end of the mountain to approach. Hours could be wasted to find the correct approach. We wanted to be near the location where Olena (Yarema) Kuz executed her courageous attack on the Russian tsar's fortification. At the southerly end of Mount Makivka, we were at a fork in the road, and heeding Yogi Berra's advice ("When you come to a fork in the road, take it"), we took one road and within twenty minutes reached a small bridge with a sign showing an eleven-kilometer hike to reach the summit, which was in the direction we had just come from. We doubled back and took the other road. A cluster of homes and a few more enquiries led to two more possible car trails we could try. Within ten minutes, we arrived at a steel pipe barrier, which was locked. We saw a rock monument with a sign near the gate. Tanasi turned off the motor and immediately closed his eyes for a nap.

We three, with shoulder bags in hand, approached the rock monument draped with blue and yellow paint (the colour of the nation's flag). A sign showing a trail 4.5-kilometer-long would lead to another monument, where heroine Olena (Yarema) Kuz bravely knocked out the tsar's machine gun nests.

We sipped our water, adjusted shoelaces for the long, uphill walk on the narrow 4x4-wheel-drive trail, maneuverable only when free of snow and rain. At best, we could only see a few hundred meters ahead of the twisting hairpin road with its densely covered slope of tall, arrow-straight pine trees. We encountered a sign illustrating a dozen different mushrooms found on the mountain. We looked, but did not find any. Farther up the trail, another sign illustrated local birds. Screeching hawks and an eagle soared high. The trail in places with near vertical cuts was littered with rocks up to football size, and we had to be careful as we maintained a brisk pace. Some of the shale contained fossils. The Carpathian Mountains are among the oldest of all ranges.

Halfway up the mountain, we stopped to rest on a large sun-warmed boulder. The air was cool and fresh. A light breeze gently swayed the pine tops. At the end of the climb, the trail broadened into a large, leveled area. Off to the right and ten meters down was a leveled half-hectare area containing a large monument and short rows of crosses. Before walking down, the ten-meter drop, we walked to two bush-shaded wooden benches that faced each other. Not a word was spoken as we slumped exhausted into the benches, which faced each other. It was a bit past noon hour. We consumed our bananas and peanuts and sipped cool water.

The monument was surrounded on three sides with fifty short crosses. They were snow-white and in lines like those in Flanders Field. I approached the nearest cross and discovered writing in Cyrillic followed by two numbers. Ohla translated the name Havryliuk, aged nineteen. My thought immediately flashed to Edmonton where a former longtime Mayor Bill Hawrelak's parents came from Banyliv in 1899.

All seemed surreal and I was compelled to walk and touch each grave marker while Ohla translated the Cyrillic names of the boys aged sixteen to twenty, some who were brothers. Most surnames were familiar from my youth in Andrew, Alberta, and common in my ancestral village of Banyliv. Astonishingly, I viewed my mother's maiden name (Palichuk) on a cross. Powerful emotions rippled up my spine, as I imagined the several skirmishes that slaughtered the boys at this strategic location.

Mount Makivka memorial with 50 crosses 2016.

It was Olena (Yarema) Kuz who led eight boys at this fortified pass that took Mount Makivka in the dead of night and turned the tide to remove the last tsar from Ukraine in 1915. Today Putin is trying to accomplish what previous tsars and dictators failed to do. Ukraine still exists, and the world, along with twenty million in the Ukrainian Diaspora, supports Ukraine and its drive for freedom.

On the descent from Makivka, we were jovial and talkative. We collected colourful shale pieces imprinted with impressions of ancient life, some of which I have in our Ukraine room in Canada. Back at the car, we awoke Tanasi and had a snack before returning to Vyzhnytsia.

It was dark, and the humming car and soft radio music

had us three hikers sleeping. My mind drifted to what route Yarema and her eight patriots took up the mountain on their silent ascent under cover of darkness. In 1915, there was limited access to the top of strategic Mount Makivka's machine-gun nests. The route we hikers took would have been too dangerous as the easy switchbacks allowed for concealed tsar sentry stations. I concluded the youth, experienced in navigating forest terrain, elected to make a direct climb, hidden from the line of sight of the just recently invented machine guns (called Chris by the Ukrainians).

Appendix #9, page 264 has a list of names on the fifty gravestones, and if you are of Ukrainian heritage from the Cheremosh River valley or from Western Canada, you have an excellent chance of seeing your ancestral name on one of them.

4.5 Kilometer, 1996 trail to East summit of the Sich Riflemen Memorial on Mount Makivka (2.) where the last tsar's forces were removed.

Finally, WWII (Ukraine's Version)

155

To better understand today's Ukrainians, in their many geographic regions, one must know Ukraine's version of WWII. The following has been copied from the Ukrainian Ministry of Foreign Affairs website, which hosts a document by the Ukrainian Institute of National Remembrance that describes the Ukrainian experience in WWII. The entire document can be viewed at: mfa.gov.ua/en/news-feeds/foreign-offices-news/56936-ukrajina-u-drugij-svitovij-vijni

The Ukrainian nation at the start of the Second World War in September 1939 was divided among five countries: the USSR, Poland, Slovakia, Hungary and Romania.

On March 15, 1939, the Carpatho-Ukrainian Parliament elected Augustine Voloshin as its president and adopted several state symbols –the blue and yellow flag, "Ukraine has not yet perished" as its anthem and St. Volodymyr the Great's Trident as their national coat of arms.

On the same day, Budapest offered Khust a peace that would annex Carpatho-Ukraine (Transkarpathia) to Hungary. Voloshin refused and thus began the general offensive of the Hungarian troops.

The culmination of this was the Battle of Krasne Pole on 16 March 1939. Here, the Ukrainian soldiers organized their defense against the regular Hungarian army which included tanks, planes, artillery, and heavy weapons. By the evening, the Carpatho-Ukrainian capital fell.

Ukrainians were the first in pre-war Europe to defend their freedom with arms. [...]

According to [a] secret protocol [the Non-Aggression Pact between the Third Reich and the Soviet Union], Eastern Europe was to be divided between two dictators: Hitler would take Poland and the Baltic States, Finland and Romanian

Bukovyna and Bessarabia would fall into Stalin's zone of interest. For 50 years the government of the USSR denied the existence of this secret protocol.

[...] The war in Ukraine began on 1 September 1939 and 120 thousand Ukrainians met the Nazis in the ranks of the Polish army. Lviv and other Western Ukrainian cities suffered from Nazi bombings on the first day of the war.

The Soviet Union entered the Second World War on 17 September 1939 as a Nazi ally. Without declaring war, the Red Army crossed the Polish border and moved westward. The Soviet troops helped the Wehrmacht break the Polish resistance in Przemysl and Brest. On 22 September, Lviv surrendered, besieged by the Wehrmacht from the west and the Red Army from the east. The same day there was a joint German-Soviet victory parade in Brest.

During the Second World War, Ukraine lost more people than the combined losses of Great Britain, Canada, Poland, the USA and France. The total Ukrainian losses during the war is an estimated at 8-10 million lives. The number of Ukrainian victims can be compared to the modern population of Austria.

The following is taken from *Ukraine's Version of Who Won WWII* by Ukraine's Andrew Hevko.

On the territory of Ukraine in WWII, there were three combatants: The Wehrmacht German Army, the Soviet Red Army and the Ukrainian Insurgent (People's) Army (UPA). What did the German army fight for? It fought for the Third Reich. Does the Third Reich exist? No, it was destroyed. What did the Soviet Union fight for? It fought for the U.S.S.R. Does the U.S.S.R exist? No, it disappeared. What did the Ukrainian Insurgent Army fight for? It fought for an independent Ukraine. Does an independent Ukraine exist? Yes, it exists. I greet the victorious Ukraine Insurgent (People's) Army.

WWII in Ukraine saw the invading Wehrmacht German

Army fighting for the Third Reich, and the Soviet Red Army fighting for the USSR. At first, these two invaders secretly signed an agreement to divide Ukraine, but the bandits double-crossed each other. In post-Perebudova Ukraine, the Third Reich had been long gone from the face of the earth. The communist USSR also disappeared.

Ukraine won because of its early revolutionary seeds, germinated from centuries of bloodshed, producing patriotic survivors. Hundreds of Ukrainian partisan groups were formed. Partisan Ukrainians fought each other for a variety of complicated religious, philosophical and circumstantial reasons. Many of my Ukrainian relatives were divided between the main partisan groups for the last 125 years. Today, in 2017 very few partisans are divided, and nationalism is at a fever pitch. Ukraine exists because of its partisans, while the Third Reich and the USSR have both disappeared. (Appendix 2, page 227 has more information)

Putin Invades Ukraine 2014
Since WWII, Ukraine soil did not see an armed invasion on its soil until Putin came along and in March 2014 annexed Ukraine's Crimea and invaded Donbas in the East, utilizing rebel techniques previously implemented in Georgia and other areas.

I phoned Tatyana in Ukraine when the invasion occurred, and she was hysterically crying, could not sleep, and visualized her bedroom being bombed. She was terrorized. Contact with others in Ukraine confirmed that they feared an attack was imminent.

Quickly I arranged to go to Ukraine in September of 2014. Doreen remained in Canada. I was on the last leg of a flight from Warsaw to Lviv. The small plane, with two seats

158

on one side of the aisle, had me sitting next to a tall, muscular, blue jean-clad man in his fifties. I noticed he was reading a manual describing a WWII battle. When the opportunity arose, we acknowledged each other and did not stop talking until the flight ended. He was an American, stationed with NATO in northern Italy, and this was his second visit to Ukraine. Clearing customs together and exiting the building, we waved a goodbye, as he met his plainclothes driver, who was driving him immediately to the Donetsk war zone.

A few weeks later my translator Oksana required a day off and was replaced by Tatyana's childhood friend, who works at a large Lviv hotel, where many NATO personnel stayed. She worked welcoming guests. She, like most Ukrainians in their twenties, was passionate about Ukraine, readily adopting the freedoms found in the West. I found her to be very patriotic, including her burning desire to go to the front with a rifle. Among her NATO guests were two from Canada.

In Vyzhnytsia, we toured the army barracks and a cluster of buildings, formerly owned by a Jewish organization. Many of the young volunteer soldiers were students from our Lingcomp School, and they readily showed us around. When we were leaving, they presented me with one of their uniforms, which I put on and posed for photos. Most of this age group and some younger are true patriots. They are surrounded by a sea of blue and yellow flags, emblems, painted bridges, postal boxes, vehicles, lampposts and dozens of other structures. Many times, I wondered how Putin could occupy the regions I visited.

Also, 2014 saw Canadian Armed Forces' Captain Mike

Dullege deploy Operation UNIFIER. Dressed in non-military clothes, he traveled by himself from Edmonton, Canada, to Lviv and drove sixty kilometers northwest to Stari, where he worked until March 2017, establishing a training base to train Ukrainian military.

Captain Dullege made a presentation on May 4, 2017, at the twenty-fourth annual fundraiser of Edmonton's "Kyiv Konnection," attended by more than three hundred, mostly of Ukrainian heritage. All in attendance, including Doreen and I, are fierce advocates for Ukraine. In Canada, there are more than a hundred groups like the "Kyiv Konnection," and each of these groups' members have worked for Ukraine's betterment. Many individuals have given a half century of service. In addition to these many official Canadian organizations, the Canadian government and thousands of individuals quietly provided material and moral support for Ukraine. They all have a story to tell, and I hope many are being recorded.

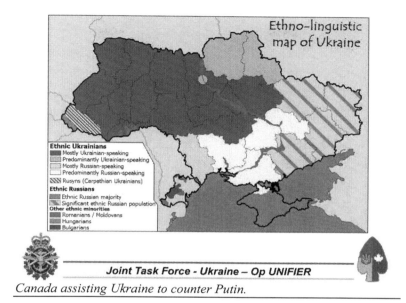

Canada assisting Ukraine to counter Putin.

Canada has a stellar reputation and a mountain of goodwill in Ukraine. All Ukrainians know this. Each dirty deed by Putin cuts to our heart, as much as it does to a Ukrainian's. Putin, the dinosaur, is a fool combating our support for Ukraine, and we in Canada represent only five percent of Ukraine's global Diaspora pulling for Ukraine's freedom.

On July 1, 2015 at 10 a.m., bully Putin closed valves delivering gas to Ukraine as the war raged in Donbas, mostly near Donetsk. Ukraine is geographically strategic for Europe's gas supply, as Europe uses Ukraine's network of pipelines to receive Russian gas. Today one-third of Europe's gas supply is from Russia, of which forty percent is transported through Ukraine. Russia, with its vindictive actions towards Ukraine, charges Ukraine a higher price, even though it is closer than Europe. Also, Ukraine must pay in advance.

Ukraine, to the surprise of Putin, stopped importing gas from Russia and cleverly reduced imports to less than half. This was accomplished by stepping up their own gas production, implementing old methods of keeping warm (sweaters, blankets, sleeping in one room) and using alternate sources of energy (primarily wood and coal).

A store and a residential home in Vyzhnytsia were in the process of installing a Latvian automatic wood-burning furnace to the exterior of their dwellings. It incorporates advancements in airtight furnaces. The furnace heated an alcohol and water hot-water system. The alcohol was distilled from grapes grown at my property, the site of our Lingcomp private school. The cost of wood required for the year was purchased and neatly stacked, for less cost than one month's previous gas bill.

Coal in Ukraine comes from Donetsk and Putin cut off the shipments to western Ukrainian thermal electric plants and diverted the coal to Russia. Putin would like the Ukrainians to freeze in the dark. In response, the US ramped up their coal production and in September 2017 the first shipment of their coal arrived in Ukraine.

Fear of Jesus
Ukrainians generally have a tougher skin than most folks as they evolved from centuries of repressive foreign control and serfdom to develop a resistance to the fear of death. Bishop Robert Barron of California wrote the following about Jesus's Final Teaching, and it speaks to me about how important it is to develop such a resistance to the fear of death:

The night before he died, Jesus gives a strange, mystical speech to his disciples. This was his last will and testament.

During this seemingly rambling discourse, Jesus is luring them, for the last time, into his vision of things, which is to say, into a world in which the fear of death has been overcome.

From the beginning of his ministry, Jesus spoke of a divine love that loves us unconditionally, that reaches out to us even when we wander far away, and that loves us even through the terror and darkness of death. Just as he moved into the shame and marginalization of sin to bring the light to sinners, now he will move into the darkness of death to show us the way through.

Jesus is about to leave this world, and he prays that his disciples might know that they are not of this world. What does this world look like concretely? Well, look around.

The fear of death is like a cloud, like a terrible shadow that falls over human life and experience. All our proximate fears are reflections of, and participations in, this primordial fear. It cramps us, turns us in on ourselves, and it makes us defensive, hateful, violent, and vengeful.

Further, structures of oppression in our world are predicated upon the fear of death. Because a tyrant can threaten his people with death, he can dominate them and perpetrate all sorts of injustice.

Whenever the strong (in any sense) overwhelm the weak, we are looking at the ways of death.

Jesus came to inaugurate what he called the Kingdom of God, God's way of being, God's order. This is an order based upon the infinite and death-defying love of God. What would the world look like under the influence of this love? It would be radically changed, revolutionized, replaced: 'A new heavens and a new earth.'

What would life be like if we were no longer afraid? We would live as the saints do – not immune to suffering, but, if I can put it this way, unaffected by it. We would know that we are loved *by a power that transcends death, and this would fill us with an exuberance beyond measure.*

Putin primarily controls his people using the fear of death. The Russian state controls the Russian media and those that show opposition are marginalized and even eliminated. This is no different than the tactics of the ancient Romans. Most I met in Ukraine do not have a fear of death from Putin. In 2017, this is especially true among the youth, who are more than willing to pick up a gun to kill Putin. Some of them know it is Better to Die a Wolf than to Live the Life of a Dog.

I receive many reports from Ukraine from various sources on Putin's invasion, and daily how many Ukrainian youth are killed and wounded. On March 28, 2015, Banyliv, my ancestral village, said goodbye to Alexander Kolotylo (a relative to my extended family). In 2014, he was in a counter-terrorist operation in Eastern Ukraine as a sergeant of the 3rd battalion, tactical groups of the 80th separate airborne brigade and mobile airborne troops of the Armed Forces of Ukraine.

A touching farewell ceremony for Alexander was held in the Banyliv Church of the Dormition. Most of the village attended. Many fighting soldiers were in attendance. Main Street was lined on both sides for the hero, everybody kneeling, most with tears and uncontrollable outbursts of grief. Officials in attendance included the head of the district administration, Mikhail Andryuk; deputy regional military commissar of educational work Valery Movchanyuk; administrator of the district council George Ivonyak; Banyliv Mayor Nikolai Andryuk, and head of the regional state administration Oleksandr Fyschuk.

All heard of Alexander's courage and heroism in defending Ukraine's sovereignty and territorial integrity. Presidential Decree No. 708/2014 was awarded posthumously to Alexander. The Order "For courage" of III degree was presented to his wife, Valery Movchanyuk. He left two daughters.

Alexander Kolotylo was one of the first to go into battle against Putin's devious invasion of Ukraine, where today in 2017, Crimea is annexed, and daily bombardments occur in Eastern Ukraine. Alexander fought and freed many small villages and the towns of Krasny Liman, Slovyansk and Seversk. He died in Luhansk. He was praised as a caring father, a loving son and a good brother, extremely humble and yet a courageous young man who did not hesitate to defend Ukraine's happy future for all.

The church ceremony, among a sea of blue and yellow flowers, mixed with tears, to the sound of the brass band playing the national anthem, culminated with shouts of "Glory to Ukraine," "Heroes of Glory," "Glory to the Nation," "Death to the Enemy." Some youth held Alexander's photo with the caption, "Heroes never die." The chant "Death to Putin" is expressed daily by elementary school children, who proudly wear blue and yellow on their apparel.

The ultimate price was paid by Alexander Kolotylo, among thousands of fighters and civilians protecting their homeland. As of 2017, nearly 10,000 have died since Putin's invasion. Ukrainian fighters are among the fiercest. They fight with inferior equipment against Putin's army, who are in unmarked uniforms with the latest of sophisticated armaments.

Six year old Jorge in centre; "Mom, buy me a gun." 2014.

Crimea

Wikipedia has the following to say about the "History of Crimea"

> *The recorded history of the Crimean Peninsula, historically known as the Tauric Chersonese (Χερσόνησος Ταυρική "Tauric Peninsula"), begins around the 5th century BCE, when several Greek colonies were established along its coast. The southern coast remained Greek in culture for almost two thousand years as part of the Roman Empire (47 BCE - 330 CE), and its successor states, the Byzantine Empire (330 CE - 1204 CE), the Empire of Trebizond (1204 CE - 1461 CE), and the independent Principality of Theodoro (ended 1475 CE). In the 13ᵗʰ century, ome port cities were controlled by the Venetians and by the Genovese. The Crimean interior was much less stable, enduring a long series of conquests and invasions; by the early medieval period it had been settled by Scythians (Scytho-Cimmerians), Tauri, Greeks, Romans, Goths, Huns, Bulgars, Kipchaks and Khazars. In the medieval period, it was acquired partly by Kievan Rus, but fell to the Mongol invasions as part of the Golden Horde. They were followed by the Crimean Khanate and the Ottoman Empire, which conquered the coastal areas as well, in the 15th to 18th*

centuries.

The modern history of Crimea begins with the annexation by the Russian Empire in 1783. [...] In 1921, the Crimean Autonomous Soviet Socialist Republic was created. This republic was dissolved in 1945, and Crimea became an oblast, first of the Russian S.S.R. (1945-1954) and then the Ukrainian S.S.R. (1954-1991). Since 1991, the territory was covered by the Autonomous Republic of Crimea and Sevastopol City within independent Ukraine. During the 2014 Crimean crisis [Putin's invasion]. the peninsula was taken over by pro-Russian forces and a referendum on whether to join Russia was held. Shortly after the result in favor of joining Russia was announced, Crimea was annexed by the Russian Federation as two federal subjects, the Republic of Crimea and the federal city of Sevastopol.

The majority of world countries, including Canada, the EU, America and the UN do not recognize Putin's annexation and in fact as of 2017 enacted severe restrictions on Putin's Russia. Putin reacted and in August of 2017 he installed international ballistic missiles (IBM) armed with nuclear bombs. Unfortunately, nuclear armaments are again on Ukraine's soil. It voluntarily gave them up to reduce the global numbers under an agreement where the USA guaranteed an invasion from Russia would be prevented. The USA under the leadership of President Obama should hang its' head in shame for not living up to its' agreement. Ukraine has asked the USA to supply defensive weapons for the Ukraine army without success. The Nuclear Non-Proliferation Treaty (NPT), signed in 1968, came into force 1970: An international treaty (currently with 189-member states) to limit the spread of nuclear weapons. The treaty has three main pillars: nonproliferation, disarmament, and the right to peacefully use nuclear technology.

Putin Propaganda

A June 6, 2015 Deutsche Welle newspaper article noted:

The lawyer Zhanna Nemtsova, the daughter of slain Russian opposition politician Boris Nemtsov, says she has left [Russia]. In an open letter, she blamed [Putin's] state propaganda for her father's death.

"Russian propaganda kills," Nemtsova wrote in a column published ... in the business daily Vedomosti, saying that responsibility for her father's death was shared by journalists working for state-controlled TV stations who had described him and other opposition figures as "national traitors."

Boris Nemtsov, 55, an outspoken critic of President Vladimir Putin, was shot dead in late February 2015 while walking on a bridge near the Kremlin in Moscow.

"Putin's information machine – similar to those in Nazi Germany and Rwanda, is using criminal methods of propaganda, and sowing hatred that generates violence and terror," she said, adding that people "infected with hatred begin committing new crimes on their own initiative."

In 2014, Ukraine had no planned national propaganda in place to counter Putin, a master at the game of deception, who had all his government departments in full swing. He controls Russia's media and the Russian Orthodox Church (ROC, a religious department of the Russian government). His propaganda, extremely effective in Russia, also extended to a few nearby countries. With the rapid annexation of Crimea in 2014, Ukraine finally awoke and created its own propaganda machine to counter Putin.

The world is now aware of Putin's charade. He rules with an iron mafia fist, using KGB tactics of fear of death. His world is one of lies and deceit, with propaganda to keep most Russians in the dark.

The following has been copied from the article "Putin and the Proxies" on the website of the Organized Crime and Corruption Reporting Project. The full article can be read here: www.occrp.org/en/putinandtheproxies/

The [Russian] oligarchs have been tamed since Vladimir Putin's arrival to the presidency. The longtime leader has struck a mutually beneficial bargain: Leave the politics to me, chip in when I need you to -- and you can keep, and even grow, your wealth. [...]

OCCRP and its long-time partner Novaya Gazeta went digging to find out more -- and pieced together the assets of some of President Putin's friends, family, and inner circle. [...] [The] Novaya Gazeta and OCCRP investigation looked into the wealth surrounding Russian President Vladimir Putin.

The Organized Crime and Corruption Reporting Project (OCCRP) is a global network of investigative journalists [...] an investigative reporting platform formed by 40 non-profit investigative centers, scores of journalists and several major regional news organizations around the globe. [Their] network is spread across Europe, Africa, Asia and Latin America/ [They] teamed up in 2006 to do transnational investigative reporting and promote technology-based approaches to exposing organized crime and corruption worldwide.

Putin has warned many times that Russia must protect itself from "colour revolutions" like those that toppled presidents in neighbouring Ukraine, Georgia and Kyrgyzstan. He uses this fear tactic to tighten his iron-fist grip on the country by personally picking the 89 regional governors and the Kremlin rubber stamps the bills they are presented. A colour revolution is the only potential obstacle to Putin's control.

According to a November 7, 2017 BBC article, the Russian news agency Tass reports that Rosgvardiya (also known as Rosguard) the elite Russian national guard now 2017 exceeds 340,000 people. They will be stationed to protect the 89 regional governors and controlled by the central Federal Security Service (FSB), the successor to the KGB controlled by no other than Putin then and now. The BBC reports that "[t]he force has some of Russia's most sophisticated military hardware and crack troops from special forces units." This force allows the Kremlin (Putin) to quickly stop an opposition to him. Political analyst Dmitry Oreshkin has observed that "The governors are now under tighter [central] control." The full text of the BBC article can be read here: www.bbc.com/news/world-europe-41900643

Chapter 6

Ukraine strives for freedom despite Putin

Jews in Ukraine

In Western Ukraine, Jews were mentioned for the first time in 1030. The following is reprinted from the *Wikipedia* page on the "History of the Jews in Ukraine."

Jewish communities have existed in the territory of Ukraine from the time of [Kievan] Rus' (one of [Kyiv] city gates was called Judaic) and developed many of the most distinctive modern Jewish theological and cultural traditions, such as Hasidism. According to the World Jewish Congress, the Jewish community in Ukraine constitute the third biggest Jewish community in Europe and the fifth biggest in the world.

While at times it flourished, at other times the Jewish community faced periods of persecution and anti-Semitic discriminatory policies. In the Ukrainian People's Republic, Yiddish was a state language along with Ukrainian and Russian. At that time [the Jewish National Union was created] ... the community was granted an autonomous status. Yiddish was used on Ukrainian currency in 1917–1920.

An army of Cossacks and Crimean Tatars massacred and took into captivity a large number of Jews, Roman Catholic Christians and Uniate Christians in 1648–1649. Recent estimates range from fifteen thousand to thirty thousand Jews killed or taken captive, and 300 Jewish communities totally destroyed. During the 1821 anti-Jewish riots in Odesa after the death of the Greek Orthodox patriarch in Constantinople, 14 Jews were killed. When part of the [Tsar's] Russian Empire in 1911 to 1913, the anti-Semitic attitudes can be seen in the number of blood libel cases. In 1915, the government expelled thousands of Jews from the Empire's border areas.

During the 1917 Russian Revolution and the ensuing Russian Civil War, an estimated 31,071 Jews were killed during 1918–1920. During the establishment of the Ukrainian People's Republic (1917–21), pogroms continued to be perpetrated on Ukrainian territory. In Ukraine, the number of civilian Jews killed during the period was between 35 and 50 thousand. Massive pogroms continued until 1921. The actions of the Soviet government by 1927 led to a growing antisemitism in the area.

[Ukraine was ravaged by Germany and Russia during WWII.] Total civilian losses during WWII and German occupation in Ukraine are estimated at seven million, including over a million Jews shot and killed by the Einsatzgruppen and by their many local Ukrainian supporters in the western part of Ukraine. [The Jews represented fifteen percent of Ukrainians killed in this brief period.]

Before World War II, a little under one-third of Ukraine's urban population consisted of Jews who were the largest national minority in Ukraine. Ukrainian Jews are comprised by many sub-groups, including Ashkenazi Jews, Mountain Jews, Bukharan Jews, Crimean Karaites, Krymchak Jews and Georgian Jews.

Ukraine had 840,000 Jews in 1959, a decrease of almost 70% from 1941 (within Ukraine's current borders). Ukraine's Jewish population declined significantly during the Cold War. In 1989, Ukraine's Jewish population was only slightly more than half of what it was thirty years earlier (in 1959). Most of the Jews who remained in Ukraine in 1989 left Ukraine and moved to other countries (mostly to Israel) in the 1990s during and after the collapse of Communism.

Ukraine's President Poroshenko, elected in 2016, and many Ukrainian elected officials are Jewish. In my thirteen visits post-Perebudova, mostly to western Ukraine, I did not see or hear of any anti-Semitic actions.

When I was seven years old in 1947 living in the small northern Canadian town of Lac La Biche, I first heard the word Jew. The town survived on fishing, trapping and logging. I was good at snaring rabbits and trapping wild animals and at age seven my father gave me a 22-caliber rifle. With Dad's help, we skinned and stretched the fur pelts. These I would take to sell to old Sam Wolff, the fur buyer. Sam paid five cents for a well-prepared rabbit pelt. He took an interest in me, always sharing a few peanuts from his jar and listening to how I set snares. The town referred to him as the Jew fur buyer, and people were wary of him, warning that he would "Jew you down" on the price of your pelts.

When in Grade Eleven in Edmonton, Canada, Steve Rankin, of Jewish descent, enrolled late in the school year. He sat directly behind me. Steve had a good physique with curly jet-black hair that contrasted with his white T-shirts he always wore. We immediately became close friends, and are still friends to this day. We skipped a lot of school classes to hunt ducks and pheasants with our trained Labrador retrievers. Steve was a good dancer and a hit with girls. He was a bit of a rabble-rouser, which contributed to good arguments and us having a lot of fun. With minimal studying, he had top marks in all his exams. At his home, I was well received by his Mom and saw a family focused on higher education. For example, his six-year-old sister was reading the six-hundred-page book *Ivanhoe*. Steve's father, David, was a physics professor at the University of Alberta. The family was academic compared to all the other families I knew. It was in this late stage of schooling that I first learned about universities, thanks to Steve. I also learned that Judaism is a religion. Steve and his family were not religious. Up to that point, I thought a Jew referred to a nationality and not a religion.

Later, I met Joe Sheckter, another Jew, who was very dedicated to his faith. Joe was older than my father, and became my mentor. He was my second father. His brother often said he could not understand the special relationship we developed. My friend Joe joined a Canadian government delegation to Moscow in 1971, where he met First Secretary Leonid Brezhnev. Joe kibitzed with Brezhnev and extracted documentation to travel to Kyiv. In Kyiv, Joe and Sadie met a relative. They departed the next day to the village of his father's birth. They packed a borrowed car with gasoline cans, cooked chicken and bread for the trip to the remote village. With Soviet documentation, they easily convinced Kyiv's traffic control at the exit of the city to allow them to tour the nearby countryside. On the outskirts of Kyiv, there were other armed controlled guarded stations. Sadie and Joe managed to pass two more stations and hide the car in a relative's barn. They stayed concealed for a week in the primitive conditions of a predominately Jewish village. When it was time to leave that area, Joe said they left behind most of their money, all jewelry and all packed clothing. Joe wore no shorts and socks when he left.

On returning to Kyiv after midnight, they approached a remote guard station with their headlights turned off. They zoomed past an awaking guard. At the next guarded station, they were waved to stop. Joe, smiling, waved back and skirted around the armed guard, who did not fire. At the entrance to Kyiv, the guards were alerted and waiting for Joe. A several-hours delay ensued, as Joe flashed Russian and Canadian documents. He explained that they had become lost in the countryside. Joe spoke minimal

Ukrainian. Eventually they were escorted to the airport.

Listening to Joe tell me about his adventure was when I first learned that his ancestors were from Ukraine. He was born in Vegreville, Canada, a small town inhabited mostly by Ukrainians. I never heard Joe speak a hateful word about Ukraine or Ukrainian people. Joe piqued my interest in Ukraine. When Joe died, Doreen attended his funeral as I was out of Canada. Joe's daughter Marilyn mentioned my name in the eulogy. Appendix 5 on page 250 has a "History of the Jews in Bukovina".

Religion
Sterling Demchinsky is a Canadian Ukrainian who is the author of the website "Ukrainian Churches in Canada." I copied the following sections from his webpage, which can be viewed here:

www.ukrainianchurchesofcanada.ca/history/highlights.html

Throughout this excerpt, I changed his spelling of "Kiev" to match my spelling in this book: "Kyiv".

> *Regardless of whether Ukrainians are Greek, Roman or Ukrainian Catholic, Greek, Russian or Ukrainian Orthodox, they share a religious legacy that originates two millennia ago. According to legends, the Apostle St. Andrew traveled [up the] Dnieper River in his mission to the Scythians (a people who occupied vast areas of what is now modern Ukraine.) On the hills of what is today the city of Kyiv, St. Andrew foretold that on those hills would someday arise a formidable city with a great many churches. While the evidence is insufficient to prove this legend, the 1621 Kyiv Synod passed a resolution declaring it true. Therefore, for many Ukrainians, this legend is a matter of faith, regardless of any definitive historic proof.*

While there is evidence that at least small pockets of Christians lived in the Ukrainian homelands throughout the first millennium, Grand Princess Ohla (St. Ohla), who ruled as regent during her son's minority, was the first Kievan ruler known with certainty to be a Christian. Chroniclers speak of both her beauty and wisdom. However, while she brought in political reforms, she did not attempt religious changes for her people.

Arguably the most significant event in the history of the religion of the [Eastern] Slav was the "Baptism of Rus". In approximately 988, Ohla's grandson, Grand Prince Volodymyr the Great (St. Volodymyr) converted to Christianity, married the Byzantine emperor's sister for dynastic reasons, and demanded of his entire realm that all people convert to Christianity. Chroniclers state that Volodymyr directed Greek priests to take vast numbers of Kievans into the river and baptise them. Today in Canada, there are many churches named for Volodymyr and Olga [Ohla], including the metropolitan cathedral for the Ukrainian Catholic Church in Canada and the cathedral for the Western Diocese of the Ukrainian Orthodox Church of Canada.

When Volodymyr the Great died, his son Sviatopolk the Accursed killed his younger brothers, Boris and Hleb, for dynastic reasons and these two young men are recognized as the first Eastern Slavs that were glorified as saints. They are still greatly venerated by Eastern Slavs to this day. Another brother eventually in turn killed Sviatopolk. He is known as Grand Prince Yaroslav the Wise. He became the greatest ruler of Kyiv and further strengthened the institution of the Church throughout the realm. Yaroslav was responsible for building St. Sophia Cathedral in Kyiv, which to this day is arguably the greatest landmark in all of Ukraine. When Yaroslav died in 1054, Kievan Rus had reached its zenith. However, fratricide again broke out among his sons, and political stability was seldom long lived in Kievan Rus after Yaroslav's rule.

In addition to political problems, Kievan Rus fell into economic diminishment for various reasons. The final blow to Kievan Rus was the invasion of Mongols in the thirteenth century. The Metropolitans of Kyiv abandoned it and eventually moved the see to Moscow. By the fourteenth century, the Lithuanians were pushing out the Mongols on one side, while the Muscovites fought them on the other side. The Lithuanians re-instituted the Metropolitan See of Kyiv and then there were metropolitans in both Moscow and Kyiv. As Moscow rose in power, it eliminated the last vestiges of the Mongol yoke by the fifteenth century. [...]

What had once been Kievan Rus was now mostly ruled by the Russians in the east and by the Polish-Lithuanian Commonwealth in the west and there was also a devastated land in the south-central area in which bands of Cossacks lived. After the Union of Lublin in 1569, all the Ukrainian homelands conquered by Lithuania went under the Crown of Poland. Thus, most of what is today Ukraine came to be in the political control of Roman Catholic Poland.

By the end of the [sixteenth] century, the Ukrainian nobility had mostly become ethnically Polanized and religiously Latinized, while Jesuits eagerly sought to convert the Orthodox people. The Ukrainian Orthodox Church [Kievan] became poorer and under continual threat. With few nobles willing to protect them the Orthodox people began to form brotherhoods at a grassroots level. Many people flocked to the south-central [Ukraine] to join the Cossacks, as a way of freeing themselves from dominating overlords.

Eventually, several Ukrainian bishops made a bid to gain equal status for their church by entering union with Rome. The Union of Brest (1596) was an agreement between Ukrainian bishops, the Pope, and the Polish Crown, in which the Ukrainian Church would switch allegiance from

Constantinople to Rome in return for guarantees that the Eastern Rite would be protected by Rome and the Ukrainian bishops would have equal status with Roman Catholic bishops in Poland. [...]

While the Ukrainian bishops must have been convinced that the Union of Brest would be the answer to their problems, they could not have imagined that the Union would deeply divide the Ukrainian people and plunge them into centuries of bitter fighting. The Union had left faithful Orthodox people without bishops, but in 1620 Cossacks belonging to an Orthodox brotherhood escorted the Orthodox Patriarch of Jerusalem to Kyiv to consecrate a new Orthodox hierarchy. Bitter fighting broke out over the possession of churches and monasteries. Hundreds died, including the very controversial Greek Catholic Archbishop, Josaphat Kuntsevych who was later canonized and is venerated in Greek Catholic churches to this day. The violence became too much for the Polish government and it intervened to recognize the Orthodox hierarchy and divide the church property between the Greek Catholics and the Orthodox.

After the Partition of Poland in the 18th century, most of what is today Ukraine came under control of the Russian Empire. Ukrainian Greek Catholics and Ukrainian Orthodox people were eventually forced to convert to the Russian Orthodox Church. A small part of western Ukraine called Halychyna (Galicia) came under the domination of the Austrian Empire and Ukrainians there remained Greek Catholics for the most part, although some would have been influenced to convert to the Roman Catholic Church. Additionally, the Austrians had taken a small province called Bukovyna from the Ottoman Empire and it contained a great many Ukrainian people who had always been Orthodox because that territory did not come under the jurisdiction of the Union of Brest.

When the Soviets came to power, religion in general came under great persecution. When eastern Poland was annexed by the Soviets, the Greek Catholic Church came under particular persecution as the Soviets attempted to snuff it out completely. This period, which ended with the fall of the Iron Curtain and the Soviet Union, was to be a bitter time for Christians with an unprecedented number of martyrs.

The animosity between Catholic and Orthodox Ukrainians flared up intermittently over the centuries and it reared its head again in Canada, particularly during the interwar period of the twentieth century. This animosity cooled during the post-war period and today, for the most part, Ukrainian parishes have more important things to worry about than the differences between being Ukrainian Catholic or Ukrainian Orthodox. Indeed, the two churches now get along very well notwithstanding their continuing differences.

Serhiy Chyrkov reported on political aspects of religion in contemporary Ukraine in an article published in the Euromaidan Press on April 28, 2016. The article is available here:

euromaidanpress.com/2016/04/28/how-the-moscow-patriarchate-is-creating-a-separatist-lavra-republic-in-kyiv/#arvlbdata

I copied the italicized paragraphs in the next section from Chyrkov's piece:

On April 23, 2016, Petro Poroshenko invited representatives from the All-Ukrainian Council of Churches and Religious Organizations to his office [...] just before Easter.

"Under the conditions of hybrid war, when Ukraine is resisting the armed aggression of the neighboring state, our enemies are attempting to take advantage of the religious factor for their own interests," Poroshenko said. "The enemy seeks to split our country and undermine it from within."

[He] urged church leaders to pay attention to the desire of Orthodox citizens of Ukraine to have "a single national autocephalous church," as do most Orthodox countries. "A church united through the Eucharist and prayer and administratively independent from other states," he added.

The presidential message was obviously aimed at leaders of the Ukrainian branch of the Moscow Patriarchate. This Ukrainian Orthodox Church of the Moscow Patriarchate has obstructed the new Ukrainian government since Ukraine's Revolution of Dignity. When Ukraine's church leaders united in a prayer service for peace, the Ukraine Orthodox Church, Moscow branch, (UOCm) refused to join.

UOCm Bishop Pavlo (Petro Lebid) is the governor of the Kyiv Pechersk Lavra (Monastery of the Caves). He lives in luxury on an estate near Kyiv in a lifestyle like Ukraine's previous president, Victor Yanukovych, who, as a puppet of Putin, fled to Moscow during the people's Revolution of Dignity, Maidan, in 2014.

The [UOCm] danger [to Ukraine] lies elsewhere. The Bishop Pavlo has created a virtual "republic" on the territory of the holy monastery, which sometimes resembles the territorial creations of the Muscovites in the Donbas. A "republic" under the control of one person, where Ukrainian laws are reduced to the minimum. People can vanish here, secret poisonings can take place, assassination attempts on disobedient leaders, which the late Metropolitan Volodymyr became in recent years. There, at the command of the Lavra head or even with his direct participation, hands of journalists are broken [and their equipment smashed].

[...] Pavlo broadcasts previously recorded video threats to personal enemies [...] throughout Ukraine." When authorized government officials point to violations of the country's laws, he answers, "I broke the law? Well, glory be to God," and

closes the gate of his own "republic" behind him.

In Moscow, the Ukraine Orthodox Church, Moscow Patriarchate (UOCm), Metropolitan Onufriy "publicly declares his desire to see an independent Ukraine 'in a coffin in white slippers' [according to the Euromaidan Press editor, this is a "Russian curse"]. Bishop Pavlo is the most odious of the servants of the Moscow Patriarchate [...]. [H]is independent Lavra "republic" is the largest [...] that follows instructions from Moscow. [...] [T]hese territorial enclaves [receive] reinforcements from Moscow. On April 16 [2016], Gundayev's Synod decided to dispatch 1450 Russian priests and 700 seminarians to the churches and monasteries of Ukraine. [...] [Now] Putin's armed soldiers will be reinforced by Gundayev's soldiers and new waves of [Putin's] hybrid war will roll over [my ancestors' soil].

Separation of church and state are found in free, advanced countries. In post-struggling Soviet Russia, the church is effectively a department of Putin's government. Most Ukrainians do want separation of church from the state.

Not too far away in my ancestral village is the large, old Ukrainian Orthodox Church attended by most of my relatives for more than a century. This church is not associated with the Russian Orthodox Church (ROC) or the Ukraine Orthodox Church based from Moscow (UOCm). Recently, Frozena learned that the Russian-based Orthodox church (ROC) that she attends is a department of the Russian government. She was shocked to learn some priests were Russian sympathizers, providing information and money to support Putin. The smallest of villages now understand Putin's relationship to the ROC and the UOCm. These are emotional times for church attendees.

Tsars, dictators and Putin today have expropriated or

desecrated thousands of non-ROC churches in Ukraine. UOCm are under the control of Putin, via his puppet Bishop Pavlo in Kyiv. Most villagers simply accepted the theft of their church, preferring not to rock the boat. Villagers since Perebudova have constructed new churches according to their religion. One example is the new church in Ispas, twenty minutes south of Banyliv, where Doreen and I donated. The church elders placed our contribution in their acknowledgement book on page 100. Many of my Ukrainian relatives, especially the Vatrich family led and supported the church construction.

In 1994, Ivan Vatrich drove us to the nearby Anna Horade Shrine, where a miracle is said to have occurred in the fourteenth century. Legend says the Turks, attempting to capture Anna, were thwarted when the cliff collapsed and swallowed Anna, leaving behind only a lock of her hair. This shrine was maintained on the site for pilgrims to visit for hundreds of years. When we arrived at the church; no one was there. Ivan, familiar with the site, led us to the shrine at the edge of the hill. Anna's hair and assorted documents were displayed in a glass-covered case. A peaked roof sheltered the shrine. A corner of the glass was missing and I reached in touching the coarse gray hair.

Fifteen years later, Doreen and I revisited the site. A huge multi-million-dollar ROC now loomed in front of us. The structure dominated the landscape. Several resident nuns in their teens with black religious robes tried to block us from going behind the church to the site of Anna's shrine. We barged on. The shrine roof was missing, and very few of the relics we saw before remained. The shrine was intentionally left to the elements to soon be destroyed.

Today, devotees and tourists from near and far marvel at the church's opulence. Church officials claim funds to build were from an anonymous Russian donor. Frozena's grandson was recently married at the church. I am sure it was a proud moment for her. She is a Moisey and like many Ukrainians has become aware of subversive actions by the Russian based churches. Meager Ukrainian donations are supporting Putin, the effective head of the ROC and the UOCm.

Daily, news fills the airwaves, describing in detail the death of Ukrainian soldiers on Ukrainian soil. Many of those killed are neighbors, and emotional village funeral processions honoring the dead are too common. Streets are lined with mourners on their knees, their heads bent in grief. Parishioners and all religious groups are starting to question their support and tolerance of the Russian based churches. They know Putin's soldiers and his Russian-backed rebels are the killers.

Canada has a few ROC churches, all under the ultimate control of Putin. The first Russian Orthodox Church (ROC) service in Canada was at Wostok, Alberta, on July 18, 1897. It is located approximately twenty kilometers from my great-grandfather's homestead farm. That July, Theodore Nemirsky contacted Bishop Nicholas of the ROC Mission in San Francisco, requesting a priest for religious services for the area. A reverend and deacon traveled more than 1,600 kilometers by train to Edmonton, and by wagon to the Nemirsky farm. There underneath an open sky, a service was held. Theodore Nemirsky's grandson and my father John Moisey were the best of friends. My father, just before his death, gave me a five-centimeter-thick file of Nemirsky archives.

Galicia and Bukovina Ukrainians were the first to leave Ukraine, starting in 1891. The clear majority were Greek Orthodox Catholics, who preferred churches of their own religious order. Great-grandfather Stefan Moisey and his sons Nikolai and Olexsa joined neighbors and constructed a church at Shandro, Alberta, in 1901. Their names are recognized with others on a plaque as the original builders. It is said that Stefan also helped construct the church in Banyliv.

The Shandro, Alberta church is a traditional wooden Bukovinian "tripartite" of a three-sectioned design plan with angular roofs and gables, topped by three small onion-shaped domes. It has a bell tower. The cemetery is located on the same property, where Wasylena and Stefan Moisey's grave is easily located as it has the largest headstone. Their daughter, Anna Rose Moisey and husband Bill Caunt's ashes are buried at the foot of the grave. It is marked by plate-sized, red-granite stones, depicting a wild rose, the floral emblem of Alberta. Stefan Rosichuk, who could neither read nor write, from memory led the design and carpentry of the church.

The history of the Shandro, Alberta Church is well documented by Anna Navalkowsky (mother is Mary Moisey), in the magazine *Alberta History*, autumn 1982. In 1903, these first area settlers pleaded with Bukovina Metropolitan Repta of the Greek-Orthdox Church (located in Chernivtsi) to send a priest for their almost-completed church. Repta responded that he had a shortage of priests, recommending they request a priest from the Russian Orthodox Mission in San Francisco, assuring them the Orthodox faith was the same in all countries.

On August 28, 1979, the Shandro congregation celebrated their seventy-fifth anniversary of their church, which is now an Alberta historic site. In 2017, I am uncertain who the ultimate head of the Shandro Church is. In 1904, a few Moisey families are listed as parishioners. This church is located fourteen kilometers N.E. of my great-grandparents' Moisey farm, in the opposite direction from the Wostock Church.

Today, the Russian Orthodox Church (ROC) in Canada is headed by an Edmonton archbishop under the jurisdiction of the Moscow Patriarchate. I wonder what information and finances the ROC in Canada contributes to their ultimate leader Putin. In Ukraine, this vital transfer has been exposed. Most Canadians of Ukrainian descent do not know of the Church-Putin connection. In Ukraine, on April 2016, when the ROC refused to join in ecumenical prayers for Peace in Ukraine, it was understandable as Putin is the supreme enforcer of the ROC. He does not want to pray for peace. He wants Ukraine. Under Putin, the State is head of the Church. The ROC in Canada, headquartered in Edmonton, did not and does not pray for peace in Ukraine either. It is obvious they take marching orders from Putin without question.

My mother, Nell Moisey, attended Edmonton's St. Barbara's ROC. Mother, after visiting Ukraine, was shocked to learn first-hand of Putin's killings in Ukraine. Mother abandoned St. Barbara Church shortly before her death. She was proud to leave the ROC and spread the word of Putin's control.

Banyliv Kolhosp and Farming
In 2017 most farmers have left the Kolhosp system. Some rent large sections of the former, unproductive collective

farms and are producing good profits. Most Kolhosp former members rent smaller parcels and are deriving a better standard of living than when in the Kolhosp. The land now is well cared for and productive. The Soviet agricultural system was an absolute failure, causing unnecessary suffering and death to millions.

In 2017, Putin continues attempting dinosaur tactics in Eastern Ukraine that he employed in Georgia and other nearby countries. His thirst for reinstating the former Soviet system is insatiable. He enriches his personal treasury by depriving rural Russians and annexing parts of adjacent countries. It does not bother him to shed innocent blood. He is evil, destroying thousands of lives and creating millions of refugees.

In Ukraine, Putin has encountered resistance that will never submit to his tyrannical daily actions. He has encountered Wolves, while expecting Dogs. Most Ukrainians today, and almost all youth, know it is "Better to Die a Wolf than to Live the Life of a Dog". Ukraine's recent propaganda machine is now opened full throttle. Coupled with modern digital communications, they will grind down the repressor Putin. More than a thousand years of overcoming invasions has produced a resilient population. Like the boxing champion Klitschko brothers, Ukraine knows how to handle punches and deliver the knockout. Ukraine has done this more often than the Klitschkos have won in the ring. Aggressive Putin keeps bullying Ukraine, but he is failing. He will be knocked out, to the cheering crowds of the global community, including the good folks of Russia, who in 2017 must stay silent or be prosecuted.

Son of a Kholhosp Member

On one of our first visits, Ivan Moisey, a Banyliv student, took me to his high school computer room. He proudly formatted the computer's eight-inch diameter floppy-disk. This is just an initial operation to start the computer. Bright and optimistic, Ivan started giving computer lessons in Banyliv with three retired computers donated from our Lingcomp Computer and English school in Vyzhnytsia. Ivan eventually sold the computers and gravitated to farming, where today he and his family are thriving farmers. In my September 2014 visit to his and his nearby father's farm, Ivan, sister Svetlana and their beautiful children, covered with field dust, quickly joined in for lunch. The young boys rapidly consumed the tasty meal prepared by efficient grandmother Maria and daughter Svetlana. This extremely productive family incorporated the latest technologies and farm equipment they can afford. I sensed the optimism about their financial future, as opposed to my first meeting in 1994 at this same table, when the biggest wish was to acquire a workhorse and hope for the good old days.

Farming was a natural progression for most of the approximately four hundred Banyliv Kolhosp families, who struggled with archaic farming practices. Touring this Kolhosp in 1994 with welder Wasyl Paraniuk, I was shocked to see dilapidated combines and other farm equipment. Wasyl was given a single welding rod each day to repair the equipment. He told me, the general rule was for the Kolhosp to have four hundred cows and four hundred pigs, along with other questionable guidelines. Today, the average Canadian and American farm family operate four hundred hectares of grain, or own four hundred cattle or four thousand pigs. Ukrainians will eventually be competitive, and they are building it on a sound foundation to become again known as the bread basket of Europe. I predict the Ivan Moisey family will increase their wealth to compete with large western hemisphere farms. Their only potential obstacle is the threat from the Russian bear, tyrant Putin.

The following appeared in the "Crisis in Ukraine: Daily Briefing – 14 October 2016, 3PM Kyiv Time" available on the website of the Ukrainian Canadian Congress at the following address:

www.ucc.ca/2016/10/14/crisis-in-ukraine-daily-briefing-14-october-2016-3-pm-kyiv-time/

The piece is based on an October 13, 2016 *Bloomberg* article called "That Boom You Hear Is Ukraine's Agriculture." Those with a subscription to *Bloomberg* can view the full report at

www.bloomberg.com/news/articles/2016-10-14/that-boom-you-hear-is-ukraine-s-agriculture

> *Bloomberg reported, "Ukraine sold $7.6 billion of bulk farm commodities worldwide in 2015, quintupling its revenue from a decade earlier and topping Russia, its closest rival on world markets. By the mid-2020s, 'Ukraine will be no. 3 after the US and Brazil,' in food production worldwide, says Martin Schuldt, the top representative in Ukraine for Cargill, the world's largest grain trader. [Cargill] is investing $100 million in a new grain terminal in Ukraine. Bunge, the world's biggest soy processor, opened a port [in 2016] at a ceremony with Ukrainian President Poroshenko. [...] [In 2017] [a]bout 1 in every 6 acres of agricultural land in Ukraine isn't being farmed. Of land in production, John Shmorhun [CEO of AgroGeneration] says only a quarter is reaching yields on the level of those in the developed world. because of lower-quality seeds, fertilizers, and equipment. 'It's a huge upside. It's mind-boggling,' he says. [President] Poroshenko supports creating*

a market for farmland, but the Parliament regularly extends the ban on selling agricultural property. Earlier in October, legislators backed a bill prolonging the moratorium through 2018, but the president has yet to sign it. The fear is that large Ukrainian companies and foreign investors will gobble up the land and displace small farmers. [...] Despite the difficulties, Ukraine's emergence as a global agro powerhouse may be a safe bet for a simple reason: the world needs more food, and Ukraine can produce it."

Holodomor

The following section is excerpted from the Ukrainian Canadian Congress (UCC) President Paul Grod's Statement on the 82nd Anniversary of the Holodomor, delivered November 2015 in Kyiv. The full statement can be viewed at: www.ucc.ca/2015/11/28/ucc-presidents-statement-on-the-82nd-anniversary-of-the-holodomor/ The UCC can be visited online at www.ucc.ca; followed on Twitter at @ukrcancongress; or on Facebook at www.facebook.com/ukrcancongress.

This week we remember and commemorate the tragedy of the Holodomor where countless millions of men, women and children were senselessly murdered through starvation by the communist regime of Joseph Stalin. Today the Holodomor remains an incredibly important and relevant human rights story.

In trying to understand genocide, I have often asked myself why did dictators like Joseph Stalin or Adolph Hitler seek to destroy an entire people and why would countless collaborators do their bidding? And – why is this relevant to us today? It seems so long ago.

Unfortunately more than 80 years later, the Holodomor has more relevance to the people of Ukraine and the world than it has ever had before. At a recent Annual Toronto Ukrainian

Famine Lecture, Pulitzer prize winner Anne Applebaum discussed how Stalin saw in Ukraine an existential threat, as Putin sees in Ukraine today. Stalin launched his assault on Ukraine because he knew that Ukraine was resistant to centralized rule, that Ukrainians were attached to their land and their traditions, and that Ukrainians could challenge Bolshevism and even cause it to collapse. Today Russia's President Vladimir Putin fears the attachment of Ukrainians to ideas of freedom, democracy, and western values like human rights. In fact Putin's regime as did Stalin's, cynically denies the very existence of a separate Ukrainian people. As Anne Applebaum said in her lecture, "If Stalin feared that Ukrainian nationalism could bring down the Soviet regime, Putin fears that Ukraine's example could bring down his own regime, a modern autocratic kleptocracy."

Ukraine today is under military, economic and political attack by the Putin regime, much like it was under Stalin over 80 years ago. There is no civil war nor was there ever any separatist movement in eastern Ukraine. This is conflict, which has resulted in more than 8,000 deaths in the past two years [10,000 deaths to 2017], is entirely engineered, organized and run by Putin's regime and is driven by an evil propaganda war.

The peace and freedom loving people of the world must boldly and actively stand up together against this great threat to global peace and security.

Ukrainians have learned their lesson from the Holodomor and will not roll-over to the Putin's attempt to eradicate the Ukrainian nation. Around the world Ukrainian communities are working in their respective countries to gain support for the plight of the Ukrainian people [who] desire nothing more than to live in a country that is free from foreign aggression and respects the human dignity of its people.

[Now] we look at today's plight of the Ukrainian people

through the historical lens of the Holodomor. Many initiatives are underway in Canada, including the recent launch of the National Holodomor Awareness Tour, an innovative mobile classroom; the Memorial to Victims of Communism scheduled to be built in Parliamentary Precinct of Ottawa; and many valuable teaching tools are available such as the very moving online video testimonials of Holodomor survivors at www.holodomorsurvivors.com.

Teaching the human rights lesson from the Holodomor will help ensure we stay vigilant and willing to stop modern day tyrants like Vladimir Putin who today has unleashed a war to eradicate the Ukrainian people.

May God inspire us to do charitable deeds, and may the memory of the victims of the Holodomor be eternal — Вічная Їм Пам'ять".

In 2017, Canadian movie director George Mendeluk premiered the Holodomor movie "Bitter Harvest." It is a must-see film to experience the brutality testified to Doreen and me by Moisey survivors of the Ukraine Holodomor. Video testimonials from actual Holodomor survivors can be seen at www.holodomorsurvivors.ca/Survivors.html

Canada 150 Years Old
One hundred and fifty years ago, Canada had a population of about three million, eighty percent of whom lived in a small area of Central Canada. A hundred and twenty-five years ago, the first few Ukrainians came to Canada and settled in the uninhabited bush lands of Alberta. Fourteen years later in 1905, Alberta became a province. Today in 2017, Alberta is by far the largest contributor of money to equalize the standard of living in other Canadian provinces.

Canada, a young country, has one of the highest standards of living. Ukraine is an old country and, by the last years of the Soviet Union, had a deplorable standard of living although Ukraine is rich in resources, with hardworking and highly educated people.

How did rapid prosperity and peace become possible in Canada? Most of Canada's population, comprised of "hungry" immigrants, arrived from dozens of countries before the twentieth century and simply wanted to work and raise their families. They desired peace and freedom. What they earned belonged to them.

In the first third of Canada's 150 years as a country; immigrants in Western Canada were left to survive and thrive on their own. There were little to no governments and few landlords in their lives. Western Canada, where most Ukrainians settled, lacked police, jails, schools, roads or basic infrastructure. The folks were left alone and established a solid base to help create one of the most prosperous countries on planet earth.

In 2017, new immigrants' desires are much the same as earlier immigrants' dreams, but today's immigrants are not as lucky. They have landlords, stifling regulations and a self-serving government, coddling to their every desire. Canada's government of today, with its surrogates and consultants, falsely believe they know what is best for new immigrants.

There is no doubt Ukraine is now shedding the yoke of foreign, oppressive dictators, and is working to remove corruption. Ukraine is an excellent example for its neighbors, including Russia, to show how it rose from a low standard of living by moving toward freedom from oppression.

Putin would be a global hero of the twenty-first century

if he shed his pride and followed Ukraine's lead. Does Putin have the intestinal fortitude to change? It is possible, but such a change would take a truly great man. He has the ability and power, and with clues from past- President Gorbachev, he would become a real hero. Putin can do it. I wish him luck.

Otpor

Steve York directed Orange Revolution, a 2007 feature-length documentary on the large protests following the Ukrainian presidential elections in 2004. It won several awards from film festivals, and has screened at many prestigious festivals since its release. The film's producers, the company York Zimmerman company, have even produced a study guide, hoping that the film will be used in schools. The following section has been copied from the study guide, which can be viewed in full at: www.orangerevolutionmovie.com/pdf/orange-revolution-study-guide.pdf

> *The Orange Revolution was the third time in just four years that a nonviolent civil resistance movement defeated corrupt or authoritarian regimes in central Europe. The first was in 2000 when Slobodan Milosevic was toppled in Serbia. Next was Georgia's "Rose Revolution" in 2003 which removed Eduard Shevardnadze from power. In all three countries, the spark was a fraudulent election [like that in recent Russian history] followed by massive civil resistance.*

> *Each of these stories featured an unpopular leader, a large and well-organized opposition, and a system to detect and rapidly publicize vote fraud throughout the country. Student and youth resistance groups also played a crucial, although not identical, role. All three opposition movements were influenced and inspired by successful nonviolent struggles of the 1980s – the Solidarity trade union movement in Poland,*

the Velvet Revolution in Czechoslovakia, and the "People Power" movement which defeated Philippine dictator Ferdinand Marcos.

Many political scientists consider these episodes to be "democratic breakthroughs," whose common goals were free and fair elections, responsive and transparent democratic institutions, and adherence to the rule of law, respect for human rights, a free media, and judicial independence.

In Serbia, opposition political parties squabbled and fought among themselves for at least a decade, finally uniting behind a single candidate to run against Milosevic in 2000. Along the way, Serbian youth, led by university students, acquired organizational and strategic skills over a period of several years, which led them to found Otpor! (the Serbian word for resistance), a movement which established branches in over 70 cities and towns. Known for their clenched-fist symbol, spray painted on walls, and printed on t-shirts, posters, and stickers, the group mobilized not just young people, but the whole population. Relying on humor, ridicule, and rock music, Otpor members helped people overcome fear, the key to building participation. Many young people were arrested, which mobilized their previously apathetic parents. Otpor was also effective in undermining police and security force loyalty to the regime. Many of its techniques were adopted by youth resistance groups in Georgia, Ukraine, and other countries, where Otpor activists sometimes acted as advisors and trainers.

Otpor's strategies and tactics couldn't simply be copied by other movements, but the mere fact that Milosevic, a man widely believed to control all conventional sources of power, was removed by a civil resistance movement without resorting to violence, inspired and empowered others. In Georgia, the Kmara ("Enough") movement was modeled on Otpor; in Ukraine, the movement was called Pora! ("It's time!"). By late 2004, the phrase "colour revolution" had entered the

194

popular vocabulary, and potential for a well-organized nonviolent movement to succeed against an entrenched authoritarian had been widely accepted. Lebanon experienced the Cedar Revolution; Kyrgyzstan, the Tulip Revolution; Iran, the Green Revolution. While none of these brought the conclusive or satisfactory breakthrough achieved in Serbia, Georgia or Ukraine, nonviolent movements are at the forefront of bringing change in the world today. [Are there similar infant movements in Russia? Yes there are.] [...]

In a matter of months, the Orange Revolution seemed to have transformed Ukraine irreversibly. Electoral reform brought free and fair elections; a lively and independent media emerged, and constitutional reform brought a healthier balance between executive and legislative power. These achievements were soon overshadowed by personal power struggles, and the continuing domination of parliament by the oligarchs. By late 2005, the Orange coalition had splintered. Yulia Tymoshenko, who had been a Yushchenko ally during the revolution, became his rival. He dismissed her as prime minister in September 2005; she was succeeded by Viktor Yanukovych for 16 months. The Orange camp reunited to win parliamentary elections in 2007, which brought Tymoshenko back as prime minister.

Disappointed by Yushchenko's weak leadership, Ukrainians have become cynical about politics. A devastating economic downturn in 2008 contributed to the despair. At the end of his presidential term in late 2009, Yushchenko's popularity slipped below 5%, leaving Tymoshenko and Yanukovych as the only viable candidates to succeed him in 2010. It could be said that unrealistic expectations guaranteed the Orange Revolution would disappoint its followers, but weak leadership, a polarized country, persistent corruption, and Russian efforts to reassert regional supremacy have played their parts.

Ukraine's democratic transition remains incomplete, but since the Orange Revolution, no elections have been stolen, and no journalists have been killed by the state. While the goals of those who forged the revolution and endured the cold and snow have yet to be reflected in policy, the political system and the rules by which political decisions are made have been transformed -- to one that, despite its flaws, is more democratic and respectful of the rule of law than it was under former Kuchma's rule.

Pora

The following comes from the same "Study Guide" available at the website of the Orange Revolution movie.

Pora! (It's Time!), appeared in late 2002, as a youth organization modeled loosely on the student groups which played visible roles in the defeat of Milosevic in Serbia. [...] Pora was really two separate organizations, known informally as Black Pora and Yellow Pora for the colours of their banners, stickers, and leaflets. Despite some rivalry, they worked together, especially in late 2004. Pora was smaller than [Serbia's] Otpor, not as tightly organized, and could only estimate its membership – at about 10,000. Many were students, and many had been active in the Ukraine Without Kuchma movement of 2001. Beginning in 2003, Pora activists consulted with, and received training from, veterans of the Otpor and Kmara groups. Pora activists were called terrorists and criminals by their government, and they were sometimes physically attacked. They were the first to erect tents in Maidan, on the night of the fraudulent runoff election, and they played a key role in organizing and maintaining order for the tent cities and crowds on Maidan throughout the revolution.

Electronic Media in Ukraine: Temnyky is the name given to secret email messages sent daily by Ukraine's presidential administration to television stations, telling them what to report, how to report it, and what to ignore. This system of media censorship was inaugurated in 2002 by Russian political consultants employed by then-President Kuchma. During the 2004 election campaign, TV news programs were ordered to portray the president, the pro-presidential parties, and Viktor Yanukovych in a positive light, to give minimal coverage to the Yushchenko campaign, and to discredit him whenever possible. In covering Yushchenko's first campaign rally, one temnyk ordered: "... do not show wide shots of the rally and shots of the crowd; show only groups of drunk people with socially inappropriate, deviant behavior."

Ukraine's TV stations: UT1 is the state-controlled broadcaster. 1+1 and Inter are networks owned by Viktor Medvedchuk, an oligarch who headed President Kuchma's presidential administration in 2002-2004. Three other TV channels are owned by Kuchma's son-in-law, Viktor Pinchuk: STB, ICTV, and Novy Kanal. During the 2004 presidential campaign, all these stations showed a strong bias towards Yanukovych. Only two stations produced balanced news. The first was Channel 5, a small station with a weaker signal, covering only about 15% of the country, with no coverage at all in Eastern Ukraine. Channel 5 is owned by Petro Poroshenko, an oligarch friendly to Yushchenko. ERA-TV provided similar coverage, but was only on the air for portions of the day, and not in the evening. After the electoral fraud was revealed, journalists and the news staff at UT1 and 1+1 threatened a strike to protest censorship. They declared to management, "Either you let us broadcast what's happening in the country, or we all walk out." Management gave in, and at 9pm they carried the first uncensored news reports.

Russian leaders [i.e.: Putin] saw the 2004 election as a turning point: Would Ukraine take a pro-Russian or a pro-Western direction after Kuchma? A year before the election, they [Putin] decided to support the candidate picked by Kuchma. Expensive Russian political advisors and spin-doctors managed the Yanukovych campaign, which also received cash contributions from the Kremlin. The total sum is

197

not known. Fifty million is the lowest estimate; the amount most widely cited is $300 million. Russian political consultants used strategies common in Russian elections including putting massive pressure to vote for Yanukovych on state employees, pensioners, and others whose livelihood depends on the state. They developed a pro-Yanukovych advertising blitz, which ran prominently in Russia, aimed at the million eligible Ukrainian voters living there. Russian President Vladimir Putin personally visited Ukraine to endorse Yanukovych. Later, Putin congratulated Yanukovych on his victory three times before the votes had even been counted. Altogether, the Russian role came off as heavy-handed, a transparent attempt to re-impose Russian influence in Ukraine. Some analysts believe the Russian efforts hurt Yanukovych. Russian leaders were shocked and surprised by the massive protests in Ukraine. In response, they have given a high priority to preventing similar "colour revolutions" in Russia or other countries. [...]

When the Soviet Union disintegrated in 1991, Ukraine became independent. Within a year, former Soviet officials and ex-managers of state-owned enterprises emerged as "oligarchs," purchasing former state companies such as heavy industry, coal mines, and media outlets, at bargain prices. These overnight tycoons, who owned huge businesses and conglomerates, enjoyed close ties with the president and controlled large factions in parliament. Their political connections allowed them to win such benefits as regional monopolies, tax exemptions, subsidies, and trade preferences.

Despite occasional anti-corruption programs, the oligarchs remain key power centers in Ukraine. As prime minister (2000-01), Viktor Yushchenko withdrew many of the tax exemptions and privileges enjoyed by the oligarchs, while turning Ukraine's deficit to a surplus and growing the economy for the first time since independence. In 2002, President Kuchma replaced his cabinet with ministers drawn entirely from the oligarchic factions in parliament. In the position of prime minister, Viktor Yushchenko was out, and Viktor Yanukovych was in.

As the presidential election approached in 2004, the oligarchs were dominant – but not unified. Among the more than twenty presidential candidates, only two were true contenders: Yushchenko, the reformer, and Yanukovych, the candidate of the oligarchs and the status quo. To be fair, Yushchenko enjoyed the support of some oligarchs too, but Yanukovych had a unique advantage. He was endorsed by the incumbent president and supported by the entire administrative branch of government. He was also supported by Russia.

Maidan and Wasyl Мойсей (Moisey) renew Nationalism
The Maidan uprising of February 2014 resulted when Ukraine's President Yanukovych unilaterally, and at the last moment, did not sign an economic European Union agreement. He simultaneously proclaimed closer ties with Russia. Maidan was a popular public outcry, facing a well-entrenched Yanukovych police system to protect him, which in turn gained control over municipal and city police forces. Blood began to flow as Yanukovych's special Russian-trained snipers began picking off demonstrators in the central square of Kyiv.

The fifth protester to be killed by a sniper was Wasyl Moisey, a distant relative of mine. The shooting was captured on film and featured in the documentary "Winter on Fire". You can hear Wasyl's name called out twice as he lay dying. This young Moisey boy said before he died, "Better to Die a Wolf than to Live the Life of a Dog." His burial and that of others of the "Heavenly 100" drew the largest attendance to funerals to ever occur in Ukraine.

Yanukovych was quickly exposed to the world; his

lavish property and personal holdings in the billions of dollars were revealed. He left for Donetsk and was quickly escorted out of the country by Russians to Moscow. It was February 2014, and now Putin gave the command to the armed forces to take control of Crimea. Putin acknowledged this on the Russian government-owned media during the second week of March 2015. During this time, Russian rabble-rousers involved in stirring initial unrest in Georgia and Northern Moldavia were also stationed in Donbas. Photos of some of these Russian goons previously appeared in media coverage while causing trouble in three other countries and appeared regularly in Donbas in 2014. In 2016, Putin still claimed Russia had nothing to do with the problems in Eastern Ukraine, which had by then claimed more than 6,000 Ukrainian lives. In 2015 Yanukovych's wealth was estimated by Forbes to be more than a billion dollars, and Putin's at $40 billion. Putin's wealth in 2016 was said to be $200 billion. Where is his personal wealth coming from?

2017 Ukraine Crisis Created by Putin

The following timeline is taken from a BBC article about a documentary film made by Andrei Kondrashov, "a journalist with state-run channel Rossiya-1", which offers the Russian view on how Crimea was annexed. Kondrashov's film, called *Crimea. The Way Home* appeared on Russian television and YouTube on 15 March 2015. The BBC article can be viewed at: *www.bbc.com/news/world-europe-31796226*

- *22 February, [2014] former Ukrainian President Viktor Yanukovych flees [Kyiv] after violent protests*

- *23 February, Russian President Vladimir Putin plans to*

rescue Mr. Yanukovych and annex Crimea

- *27 February, pro-Russian gunmen seize Crimea's Parliament and other key buildings*

- *28 February, unidentified soldiers in combat fatigues occupy two airports in Crimea*

- *1 March, Russian Parliament approves Mr. Putin's request to use force in Ukraine*

- *16 March, 97% of voters in [a Russian-sponsored referendum in] Crimea agree to join Russia*

- *18 March, Mr. Putin signs a bill absorbing Crimea into the Russian Federation*

All this was accomplished in 26 days by the incredibly surgical Putin. The same timeline appeared in other BBC articles, including one dated March 15, 2015 describing some of the details that emerged from Kondrashov's documentary. The following is taken from that article, which can be viewed at: www.bbc.com/news/world-europe-31899680

The Ukrainian government, Western leaders and NATO say there is clear evidence that Russia is helping the separatists with heavy weapons and soldiers. Independent experts echo that accusation. Moscow denies it, insisting that any Russians serving with the rebels are "volunteers" [...doing a...] "good deed".

Full details of Mr. Yanukovych's escape from Ukraine are unclear although Mr. Putin spoke of Russian efforts to evacuate him and threats against [Yanukovych's] life.

"For us it became clear and we received information that there were plans not only for his capture, but, preferably for

those who carried out the coup, also for his physical elimination," Mr. Putin says in the film. He said preparations to extract Mr. Yanukovych were made by land, sea and air, saying "heavy machine guns" were placed in Donetsk "so as not to waste time talking." Russia's Interfax news agency quoted Putin as saying that saving the life of Ukraine's former leader and his family was a "good deed".

Ukraine and Russia on Different Paths

The following is taken from a February 24, 2015 article called *"Separated at Birth: Ukraine's and Russia's Divergent Paths,"* written by Brian Whitmore, and which appeared on his blog *The Power Vertical* on the website of Radio Free Europe / Radio Liberty. The full article can be viewed here:

www.rferl.org/a/separated-at-birth/26867185.html

[...] Two days in two countries more than two decades ago. Two days, nine months apart, set Russia and Ukraine on the radically different trajectories that culminated in the conflict we are witnessing today. As the Russia-Ukraine conflict drags on, as we watch with trepidation as the Minsk-2 ceasefire crumbles, as Mariupol and maybe Kharkiv brace for separatist assaults, it's worth recalling how and why these two countries arrived at the place they are today.

The immediate cause of the current crisis, of course, is Russia's determination to prevent Ukraine from integrating with the West. But the underlying cause can be found in the divergent paths they took after 1991.

And those different courses are encapsulated in two fateful days in the early formative years after the Soviet breakup.

[...] The first day is October 4, 1993, when Russian President Boris Yeltsin resolved his longstanding conflict with Parliament by sending tanks and shelling it into submission.

202

At the time, it looked like a victory for Yeltsin's team of reformers over a retrograde and reactionary legislature. Supporters of Yeltsin called it one of those times when it is necessary to use illiberal means to achieve liberal ends. But, it was post-Soviet Russia's original sin.

The shelling of the Russian Parliament established the dangerous precedent that political disputes could be resolved by force. The Russian presidency turned into an unaccountable behemoth – one that Vladimir Putin would ultimately use to the fullest.

The executive-heavy power vertical, the unaccountable super presidency and the decorative pocket parliament otherwise known as the State Duma were the direct result of the way the 1993 crisis was resolved. So is the fact that the rule of law in Russia is an illusion at best, consistently trumped by a much older principle: Might makes right.

"For the last 20 years, we've continued to use the same methods," Sergei Filatov, Yeltsin's chief of staff at the time of the crisis, told RFE/RL's Russian Service in October 2013, on the 20th anniversary of the shelling.

"We survived that time and we should have learned something from it, but unfortunately we didn't learn anything. We all had that Soviet, imperial mentality, where strength will always better solve the problem, as opposed to negotiations and compromise. If we're ever going to become a democratic society, we need to change our methods of managing the country and the methods of interaction among the authorities."

The Ukraine Alternative

Fast-forward to the following summer -- July 10, 1994 -- in Ukraine.

On that sweltering summer day, in the second round of Ukraine's first post-Soviet election, voters rejected incumbent

President Leonid Kravchuk and elected his challenger, Leonid Kuchma.

And Kravchuk did something remarkable for the former Soviet Union. He stepped down without incident and allowed Kuchma to take power.

The election of 1994 came in the wake of a political crisis in Ukraine that was similar to the one Yeltsin had faced in Russia.

[Ukraine] was in an economic collapse and a debilitating series of coal-miners' strikes. Kravchuk was locked in a bitter dispute with the Ukrainian parliament, the Verkhovna Rada. But in contrast to Russia, the crisis in Ukraine was resolved peacefully with an agreement to hold early presidential and parliamentary elections.

Initially the conventional wisdom about the 1994 election was that it was a victory for Moscow because Kuchma, who hailed from eastern Ukraine, was friendlier to Russia than Kravchuk.

But the precedent that was set by a peaceful transfer of power proved to be more important and more enduring.

It's worth noting that in the five presidential elections Ukraine has held since independence, the incumbent or the incumbent's handpicked successor has lost three times. Only one incumbent, Kuchma in 1999, won re-election.

By contrast, in Russia, the incumbent or the incumbent's chosen successor has won each of the five presidential elections since the Soviet Union broke up. Machinations to subvert and manipulate the democratic process -- like Yeltsin handing the Kremlin to Putin with his New Year's Eve resignation in 1999 or the "casting" move Putin and Dmitry Medvedev pulled off in 2011-12 -- have been the norm.

A Study in Contrasts

Not only have Ukraine's elections always been more

competitive than Russia's; its political and economic elite has always been more pluralistic.

On [a] Power Vertical Podcast, Sean Guillory of the University of Pittsburgh's Center for Russian and Eastern European Studies, noted that "the taming of the elite in Russia as opposed to Ukraine" was a key factor in determining the different paths the two countries followed since independence.

In Russia, "the state stepped in and obliterated the political power of the oligarchs in the early 2000s and set Putin up as the center of the state system. All of them agreed to have a strongman in charge", Guillory said. "We didn't have this in Ukraine. Nobody came out on top in Ukrainian elite politics. It was always a contest among various oligarchs based in various parts of the country".

It was the shelling of the Russian Parliament in 1993 and its political aftermath that set the stage for Putin's authoritarian rule. "The creation of a very strong presidency is what allowed all this to happen", Guillory said.

And perhaps most importantly, from the 1994 election and onward, Ukraine's civil society has always been stronger and more independent than its Russian counterpart.

In Ukraine, independent civic groups and NGOs thrived, flourished, and multiplied and ultimately became a force to be reckoned with in the country's politics.

In Russia, they were alternatively marginalized, co-opted, and manipulated by the authorities, or harassed out of existence. They have been called a fifth column and branded as foreign agents.

Ultimately, Ukraine's civil society became the Third Force as Kyiv's and Moscow's political paths diverged and the Kremlin schemed and battled to keep its neighbor in its political orbit.

Irreconcilable Differences

So it is fair to say that since the Soviet collapse, Ukraine has progressively become more democratic. Russia, less so.

But Ukraine's development since 1991 has been far from perfect. Corruption was rampant and oligarchs ruled. But by the summer of 2013, Ukraine's increasingly confident civil society wanted something better. And the first step toward something better was Ukraine signing an association agreement with the European Union.

"If you are a student or a small business owner in Ukraine, you understand Europe in the following way: Europe is part of our history, and Europe today means the European Union. And the European Union means bureaucratic predictability and the rule of law," Yale University historian Timothy Snyder said in a recent lecture.

Snyder added that the Euromaidan uprising was "a middle-class revolution" to move the country "from oligarchic pluralism to real pluralism".

What made this decisive was that top oligarchs like Rinat Akhmetov and Ihor Kolomoysky calculated that they had a better chance of protecting their wealth in a European-style system than in a Ukraine that was essentially a colony of Russia.

And once that happened, the divergent paths that Ukraine and Russia had taken since 1991 became irreconcilable differences.

Writing in [...] Foreign Affairs, Princeton University historian Stephen Kotkin notes that Ukraine is "a nation that is too big and independent for Russia to swallow up", while "Russia is a damaged yet still formidable great power whose rulers cannot be intimidated into allowing Ukraine to enter the Western orbit. Hence the standoff."

Spontaneous Revolution: Maidan

Nov. 22, 2013 a crowded tent city occupied Maidan Square

tent city where an evening performance was staged. The following section is also from the Orange Revolution movie's "Study Guide":

Away from Maidan, a less visible battle was being fought. Lawyers for Yushchenko and his political party filed over a hundred court cases citing election irregularities. Three hundred lawyers worked without pay to prepare the legal cases. The key action was at Ukraine's Supreme Court where the pressure of mass action and the rule of law converged. In the end, recalls Mykola Katerynchuk, the lawyer who supervised the cases, "We proved that the results of the election second round were falsified, and revealed the methods and participants in these falsifications. The judges realized that the people in the streets might try to seize power at any moment, and this may have prompted them to make their decision quickly – in just a week. Because the Supreme Court performed its historic role, a violent scenario was avoided. It transformed the revolution from a crisis of illegitimacy into one of legality. It legitimized a transition from fraud to the establishment of democratic elections. It was a ruling that favored politicians, favored voters, and favored the democratic future of Ukraine. And this one case washed away all the dirty money and the power of those oligarchs."

A member of the campaign staff who helped organize the events on Maidan explained, "I imagined this campaign as a war. I couldn't think of it any other way, and we couldn't organize it any other way. We would have to work in a strict discipline, otherwise it would be impossible to win".

The [illegitimate] regime assumed that after a few days the frigid temperatures would force protesters to go home. But as one of the organizers observed, "These people were really prepared to do anything, to give everything, to be rid of this criminal government." Night after freezing night, they stayed.

To manage the mass of people in the tent cities, in Maidan, and around the Parliament and Presidential administration buildings, strict rules were established. Members of Pora!, the youth resistance organization, were the enforcers. Alcoholic beverages and drugs were prohibited in the tent camps. Trash was hauled away daily. Pora volunteers controlled the checkpoints, patrolled the encampments, and kept order. [...]

All of Ukraine's senior politicians were born, educated, and began their careers when Ukraine was a Soviet republic. Viktor Yushchenko [was born in] 1954, in northeastern Ukraine. By 1991, when Ukraine became independent, Yushchenko had earned degrees in economics and finance, and established himself as a respected economist, employed by local, regional, and national banks. In 1994, he became the first governor of Ukraine's central bank, where he earned high praise for stabilizing the currency and reducing inflation. President Kuchma appointed him prime minister in 1999, but his aggressive anti- corruption programs made him unpopular, and he was pushed out of the prime minister's office in 2001. Within a year, he became leader of Our Ukraine, a reform- oriented political coalition. Our Ukraine won more parliamentary seats than any coalition in 2002. His run for president in 2004 energized the millions who saw it as a chance to break, or at least loosen, the oligarchs' grip on their country.

Leonid Kuchma [was born in] 1938, in north central Ukraine. Educated as an engineer, Kuchma was successful in Soviet industry and recognized for his design and development of rocket and space technology. He entered politics in 1990, first as a member of parliament, then briefly as prime minister. He was elected president in 1994, promising to reverse a serious economic decline through closer cooperation with Russia. Targeted by accusations of criminality and corruption throughout his presidency, he maintained close ties to the wealthy oligarchs who controlled much of Ukraine's economy. As his popularity plummeted, he lashed out at the media,

208

especially television. Tape recordings allegedly made in his office were widely accepted as evidence of his involvement in the murder of journalist Georgiy Gongadze and other crimes. Following the fraudulent election of 2004, he was pressured to declare a state of emergency and inaugurate Viktor Yanukovych, but he refused to do so.

Viktor Yanukovych [was born in] 1950, in the Donetsk province in Eastern Ukraine. After eight years as an electrician at a local bus company, he earned an engineering degree by correspondence courses. Later he held management positions in the transport sector. He was vice- governor, governor, and head of the province council of Donetsk between 1996 and 2001. His political career has been marred by charges of criminality and corruption. He was convicted of robbery in 1967 and of rape in 1970, crimes for which he served a total of five years in prison. President Leonid Kuchma named him prime minister in 2002, and supported his run for president in 2004. Coming from a Russian-speaking region, Yanukovych favored close relations with Russia. During the campaign, he advocated making Russian an official language of Ukraine.

Yulia Tymoshenko was born in 1960, in south-central Ukraine. During a successful and controversial business career, she joined the ranks of Ukraine's oligarchs, doing business with many of the country's most famous (and infamous) tycoons. As president of United Energy Systems of Ukraine, the main importer of Russian natural gas at that time, she was accused of selling large volumes of stolen gas and of evading taxes; her nickname became "the gas princess". She was elected to Parliament in 1996, and served two years as deputy prime minister for fuel and energy. As a leader in the 2001 Ukraine Without Kuchma movement, Tymoshenko was known for her passionate, sometimes inflammatory, rhetoric. That same year, she formed the Yulia Tymoshenko bloc, a political coalition that joined the Orange forces working for

Yushchenko's presidential campaign in 2004. She became Ukraine's first female prime minister in early 2005. Many Ukrainians accept her as a reformer, ignoring or forgiving her problematic history. She speaks for the rule of law, against corruption, and for a balance of relations with Russia and the EU. In 2009, she announced her intention to run for president of Ukraine.

Protesters remained in the bitter cold tent city all winter with angry crowds and a few small deadly skirmishes until Feburary 20, 2014 when all hell broke out with Russian trained snipers from roof tops killing what is now known as the "Heavenly 100" (approximately one hundred and thirty civilians and eighteen police). The fifth civilian to die was a distant relative, twenty-one-year-old Wasyl Moisey, shot in the chest. He was well known for saying it is "Better to Die a Wolf than to Live the Life of a Dog".

A year later on February 20, 2015 President Poroshenko posthumously proclaimed these "Heavenly 100" be awarded the "Hero of Ukraine" honor. Amazingly this proclamation is one hundred years to the month when my third cousin removed, Olena (Yarema) Kuz in 1915 led a group of eight men and tossed grenades to remove the last Russian tsar's forces from famous Mount Makivka, for which she was honored with two medals of bravery.

I deeply feel these two-distant relative's sense of duty for our beloved Ukraine and would gladly give up my life to dispose of the current tyrant Putin for his murderous war now raging in Ukraine as this book is being published.

After Maidan; my 12th Visit to Ukraine
In September 2014, I prepared for the twelfth visit to Ukraine, seven years since the last visit. Contact with friends

and relatives during this time revealed no one was particularly worried about the advancement of Ukraine. They were generally pleased that the country was shifting to be more European and abandoning the Soviet system. The Maidan protests in early 2014 clearly exposed the meddling and viciousness of Putin. They were optimistic Putin would eventually be driven out of Ukraine. On the night before leaving, as I prepared to go to bed early to be fresh for the long trip, Doreen called me to the television to watch an Omni documentary on Canadian-Ukrainian artist Mykola Bidniak.

Mykola lived most his life less than two hundred kilometers from our Alberta home. He was born in Ontario, Canada in 1930, the son of immigrants from Bukovina. I planned to watch the long documentary for a few minutes. Immediately, we both were captivated with this talented man's accomplishments and his love for Ukraine. While visiting Ukraine with his parents during WWII, at age fifteen, Mykola lost both arms and an eye in a land mine explosion. After living in central Canada, he had art training in Calgary, Alberta, where nearby he maintained a small farm with his physical disability. He was an independent soul, and his modern icon paintings are spectacular. The documentary told various stories about Mykola's life and showed him painting by holding a brush in his mouth.

Doreen and I discussed the documentary for another hour as we Googled more about Mykola Bidniak. His love for Ukraine was contagious. He lived his last ten years in Ukraine and was buried in Lviv's Lychakiv Cemetery. I did not sleep well and was up before daybreak, to fly to Lviv. In my dream, I was compelled to visit his grave. I visualized support through art, and not shooting, to bring peace to

Ukraine. I had to visit patriot Mykola Bidniaks's grave. I just had to.

I emailed Valentyn to inform faithful driver Tanasi (his mother was a Moisey) to locate the cemetery so I could make a visit before nightfall, as I was arriving in Lviv late in the day. After clearing customs, Tanasi and I set off for Lychakiv Cemetery. Tanasi parked at the entrance and was greeted by the caretaker, whom he befriended earlier in the day. The smiling caretaker led us through the elongated shadows of the main entrance. The cemetery gates were closed behind us, as visiting hours were over. Led by the caretaker in friendly conversation with Tanasi, we approached five nearby raised coffins, embedded in a mountain of fresh cut flowers. Next to each coffin was a metal and glass-framed photo of each man, some in uniform. Quickly Tanasi explained they were recent heroes killed fighting Putin's puppets near Donetsk, Ukraine. Suddenly I sensed what most of my friends feared about the war now raging on Ukraine's soil.

The sun had set as we walked a few dozen steps across the main walkway towards the main cemetery, and there, suddenly, loomed Mykola Bidniak's grave marker, a bronze angelic sculpture. There he was in the first row, in the middle of Ukraine's most esteemed artistic and honored community members. Wow!

I placed a Canadian flag on the salt-and-pepper-coloured granite slab. We three stayed and talked for a long time, long past the caretaker's working hours. He walked with us to Tanasi's car, and we left for the five-hour drive to sleep at Maria and Valentyn's Vyzhnytsia home. See Appendix 7, page 256 for more on Bidniak, who, beyond his vocation, embodies the passion Canadians of Ukrainian heritage hold for their motherland. I now better know why I love Ukraine.

The next morning with translator Oksana Chorney and Tatyana Krasniuk (her grandmother Frozena was a Moisey) we visited the Banyliv house where metal sculptor, Roman Paraniuk lives. Roman showed considerable interest when I told him about artist Mykola Bidniak, who so dearly loved Ukraine. I mentioned my dream of bringing peace to Ukraine by using art and not guns. Suddenly Roman broke into tears as a friend of his was recently killed in the war. He asked his

mother and family to leave the room, and we discussed
Bidniak and the war.

Zen at Canadian Mykola Bidniak's grave in Lviv, 2014.

Roman wanted to discuss with his artist friends the concept of presenting a large sculpture of friendship between Eastern and Western Ukraine. Three days later he had a design for a two-meter high, 3,500-kilogram peace sculpture, which I then commissioned him to build. It would be completed in less than a year.

Eight of us, mostly young family members (I was double to triple the age of most members), formed an informal group. We found community support in Banyliv to have school children parade the sculpture, draped with the Ukrainian blue and yellow flag, through villages from Ukraine's western border toward Donetsk. Children from one village, with their flags, would lead the parade of the sculpture entering the next village. A transfer to new students would march the sculpture through their village. Ivan Vatrich would purchase a vehicle to pull a trailer with the mounted sculpture. Tanasi, with his street and road smarts, would be the driver on the year-long journey. This slow march would eventually capture media attention, and the peace initiative would bring awareness of friendship from Western Ukraine to the Donetsk region.

Now, one of my relatives in Kyiv contacted a school in Eastern Ukraine to receive the sculpture. I talked with and emailed this excited contact on many occasions. After several months, the situation became so dangerous in the Donetsk region that the contacts feared for their lives. I agreed to stop the project as none of us wanted innocent blood on our hands. The peace project died. Now in 2017, it is too dangerous to mention this peace-minded contact's name. Hopefully one day we will meet.

Survival rates in Ukraine and Canada

Survival was extremely difficult in Ukraine's 19th century. In addition to killings from five occupational forces, the birth rate was brutal. Mary Ann (née Moisey) Tymchuk, my Canadian cousin, researched the Chernivtsi archives to reveal the following statistics of a few of our ancestors' survival rates:

Stefan's father, Tanasi Moysey (1821 – 1881) had seven children; three died as babies, a forty-three percent death rate). Stefan (1846 – 1918) had eight children; two girls died at ages three and five, a twenty-five percent death rate). Stefan's older brother Ignati (1843 – 1893) had nine children; five died before the age of five, a fifty-six percent death rate). In Canada, Stefan's son, my grandfather Gregory (1887 – 1974) had ten children in Canada; first-born Helen died at birth, a ten percent death rate. Of Gregory's twenty-nine grandchildren (including me) only one set of twins died at birth, a six or three percent death rate if the twins are counted as one birth. My children and grandchildren have all survived.

In the year of Stefan's birth, when oppressive foreign landlords controlled the people, the seeds of revolution were planted. This revolution slowly but surely resulted in today's post-Perebudova Ukraine. As oppression increased in Ukraine and the population grew on non-available lands, pressures boiled, and leading to migration in the late nineteenth and early twentieth centuries. Migration was primarily to Canada, Brazil, Europe and the United States. In the 1930s and 40s, brutal dictator Stalin forcibly removed millions of Ukrainians to the Siberian Gulag, which partly explains the large Ukrainian population in today's Russia.

Chapter 7

My Last Visit

Three Apartments Purchased

In the 1990s, I purchased three adjacent apartments of five in a palatial building on 75 Ukraine Street, Vyzhnytsia, Chernivtsi Oblast to start Lingcomp, a private school. The purchase from Mila cost $8,500 US, from Klym $10,500 US, and from Orletsky $11,500 US. The apartments were purchased in the name of Valentyn and remained in his name for several years. They were subsequently transferred to my name.

Cash was given to Valentyn, as we did not trust a bank to handle the money. Banks could not be trusted immediately after Perebudova, as they were known to go broke often. Valentyn's pockets bulged with cash, and he worried about being robbed.

The three apartments were renovated with tender love and care by Maria's family and friends. They then purchased furnishings and equipment for the Lingcomp Computer and English schools. After more than a decade of operating as a school, Valentyn's family continue to maintain the apartments, operate their two stores and laser manufacturing center, as well as Valentyn's law office.

On my thirteenth visit in 2016, Doreen and I decided to will the three apartments to distant family members. The Klym apartment is willed to Tatyana Krasniuk, Mila's to Svetlana (née Moisey) and Orletski's to Valentyna Moisei (her passport says Мойсей). The three women signed a registered contract allowing Tatyana to operate her businesses to a specific date. To will the apartments was the cost-effective method to pass them on to avoid immediate prohibitive gift taxes. The women are descendants of my great grandfather's brother Ignati Moysey (spelling imposed by the then occupying Austrians). Doreen and I received much joy from my long-lost Ukrainian family and felt sharing our good fortune was the least we could do to express our gratitude. See Appendix 3 for more on history of the three apartments, page 245.

Svetlana, Tatyana, Zen, Valentya and translator Ohla in Chernivtsi,

2016.

My Thirteenth 2016 Visit, Nikolai the 3rd, Luba and Mount Makivka

On the last day at the Lingcomp building, a woman smiled as I walked around her to enter the store in the building. On leaving to enter Valentyn's law office, she again smiled; I hesitated, knowing I had met her before. Smiling, she said "I am Luba". A man stepped forward, saying "I am Nikolai" (Nikolai the 3rd, the grandson of the first Moisey we met in Ukraine). What an unexpected and pleasant encounter.

Valentyn knew of the many times I enquired about the boy Nikolai's activities, and he had arranged this surprise meeting. Valentyn, in his quiet way always thought of others and is extremely effective in achieving results for others. We entered Valentyn's law office with translator Ohla. He left to give us privacy.

The boy, now thirty-two years old and married, told us he had a seven-year-old daughter with a severe thyroid problem from birth. They all live in Luba's house, where the daughter was born. It is the house my father and I visited twenty-one years earlier, when the boy Nikolai the 3rd was living at the Yabluniv Internat School for homeless children.

We talked for more than an hour, at times emotionally holding hands. Life for them, although better, was still difficult. We were sitting below a copy of one of Ukraine's most famous paintings, in what was once Orletski's large living room.

We were discussing the painting as Tatyana walked in for some documents. She removed the painting from the wall and later gave us the rolled-up canvas for our Canadian Ukraine room. Tatyana, like her father, always went out of her way to please us.

Luba responded to my enquiry of how she lived in Ukraine's Perebedova times. During the 1970s, 1980s and early 1990s, she travelled to all the Soviet and a few neighbouring countries, making a living by selling fruit in season, clothing and woodcarvings she purchased primarily from Stari Kuty and Vyhznytsya. She travelled with a friend

 or two, and at times with large groups by train on more than a hundred occasions. These travelers are among the wisest street people one can encounter. Luba now does not travel abroad, instead focusing on creating art works for sale. She presented me with a cleverly decorated liquor decanter made for almost no-cost from recycled materials, which we use on every possible occasion. Nikolai the 3rd works closely with his Mom, and he is back at work after falling while repairing their leaky roof and sustaining two broken legs.

Nikolai related experiencing a few other sad moments. Again, he avoided mentioning his alcoholic father and a few other relatives who treated his family meanly. Luba and Nikolai are friendly and happy survivors, who are typical of many remaining in

remote Ukrainian villages. The amenities of the big cities will take decades to reach these folks.

Poet Stefan Kuz and author Zen with books 2016.

Through the glass door, Tatyana and a man were waiting, as I hugged Luba and Nikolai. As they left, Tatyana entered

the office with poet Степан Кузъ (Stefan Kuz), a relative of my great-grandmother Wasylena and Heroine Olena (Yarema) Kuz.

Tatyana brought in fresh herbata, as I excused myself for a bathroom break, and upon returning Stefan was busily writing poetry in a thick, well-worn scribbler with a short, yellow pencil. He appeared to be a compulsive writer, and I later learned he often carried a scribbler wherever he went.

I met Stefan's wife on September 22, 2014, while he was working in Kyiv. She presented me with his just-published poetry book, *Не Ділітъ Україну (Ukraine Do Not Believe)*. He is no fan of the past communist system and takes several pokes at Putin's eyes. Stefan liked the title and first draft of my book cover. He agreed it was "BETTER to DIE a WOLF than to LIVE the LIFE of a DOG."

Conclusion

In the last twenty-five years since the failure of the Soviet Union, I noticed great increases in Ukraine's standard of living, a pride of language, an explosion in the arts, and a surge in nationalism, patriotism and the confidence of the youth to reach for the stars. The arts have blossomed. Singers win European competitions, and Ukrainian clothing design is witnessed throughout Europe and rapidly spreading to the Americas. Traditional folk dancing, regional costumes and decorating have reemerged from near oblivion. The standard of living in many villages went from bartering and subsistence to cash and smart phones in pockets. Houses progressed from burning wood to gas. Gas is no longer imported from Russia. Putin's cronies in Ukraine's Rada have been exposed for receiving his bribes.

Tsarist and previous occupiers often tried to change Ukraine's rich history, to keep the locals as serfs. A wave of nationalism has and is sweeping the country. Schools are modern and clean. Most old commies have died off. The youth are super confident and fight to root out the last vestiges of communism and corruption. They are hungry for freedom and have embraced the European Union. Nothing will stop them from participating in the ways of the West. The Soviets forced the use of the Russian language. Today the country has reverted to Ukrainian being spoken in households and on streets. This has also occurred in Eastern Oblasts, where the majority spoke Russian, and now speak Ukrainian, except for small areas.

Ukrainian youth have embraced their almost lost culture, and no occupier will ever get them to change. The memory of two six-year olds emphatically wanting to kill Putin in my

2014 visit is still fresh. Today's Ukrainians have turned their backs on the stifling Soviet Union and the yoke of Russian domination and corruption.

Ukraine's Ministry of Economic Development and Trade reported Ukraine's 2017 exports grew by 24.2% (or $4.3 billion) when compared to the first half of 2016. Agricultural exports grew by 28.9%; metallurgy exports by 23.4%; mineral exports by 61.4%; machine building products by 14.2%; various industrial products by 23.1% and light industry products by 9.7%. Ukraine is on a positive move and will become a key contributing cog in the European Union.

Most houses we first stayed at had outdoor toilets; not so in 2017. Most rural folks walked before, but now own cars. We were shocked on our first visit that bus service did not exist. Today, the roads are plied by buses. Electricity in rural Ukraine was available only hours per day, if lucky. Ukraine in 1991 was like rural Canada of the 1930s, at best. Soviet Ukraine had an extremely low standard of living, contrary to the boastfulness of the lying Kremlin and its dictators. Today, some of my relatives are owners of corner stores, restaurants, hotels and participate in owning paintbrush, plastic and brick factories. They are sculptors, clothing designers and fabricators. The average Ukrainian relies less on government than we do in Canada. They are much more self-reliant than Canadians.

Ukraine a Part of Europe for a Millennium

Ukraine has been part of Europe for nearly a thousand years. It is once again at the center of European discussion, and in 2017, an agreement was signed to join the EU (European Union). This is the same agreement that sparked protests and upheaval throughout Ukraine in November 2013, when then President Viktor Yanukovych (Putin's puppet) refused to sign it. In June 2014, newly elected President Petro Poroshenko signed the agreement, taking Ukraine's first step towards full EU membership.

To understand present-day Europe, we need to understand European history. A look at medieval maps and family trees reveals that Ukraine has always been part of Europe.

Early Kievan Rus lands were part of Bukovina unions of tribal principalities related to the central government duty to participate in military campaigns of the Kievan princes and to pay tribute to them. From the 10th century, modern Bukovina territory was part of the Kievan state, and in the 12th century of the Galicia-Volyn Principality. In 1241, it was under the rule of the Tatar khans. In 1514, Bukovina was under Turkish domination.

Because of the Russo-Turkish War of 1768-1774, Russia occupied Bukovina and a year later in 1775 Austria annexed it. Bukovina was under military control, and in 1786, it was connected to Galicia, and in 1849, Bukovina became a separate province; three years after the birth of my great-grandfather Stefan Moisey. At that time, most of Bukovina had little written law. After the collapse of the Austro-Hungarian Empire, Bukovina became part of Romania, and in 1940 became part of the USSR.

WWII Finally Ukraine's Version

The Ukrainian Institute of National Remembrance has published a booklet presenting Ukraine's version of World War II. The booklet can be viewed in English at: issuu.com/memory.ua/docs/ukraina_u_2_pdf_eng_inter/2 The following several pages of italicized sections have been copied from that booklet.

The Ukrainians in the Transcarpathia were the first during the interwar period, who in March 1939 did not wait for the annexation of their region by foreign powers but stood up with arms for their freedom against the aggression of foreign countries.

From September 1, 1939 onwards, the Luftwaffe bombed Galicia and Volynia.

During the Second World War, the front passed the whole of the Ukrainian territory twice. Through Kharkiv, the second largest city in the country, the front passed by four times.

Ukrainians became cannon fodder for two dictators – Hitler and Stalin. Every third man in the Red Army was lost (compared to every 20th in the British army). The reason for this terrible situation was simple – Stalin did not count losses because, as he said: "Women can give birth to more children!"

The victims of this clash of two totalitarianisms were both the military and civilian Ukrainians, the area between the Carpathians and the Don River became known as the "Blood Lands." That was the price Ukrainians paid for a lack of their own independent state.

The Ukrainians fought against Hitler and his allies in the Polish, Soviet, Canadian and French armies, along with those of the American and Czechoslovakian and in the European, African and Asian theatres of war and on the Pacific and Atlantic oceans.

Ukrainian Alexei Berest was one of those who put the Soviet flag on the Reichstag in Berlin, the Ukrainian Michael Strank – was one of the American Marines who raised the American flag at Iwo Jima. But only one army formation fought under the Ukrainian flag during the war – the Ukrainian Insurgent Army (UPA).

[World War II's] approximate losses according to the United Nations [were:] China 15 million, Russia 14 million, Ukraine 8-10 million, Poland 6 million, Yugoslavia 1.1 million, France 550,000, Great Britain 450,000 [and] USA 420,000.

Ukrainians – the Heroes of Second World War:

Olena Viter: Mother Superior of a convent in the Lviv province. During the German occupation, she hid people against severe repression. By saving the Jews during the Holocaust, she was awarded the title of a "Righteous Among the Nations."

Kateryna Zarycka: Organizer of the Women's underground activities network, Head of the Ukrainian Red Cross for the UPA. Awarded the Silver Cross of Merit.

Stefan Vaida: Lieutenant of the 1st Czechoslovak Army Corps. Participant in the Battle of the Dnieper and the battles in the Carpathian Mountains. Killed in Poland. He was awarded the Czechoslovak War Cross 1939-1945 and the Hero of the Soviet Union.

Michael Oparenko: Polish bomber pilot. He participated in the battles against the Nazi aggressors in Poland and later in France and the UK. Was awarded the Polish Cross of Valour twice.

Alex Diatchenko: Sailor U.S. Navy. By the price of his own life

228

tried to save captured German ship from destruction. For his feat of arms he was rewarded by the Silver Star. American military transport ship was named after him (USS Diachenko (APD-123)

Nicholas Oresko: Master Sergeant U.S. Army. For a daring attack on the enemy's fortified position in Germany, he was awarded the highest American honours: the Medal of Honour, the Bronze Star and the Purple Heart.

Peter Dmytruk: Canadian military pilot. He was shot down and joined the French Resistance. Saved civilians from German repression. Awarded the Cross of War.

Ivan Kozhedub: Soviet fighter pilot. The most effective Allied ace. Had 64 air victories. Awarded the Hero of the Soviet Union three times.

My Father's brother, my Canadian uncle Steve Moisey from Andrew, Alberta, also fought in World War II, shed blood, and was lucky to survive.

During the Second World War, most Ukrainians fought on the side of the Allies.

The war began on 1 September 1939 and 120 thousand Ukrainians fought against the Wehrmacht as part of the Polish Army. Most were Polish citizens who came from Galicia and Volynia, which was a part of interwar Poland.

In addition, there were a few dozen veterans of the Ukrainian Army from 1917-1920 serving in the Polish armed forces. These officers also defended Poland in 1939.

After the defeat of Poland in 1939, Ukrainians also fought as part of the Polish armed forces under Soviet and British command. Entering the Polish formations under the USSR, Ukrainians saved themselves from the death sentence that came in the GULAG camps. For this reason, Ukrainians born in Transcarpathia, also joined the 1st Czechoslovak Army

Corps under the command of Ludvik Svoboda

My father's brother Steve Moisey, WWII Canadian Army

On 17 September 1939, the Red Army crossed Poland's eastern border. This was how Soviet Ukrainians entered the Second World War.

Many Ukrainians fought on the Soviet side against Finland in 1939-1940.

More than 6 million Ukrainians fought in the Red Army during the 1941-1945 German- Soviet War.

In the summer of 1945, Ukrainians as part of the Soviet army took part in the defeat of Japan.

At the front from the Atlantic to the Pacific and Norway to Egypt, Ukrainians fought in the Armed Forces of the United States of America (80 thousand), the British Empire (45 thousand), France (6 thousand) and other countries. These were predominantly members of the Ukrainian Diaspora.

During 1942–1950 the Ukrainian Insurgent Army fought in Ukraine, with approximately 100 thousand people moving through its ranks.

Some Ukrainians did fight alongside Germany's allies. Most of them were forced to take this step by trying to survive the German occupation. Some associated with Germany, expecting independence from Soviet Ukraine. Playing on these national feelings, the German invaders created Ukrainian military units during the final stages of the war.

In June 1940, a Soviet Union ultimatum demanded that Romania transfer all of Bessarabia and northern Bukovyna. Without the support of Berlin and not wanting a war, Bucharest gave their territories to the Soviet Union without a single shot fired.

On these newly-occupied territories, the Soviet regime implemented a large-scale repression. In Western Ukraine in 1940 and the first half of 1941, over 10% of the population was deported. In the newly established Ukraine, there were 25 prisons created where tens of thousands of residents were imprisoned.

Even before the end of war with Poland, on 28 September 1939 the German-Soviet Treaty of Friendship, Cooperation and Demarcation was signed, in which a secret protocol was included that specified the spheres of influence in Europe. Afterward, trade agreements were concluded because of which Germany received critical raw materials and supplied the Soviet Union with modern techniques and technology. Because of this cooperation, the Third Reich was able to wage war in the West and could not declare war against their Soviet allies in 1940.

Hot Summer of 1941

Blitzkrieg. *At dawn on 22 June 1941, German troops crossed the USSR border. During the fighting along the border region of Dubno, Lutsk and Brody, Soviet troops were defeated. The Red Army lost their command and began the retreat to the Dnieper River.*

At the same time, in Lviv, Lutsk, Stanislav, Dubno and in dozens of other cities in Western Ukraine there began a mass execution of political prisoners. During the first two weeks of the war, more than 21 thousand people were shot by the NKVD in the prisons of Western Ukraine. With the eastward departure of the Red Army, mass executions took place in Vinnytsia, Uman, Kyiv and other cities.

"Scorched Earth" *The retreat of the Red Army was accompanied by the use of the "scorched earth" tactics. Its need was declared by Stalin in a speech on 3 July 1941. Numerous resolutions of the Council of People's Commissars of the USSR and the Central Committee of the Communist Party of the Soviet Union ordered the destruction of everything that could not be evacuated to the eastern regions of the USSR including plant equipment, machinery, grain etc. One of the horrific crimes of the Stalin regime was the destruction of the Dnieper Dam by NKVD troops in August 1941. This resulted in the death of tens of thousands of Red Army soldiers and civilians who were nearby.*

Military Disaster. *The Red Army's fight in Ukraine in 1941 turned into a disaster. In August-October 1941, the Red Army in Ukraine was destroyed. The number of dead Soviet soldiers is still unknown. In encirclements ("pockets") near Uman, Kyiv and Melitopol about 1 million Red Army soldiers were lost.*

Only at the beginning of 1942 did Soviet command try to begin offensive operations, but they all ended in a crushing defeat for the Red Army. In May-July 1942, Soviet troops were defeated in

232

Kerch, Sevastopol and Kharkiv. The Red Army lost 500 thousand soldiers as prisoners of war. By 22 July 1942, the entire territory of Ukraine was occupied by German troops and their allies.

[...]

Battle for Kyiv

The Battle for Kyiv lasted from early July to 26 September 1941. In August, Hitler rejected the proposal of his General Staff to concentrate all their strength in the direction of Moscow. A directive was quickly signed which moved the offensive south. In early September, Kyiv was "in a vice."

The Soviet garrison in the fortified Kyiv area continued their struggle. The Kyiv resistance lasted for 6 weeks – longer than the resistance for the whole of Poland in September 1939. Only on 19 September, when the Nazis closed their encirclement to the east of Kyiv, did the Red Army leave the capital of Ukraine.

In the pocket at Kyiv, according to German data about 665 thousand Red Army soldiers were captured.

Adolf Hitler stated on the Battle for Kyiv: "The greatest battle in the history of the world!"

According to David Stahel, author of "Kyiv 1941, Hitler's Battle for Supremacy in the East," this offensive was a triumph for Hitler, but it was here and not in Moscow or Stalingrad, that he lost the Second World War. Hitler lost time for his Blitzkrieg, miscalculated the extent of resistance from the enemy, failed to predict the weather and had difficulties supplying ammunition, fuel and refreshments to the occupied territories. These factors were fatal to the war.

Crimes of the Communists in Kyiv

Before their departure from the Ukrainian capital, the Soviet government had mass executions of political prisoners in Kyiv prisons. Many houses were mined by the NKVD and then destroyed. Eighteen months after the fall of the city, there was a crime against culture: Soviet commando units blew up the 11th century Cathedral of the Assumption, the main church of the Kyiv Pechersk Lavra.

On 24 September 1941, NKVD detonated radio- controlled mines that they laid in advance in houses along the central streets of the Ukrainian capital.

NKVD saboteurs destroyed the center of Kyiv, along with its people. Explosions and fires destroyed 324 old houses. Thousands of people in Kyiv were killed and 50,000 were left homeless.

The occupational authorities used the destruction of central Kyiv as an excuse for their accusations against the Jews and soon began their mass killings at Babi Yar.

[...]

Prisoners of War

During the 1941-1942 retreat, the Red Army lost almost 70% of its personnel in Ukraine. Millions of Red Army soldiers were taken to German captivity, a significant portion of which went voluntarily. During the war, there were 180 concentration camps in Ukraine where nearly 1.8 million POWs were killed.

Holocaust

During the occupation, Ukraine lost more than 5 million civilians, of which 1.5 million were Jews. Mass executions began from the first days of the German-Soviet war. Nazi Einsatzkommando groups almost completely destroyed the

234

Jewish community in Lviv, Drohobych, Lutsk, Rivne, Zhytomyr, Kharkiv and dozens of other cities in Ukraine.

Babi Yar

During the 1941-1943 Kyiv occupation, Babi Yar became the place of mass executions of civilians, prisoners of war and resistance movement members. In only two days – 29 to 30 September 1941 – the Nazis shot almost 34 thousand Jews at Babi Yar. The mass shootings at Babi Yar and the neighbouring Syrets Concentration Camp were continuously held until the liberation of Kyiv. During the years of the occupation, there were approximately 70-200 thousand people shot at Babi Yar.

Koriukivka

On 1-2 March 1943, in response to the actions of the Soviet partisans, the German and Hungarian units held punitive actions against the civilians of Koriukivka in the Chernihiv province. They shot several thousand residents and burned almost all the houses. On 9 March 1943, the invaders again came to Koriukivka. On this day, they assembled all the surviving villagers and burned them alive. In three tragic days, the invaders killed 6700 people and burned 1290 houses. It was the largest settlement in Europe that was destroyed by the Nazis as part of their punitive operations during the Second World War.

During the German occupation of Ukraine, there were more than 1370 settlements destroyed. The number of victims of these punitive operations were at least 50 thousand people.

Righteous

According to Yad Vashem, the nation- al Holocaust memorial, 2472 Ukrainians are recognized as saving the lives of the Jews during the Holocaust and given the title "Righteous among the Nations."

During the Nazi occupation of Kyiv, Father Alexander Glagolev and his family saved the Jews of Kyiv from destruction. He hid them in his apartment and in the buildings that belonged to his parish. He also gave them a certificate of baptism on old certificates that remained from the time of his father. In the autumn of 1943, he was arrested by German police and sent to Germany. Along the way, he managed to escape and returned to Kyiv. The "YadVashem" Institute awarded him and his wife and children the title of "Righteous among the Nations."

Trying to save the Jews from extermination, Father OmelyanKovch gave them baptismal certificates. Overall, he released more than 600 certificates. He wrote a letter to Hitler, which condemned the mass killings of Jews and sought permission to visit them in the ghetto. For this, in the spring of 1943 he was arrested by the Gestapo and imprisoned in the Majdanek Concentration Camp, where he secretly continued his priestly activities until his death in 1944. In 1999, the Jewish Council of Ukraine gave him the title of "Righteous of Ukraine."

Guerillas

The lack of political rights, the economic exploitation and the terror against the civilians and prisoners of war caused people to hate the invaders. Hundreds of thousands of Ukrainians took part in the resistance against the Nazi occupation regime.

Soviet Partisans

The underground network was organized by the intelligence agencies of the USSR and the Communist Party. Trained commandos were thrown across the front lines. The Red partisans were formed from emissaries of the Soviet command, residents and soldiers of the Red Army who escaped captivity. Leadership and arms for the Red partisans was provided for by Moscow. Large guerrilla groups were formed in military units, which carried out raids in the German rear. The Red partisans fought against the occupation's forces and administration, committed sabotage operations of communication lines and conducted intelligence activities.

Polish Partisans

In western Ukraine, in addition to the Red partisans, there was also the Polish underground. The Polish government-in-exile sought to restore their pre-1939 eastern border. To do this, they set up the basis of the Home Army (AK). They relied on Polish settlements that were scattered among the Ukrainian population.

Apart from Soviet and Polish partisans, the fight against the German occupiers was also carried out by the Ukrainian Insurgent Army (UPA).

Ukrainian Liberation Movement

The Ukrainian liberation movement existed in western Ukraine before the Second World War. The Organization of Ukrainian Nationalists (OUN) fought for Ukrainian independence against Poland until 1939, from 1939-1941 against the Soviet Union, and after that against Germany.

The summer 1941 attempt of the liberation movement to try to restore Ukrainian independence was suppressed by the German occupiers. The OUN leaders were imprisoned in concentration camps.

During the German occupation, the OUN underground operated across Ukraine from the Carpathians to the Donbas. In eastern Ukraine, raids were organized by members of the OUN who made their way from Galicia and Volynia. Members of these groups found allies among the local population in Kyiv, Dnipropetrovsk, Donetsk, Simferopol and other cities.

Halyna Kuzmenko: born in Chernihiv, grew up in the Donbas, fought with the UPA in the Carpathian Mountains.

In the wooded areas of western Ukraine, Ukrainian nationalists created the Ukrainian Insurgent Army in 1942. The UPA was made up of local people opposed to the German plans for the economic life of their country and the export of the population to the Reich for forced labour. The UPA disorganized the German occupation's administration in Volynia: some areas were temporarily liberated from the Nazis. In the liberated territories, the Ukrainian self-government acted under the protection of the UPA. An example of this territory the area around the Kolky settlement – the insurgent's "Kolky Republic".

In their battles against the German occupiers, the UPA destroyed almost 13 thousand enemies. The objectives of the UPA, AK and the Red partisans were different, which is why in 1943-1944 there were bloody battles between them. A particularly cruel form of conflict occurred during the Polish-Ukrainian conflict, the victims of which became civilians from both sides.

The Expulsion of the Nazis from Ukraine and Central Europe

In 1943, the armies of the anti-Hitler coalition, after their victories in Stalingrad and Al Alamein, began to release territory from Nazi occupation. In the second half of 1943 to the end of 1944, Ukraine became the main theatre of operations in the Eastern Front. In 1944, of the Red Army most were concentrated infantry, armoured and mechanized formations.

Ukrainian Fronts

On 20 October 1943, four Ukrainian fronts were formed based on military units which fought in Ukraine. Henceforth, they especially recruited Ukrainians who were mobilized into the Red Army. From only February 1943 to October 1944, nearly 3.7 million people were mobilized in Ukraine.

Black Infantry ("Chornosvytnyky")

During the offensive, Soviet command started the total mobilization of the civilian male population in Ukraine. A special field army was created which even mobilized 16-17-year olds. Ukrainians, without proper training, were used as "cannon fodder". The communist regime regarded everyone in the Nazi-occupied territories as traitors. In battle, they often went unarmed and in civilian clothes and so they were called "Chornosvytnyky" or the "Black Infantry"

Battle of the Dnieper

In the autumn of 1943, Soviet troops reached the Dnieper River and Stalin ordered them to take Kyiv at any costs by 7 November, a symbolic date for the communist regime – the anniversary of the October Revolution. The

Battle of the Dnieper was the bloodiest battle operation in Europe.

To take the capital of Ukraine before the specified date, Soviet command threw all their available forces into the battle, regardless of their losses. Kyiv was won on 6 November 1943 at the cost of at least 380 thousand soldier's lives. Among them – about 250-270 thousand forcibly mobilized "Chornosvytnyky".

The Rescue of Krakow

In 1944, the retreating Nazis prepared their plans to start mining Krakow. First, transportation and industrial facilities were mined. Next, the historical city center. Soviet intelligence, which was led by Ukrainian Yevhen Berezniak from Dnipropetrovsk and Oleksiy Shapovalov from Kirovohrad, received information about this plan. With this information, engineers promptly destroyed the explosives and the city was saved.

Yevhen Berezniak *– scout, Hero of Ukraine, awarded the*

239

Polish War Order of Virtuti Militari. In 1944, he led a group of scouts, code-named "Voice", which operated in Poland. Captain Yevhen Berezniak operated in the suburbs of Krakow in August 1944. Was arrested by the Gestop but managed to escape. Operated 156 days behind enemy lines. His greatest achievement – saving Krakow from destruction. After returning home, security officers accused him of wanting to stay in captivity. He was taken to an NKVD filtration camp. After his release, he worked as a Ukrainian language teacher. By the 1960's, he was under surveillance by the secret intelligence services. He died in his 99th year.

Auschwitz Liberators

On 27 January 1945 came the end of the most terrible tragedy for the prisoners of the largest Nazi "death factories" – Auschwitz. On 24 January, the 60th Army of the 1st Ukrainian Front launched an offensive against the city of Oswiecim. Almost half of the soldiers of the Army came from Ukraine. During the attack, on 27-28 January, the following concentration camps were freed: Auschwitz-I, Auschwitz II Birkenau and Auschwitz-III Monowitz. The first gate of the main camp was opened by the soldiers of the battalion headed by Poltava-Jew, Anatoly Shapiro of the 100thLviv Division.

Anataoly Shapiro *– participant of the Auschwitz concentration camp liberation, Hero of Ukraine. Born in 1913 in the city of Krasnohrad, in the Poltava province to a Jewish family. Was a trained engineer. During the Second World War, commanded a separate infantry battalion of the 100th Infantry Division. Awarded 20 orders and medals.*

Victory, But Not Liberation

After the expulsion of the Nazis in October 1944, the Soviet totalitarian regime returned to Ukraine. Although, given the important contributions and enormous sacrifices, Ukraine was one of the founding members of the UN, there was no room for an independent Ukraine in the new world order.

The Punished People

The expulsion of the Nazis from Crimea ended on 12 May 1944 and a week later the Soviet government began the deportation of Crimean Tatars. They were accused of mass desertion at the beginning of the war and with rampant collaboration with the occupiers. There were also similar charges made against other people living in Crimea.

The Crimean Tatars contributed to the victory over Nazism. By 1941, the Red Army mobilized more than 12 thousand Crimean Tatars out of which more than 3 thousand died. The title "Hero of the Soviet Union" was awarded to 5 Crimean Tatars, 2 were with honours and one – Amet-khan Sultan – was given the "Hero" title twice.

On 18 May 1944 began the forced eviction of all the Crimean Tatars to Central Asia. By early July, 225 thousand people were deported: 183 thousand Crimean Tatars, 12 thousand Bulgarians, 9.5 thousand Armenians, 15 thousand Greeks and 4 thousand other nationalities. Another 9 thousand Crimeans were exiled from the Red Army in 1945. Due to the deportation conditions, more than 30 thousand deportees were killed before the end of the war.

The World, Divided in Half

On the eve of the final defeat of the Third Reich, the leaders of the "Big Three" – Roosevelt, Stalin and Churchill, met on 4-11 February 1945 at the Yalta Conference. According to the USSR, its decisions affirmed their right to western Ukraine and Belarus, lands that were detached from Poland in 1939.

Because of these Yalta agreements, and later at Potsdam, Europe was divided into two parts: the liberation democratic West and the communist totalitarian East.

Quote: "From Stettin in the Baltic to Trieste in the Adriatic an

"Iron Curtain" has descended across the continent." W. Churchill

Ukrainians continued to suffer losses and after the war, mass repression continued until Stalin's death. An organized resistance to Soviet rule in western Ukraine existed until 1954 and some clashes occurred until 1960. During the suppression of the national movement, about 500 thousand people were repressed (killed, imprisoned or deported).

Another 200 thousand Ukrainians who were in Western European Displaced Person's Camps were not willing to return to the Soviet Union.

Ukraine's Contribution to Victory

Ukrainians made a major contribution to the victory over Nazism, becoming one of the victorious nations.

Millions of Ukrainians, with weapons in their hands, fought against Nazism during the war. Ukraine gave the Red Army: 7 Front and Army Commanders, 200 Generals, more than 6 million soldiers, NCO's and officers.

About 120 thousand Ukrainians met the Nazis in September 1939 as part of the Polish Army. In subsequent years, more than 130 thousand Ukrainians fought in the armies of other anti-Hitler Allies (USA, British Empire, France). Hundreds of thousands of Ukrainians fought Nazism in the resistance movement.

Because of the fighting, more than 700 cities and towns were destroyed in Ukraine along with tens of thousands of villages. Kyiv was 85% destroyed, Kharkiv – 70%, Dnipropetrovsk, Zaporizhzhia and Poltava suffered great devastation and Ternopil was almost destroyed. Nearly 2 million homes were destroyed which resulted in more than 10 million homeless people. Overall, Ukraine's material losses in the war were 285 billion rubles or $100 billion.

During the Soviet retreat of 1941, 550 industrial companies, property and livestock from thousands of farms was taken from Ukraine along with farms and dozens of academic and educational facilities, cultural centers and historical valuables. Nearly 3.5 million inhabitants left the republic – skilled workers and professionals, scholars, intellectuals who gave their labour and intellectual force in the development of the military and economic potential of the USSR.

To gain support in Ukraine, in 1943 Stalin was forced to make certain concessions to Ukrainians. The Ukrainian Fronts were created, the government of the Ukrainian Soviet Socialist Republic was formed based on the People's Commissars (Ministries) of Defense and Foreign Affairs.

In recognition of this Ukrainian contribution to the victory over Germany, Ukraine was included in one of the founding states of the United Nations.

[...] Proclamation of the Third Universal [occurred] on Sofia Square in Kyiv, 20 November 1917 [led by] Ukrainian political leaders Symon Petliura, Mykhailo Hrushevksyi, and Volodymyr Vynnychenko.

[...] Declaration of Independence of Carpathian-Ukraine [occurred on] 15 March 1939.

[...] On 23 August 1939, the Non-Aggression Pact was concluded between the Third Reich and the Soviet Union (the Molotov-Ribbentrop Pact) [...]

Russian expansion by Tsars failed to conquer all of Ukraine up to WWI. Dictator Lenin, and even to Putin today have tried to erase Ukrainian culture. This was not to be; and never will be, because of the indelible Ukrainian spirit. The spirit is reflected in song, poetry, costume, dance and many family activities. It is a culture developed on the work ethic. The work ethic of dozens of previous generations was required to simply survive. Most 19th and 20th century Canadian Ukrainians inherited this work ethic.

The internationally recognized Ukrainian People's Republic just emerged from its own civil war expelling the last Tsar in 1915. Almost immediately a chaotic period of warfare ensued after the Russian Revolution of 1917. The Ukrainian Soviet-Socialist Republic (SSR) on December 30, 1922 became one of the founding republics of the Soviet Union. Initial Soviet policy attacked the Ukrainian language and culture. Russian was forced to be the official language of administrations and schools. A policy in the 1930s tried to impose everything Russian. In 1932 and 1933, under Stalin, millions of people, mostly peasants, in Ukraine starved to death in a politically induced famine (Holodomor) largely due to the "liquidation of the Kulak class." Six to eight million people died from hunger in the Soviet Union during this period, of whom four to five million were Ukrainians. Dictator Nikita Khrushchev was head of the Communist Party in 1953.

History of the Author's three apartments in Vyzhnytsia

Mila Koshovetz (had one daughter) was given the apartment for free. Estimated price in 1994 recorded as 75,400 rubles. Orletski (wife Stefa, husband & daughter), March 29, 1991 paid 3,741 rubles for their apartment. Klym apparently paid more than the others for his apartment. All the above original owners have died, except the daughters of Koshovetz and Orletski.

Zen purchased the three apartments from Mila, Klym and Orletski for $8,000 US, $11,000 US and $11,500 US respectively in the mid-1990s. The apartments were in the name of our distant relative Valentyn Krasniuk for many years and then transferred to the author's name. The apartments were used by Lingcomp, a legal Ukraine/Canada Joint Venture for a Computer and English school for more than a decade. Subsequently the Krasniuks used the apartments for a computer store.

In September 2016, Zen willed the three apartments to three Ukraine female family members. The will is registered in the central registry at Vyzhnytsia. Each recipient has a copy of the willed units. In addition, each inheritor has a hand-written copy, signed by all of us and witnessed by Ohla Sokivka, my translator from Kosiv while we lunched at a Chernivtsi restaurant on Sept 20, 2016. This hand-written document provided Tatyana twelve years of triple net, free rent, including her providing annual proof of fire insurance and use of the units for her various businesses. When I die, they will have their specified apartment in their name.

Stefa Orletski, the previous owner of one of the apartments, stated there was a main street door entrance with a carving. As a young girl living here, she heard horrible things below in the now-filled basement (beatings, shootings, bodies removed – and she told me where they were buried). Stefa asked me not to reveal more of our discussion as some Russian supporters still live nearby. I promised I would wait for many years before telling.

Our faithful lawyer Valentyn was told by Mr. Kordiak how he was beaten and woke up on a dead body in this basement. This occurred between 1945 and the 1950s. Apparently, the building was a former driving school.

Scholarships

You can learn more about the Moisey Scholarships by visiting _www.moiseyscholarship.org_. Here is a list of the Banyliv winners of the Wasylena and Stefan Moisey Scholarship:

- 2005: Maya Andryuk, Mykolaivna Doutchak Mykola Mykolayovych, Lesya Andryuk, Mytskan Petro Petrovych and Choboryak Alina Viktorivna.

- 2006: Havrysh Nadiya, Serhiivna Marchouk, Oleksandr Tanasiyovych,

- 2007: Zahul Iryna Ivanivna, Kuz Oleksandr Ivanovych,

- 2008: Dasevych Kateryna Dmytrivna, Strynadko Galyna Tanasiivna

- 2009: Terteryan Larysa Levonivna, Oleksandryuk Kateryna Ivanivna, Pylypyk Nazariy Tarasovych

- 2010: Magalyas Maryana Vasylivna, Zvarych Oleksiy Ivanovych

- 2011: Kolotylo Mariya Mykhailio, Andryuk Ivan Mykolayovych

- 2012: Chronoguz Tetyana Ivanaivna, Mandryk Ivan Gregorovich

- 2013: Godovanets Tetyana Stepanivna, Stafiychuk Ivan Olekisyovych

- 2014: Kolotylo Yulia and Ivanchuk Grygoriy

- 2015: Romanyuk Alina and Ostashek Petro

- 2016: Anna Andryuk, Mykhailo Kovtunovych

- 2017: Zinovilia and Antonolii Myronov

CUF (Canada Ukraine Foundation)

Here is a list of additional student award winners of the "Doreen & Zenith Moisey Fund" distributed by the Canada Ukraine Foundation in the Lviv office area. First, we have the winners in the Ivano-Frankivsk region:

- Bunziak Oksana, Secondary School of Obertyn, Tlumach region

- Vozniak Taras, Kolomya Secondary School #6

- Grynechko Mariana, Secondary School of Stary Lysets, Tysmenytsa district

- Grynkiv Anastasia, Ivano-Frankivsk Secondary School #21

- Drohomeretsky Yuriy, Secondary School of Pechenizhyn, Kolomya district

- Kozak Mychailo Nadvirna, Secondary School #3

- Konopka Ihor Rogatyn, Grammar School named after Volodymyr Velyky

- Melnichek Ivanna Rogatyn, Secondary School #1 specialized in foreign languages

- Semkiv Yaroslav, Ivano-Frankivsk oblast Boarding Lyceum for talented children from rural regions.

- Stasiuk Nazar, Secondary School of Dovgy Voinyliv,

Kalush District, Scholarship Awards Event, Chernivtsi Region.

Here is the winners list for the Chernivtsi region:

- Marko Olesya Volodymyrivna, Secondary School #3 of Novoselytsya

- Poturnak Kseniya Bohdanivna, Liceum #3 of Chernivtsi

- Oleksyuk Olga Serhiivna, Gymnazium of Kitsman

- Muzyka Dmytro Stanislavovych, Gymnazium of Klishkivtsi

- Dovhan Viktoriya Mykolayivna, Secondary School of Kelmyntsi

- Moldavan Volodymyr Ivanovych, Gymnazium of Zastavna

- Cherednychenko Viktor Ihorovych, Liceum of Hlyboka

- Kuzyk Oleksiy Dmytrovych, Secondary School of Zamostya

- Shvets Bohdana Vyacheslavivna, Secondary School of Sokyryany

- Yakivyuk Dmytro Yuriyovych, NVK "Perlyna Hutsulschyny" of Pidzakharychi

APPENDIX 5

History of Jews in Bukovina

The following section is an excerpt of the chapter "Rus-Banila" from the book Geschichte der Juden in der Bukowina (History of Jews in Bukovina) edited by Hugo Gold, and translated to English by Jerome Silverbush. The original can be found at:

www.jewishgen.org/yizkor/Bukowinabook/buk2_097a.html#f3

As told by Jakob Enzenberg, Kfar Ata, Israel, Published in Tel Aviv, 1962

Rus-Banila which had many Jews lay between Waschkoutz and Wiznitz. In 1888, of the 4222 residents, 818 were Jewish (19.39%) of whom 358 had citizen's voting rights. The Jews of the town farmed and raised cattle. Among these were landowners and those that leased their land. Mendl Thau, Jankel Leder, and Leiser Nagel should be mentioned. The lessee in Slob. Banila, Eisik Lipmann Eifermann was the father of the lawyer Dr. Nathan Eifermann who lives in Argentina. In the forests of Rus-Banila, engineer Schlomo Geller (died 1961 in Tel-Aviv) had a model enterprise. In 1918, a Zionist organization came into existence in Rus-Banila. Its founders were Israel Sattinger (died in Israel), Hermann Neumeier (both were mentioned in the Golden Book of the K.K.L. for their services), also Hermann Bildner the estate owner in the nearby village of Millie who together with his brother-in-law Benno Herer was deported to Siberia by the Russians. Both perished there. The Zionist organization of Rus-Banila participated in an outstanding way in all collections for the K.K.L. and the K.H. and was always at the forefront in all collection efforts. The leadership of the successful and hard working organization was in the hands of Herman Neumeier who later served many years as secretary of the regional Zionist organization in Chernivtsi, the lawyer Dr. Elias Burg (died in Transnistrien) who was in the Bukovina section of the Jewish political federal party and Moses Bildner (presently active in the Defense Ministry in Tel-Aviv). The above named were responsible for the opening of a well attended Hebrew school in Rus-Banila in 1918. Rus-Banila took active part in every Zionist campaign. The first national battle took place with the regional parliment election (1910) as Prof. Kellner and Dr. Straucher ran for office. 705 of the Jewish voters of Rus-Banila voted for Prof. Kellner. David Bildner, a good Talmud scholar and an expert on Maymonides stated at that time that it was in the interest of the national Jews to vote for Prof. Kellner's list. His example was decisive in the outcome of the election. There were 1200 Jews in Rus-Banila.

The rabbi of Rus-Banila, Rabbi Berisch Reimann and his son Elieser and family died on the way to Transnistrien. After, the occupation of Rus-Banila by the German-Romanian armies, 263 Jews were murdered by the Soldateska and the Ukrainian village residents. They were buried in two mass graves in the Jewish cemetery. About 70 families lost their lives in Transnistrien, 15 were transported over the Bug and then murdered by the SS. It is certain that we will remember their fate with great sadness.

As told by Zwi Hermann Neumeier, Tel –Aviv

APPENDIX 6A **MOISEY FAMILY TREE, CANADA**

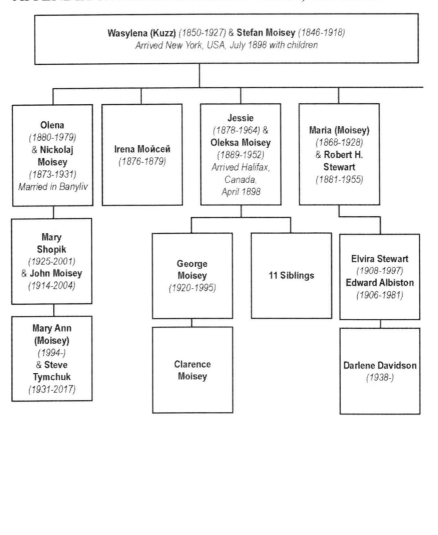

Wasylena (Kuzz) *(1850-1927)* & **Stefan Moisey** *(1846-1918)*
Arrived New York, USA, July 1898 with children

Olena
(1880-1979)
& **Nickolaj Moisey**
(1873-1931)
Married in Banyliv

Irena Мойсей
(1876-1879)

Jessie
(1878-1964) &
Oleksa Moisey
(1889-1952)
Arrived Halifax, Canada, April 1898

Maria (Moisey)
(1868-1928)
& **Robert H. Stewart**
(1881-1955)

Mary Shopik
(1925-2001)
& **John Moisey**
(1914-2004)

George Moisey
(1920-1995)

11 Siblings

Elvira Stewart
(1908-1997)
Edward Albiston
(1906-1981)

Mary Ann (Moisey)
(1994-)
& **Steve Tymchuk**
(1931-2017)

Clarence Moisey

Darlene Davidson
(1938-)

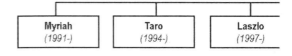

Myriah
(1991-)

Taro
(1994-)

Laszlo
(1997-)

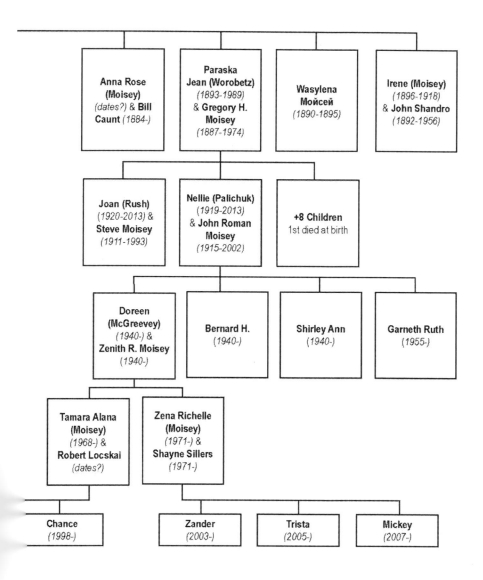

Anna Rose (Moisey)
(dates?) & **Bill Caunt** *(1884-)*

Paraska Jean (Worobetz)
(1893-1989)
& **Gregory H. Moisey**
(1887-1974)

Wasylena Мойсей
(1890-1895)

Irene (Moisey)
(1896-1918)
& **John Shandro**
(1892-1956)

Joan (Rush)
(1920-2013) &
Steve Moisey
(1911-1993)

Nellie (Palichuk)
(1919-2013)
& **John Roman Moisey**
(1915-2002)

+8 Children
1st died at birth

Doreen (McGreevey)
(1940-) &
Zenith R. Moisey
(1940-)

Bernard H.
(1940-)

Shirley Ann
(1940-)

Garneth Ruth
(1955-)

Tamara Alana (Moisey)
(1968-) &
Robert Locskai
(dates?)

Zena Richelle (Moisey)
(1971-) &
Shayne Sillers
(1971-)

Chance
(1998-)

Zander
(2003-)

Trista
(2005-)

Mickey
(2007-)

253

APPENDIX 6B **MOISEY FAMILY TREE, UKRAINE**

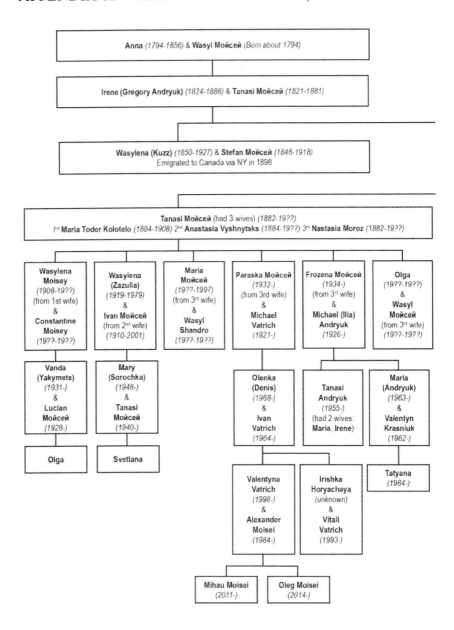

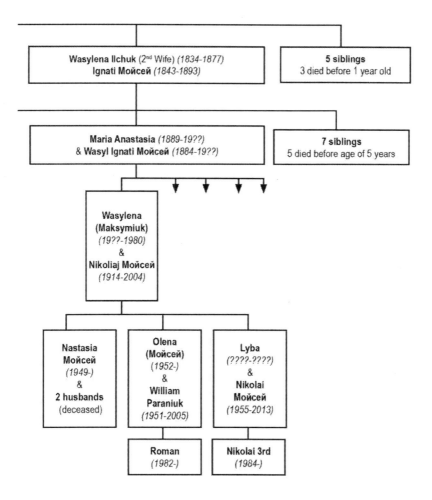

Ukrainian Sculptor Roman Paranuik & Canadian Artist Mykola Bidniak

The following has been copied from the article "Angel In Flight" by Iryna Yehorova published on December 12, 2006 in *Dyen'* (The Day). The original can be read here: *day.kyiv.ua/en/article/culture/angel-flight*

Only those who loved Mykola Bidniak and appreciated his talent were present at the unveiling of his gravestone in Lychakiv Cemetery. Perhaps this is the way it was meant to be? Maybe outsiders shouldn't go there. From now on, a bronze "Angel in Flight" will always greet those who walk down one of the central alleys of Lviv's Lychakiv Cemetery and remind them of this remarkable man and artist (see Den, March 11, 2006).

In his last will Bidniak said that he wanted to be buried in the city of lions, where he spent the last 10 years of his life. He lived most of his adult life in Canada, where he was educated, created his works by painting with his mouth, and dreamed of Ukraine, which he had left as a small boy and where he would be able to return only after it became independent. The artist's wife, the noted singer from Lviv, Mariika Maichyk, introduced Mykola Bidniak to Ukraine, while the international community learned about him thanks to the Association of Mouth and Foot Painting Artists of the World, based in Liechtenstein. Bidniak, who lost his arms at age 15, when a mine exploded, headed this organization for many years.

Remarkably, all those who learn about Bidniak's creative legacy and life since his death agree that he is the most dramatic personality of the second half of the 20 th century. His friends, who remember his infectious laughter and optimism, say that Mykola was a happy man. They valued his company so much when he was alive that they do not want to let go of him even now.

Perhaps some people would think this unimportant, but Bidniak is in excellent company in Lychakiv Cemetery. Lying next to him is Dmytro Krvavych, the sculptor and veteran lecturer from the art academy, who said of Bidniak: "He is a giant of 20th-century Ukrainian icon painting. We do not have a more spectacular personality in the sacred art of our time. I think that only a man who has access to another, higher, world can create such masterpieces. The creativity of this genius spans many genres and is unique in terms of complex techniques and rich palette. It is extremely important to study every aspect of his creativity. We still do not know who Mykola Bidniak is for us; we do not realize in whose company we are."

On the other side of Bidniak's grave is Emanuil Mysko, probably one of his closest friends with whom he shared his joys and sorrows. Prof. Mysko, rector of Lviv's Academy of Arts, marveled at the Mykola Bidniak phenomenon. He wrote: "Does not Mykola represent an enigma? He was raised and educated in a foreign modern environment but nevertheless remained Ukrainian by profession, vocation, and creative orientation. Does he not set an example worthy of being emulated by some of our homegrown aesthetes, who are trying to outstrip cosmopolitans and amaze the formalistic world?

"This world has not conquered Mykola Bidniak with his inherently creative way of thinking and national mentality. From a great distance, he clearly saw, sensed, and appreciated the native Ukrainian creative heritage that dates back centuries and has undergone natural selection, in which the finest humanistic ideas have continued to evolve."

257

To say that it is a shame that Ukraine knows so little about this artist is to say very little. Only art specialists and a handful of aesthetes know which of his creations are stored in which museums. Chornobyl Madonna is at the National Art Museum of Ukraine; Man Engulfed by Fire is in Kaniv. Some works are at the Culture Foundation and the Shevchenko Committee, but most of his creations -about 40 in all — are in the storerooms of the National Museum in Lviv. All these works are gifts.

Meanwhile, Ukraine failed to bestow citizenship on him and did not even contribute any funds to his gravestone. All the expenses — the sculpture by Mykola Posikira, the bronze cast, and installation — were paid for by Moscow businessman Valerii Levin.

"We met in the Crimea," he recalls. "I watched him work on his plein-air paintings for three years. I heard him speak English and tried to communicate in the same language, but I wasn't much good at it. And then I heard him speak Ukrainian. I was so happy! I was raised in an orphanage in Sambir and then lived in Kyiv for quite some time, so I can say that Ukraine is not a foreign land for me.

"After Mykola and I became friends, my life acquired a somewhat different meaning. For those who met him even once, Mykola Bidniak served as an example of vital strength and courage. To healthy people he gave strength and sincerity, something we so often lack in this world today. So my wife Ludmila and I wanted to do something for him."

Mykola Bidniak's widow is looking forward to publishing a monograph written by the art historian, Dr. Volodymyr Ovsiichuk. The manuscript has been collecting dust for three years. "Three times I have tried to contact the president of Ukraine, Kateryna Yushchenko, and the Ministry of Culture, let alone lower-ranking bureaucrats, asking them to help publish it, but to no avail," says Mrs. Bidniak. "There is still no money to publish it, even though Mykola donated his best works to various prestigious Ukrainian museums. The impression is that Ukraine does not need him even after his death, although his destiny and creative work may be regarded as the best example of patriotism, civic, and purely human courage."

Those who watched him decorate churches, perched high on top of scaffolding, those who heard his excellent lectures at the Chair of Sacred Art at the Art Academy of Lviv, and those who saw his works dedicated to Ukraine's liberation efforts, painted long before the 1990s or in independent Ukraine, will forever cherish their memories of Mykola Bidniak. After he was awarded the Taras Shevchenko Prize and the Order of Yaroslav the Wise, and after becoming a member of the National Artists' Union of Ukraine, the artist said, "I have been and remain simply Mykola Bidniak." Such a statement is possible only from one who has untold riches in his soul.

IMF Publishes a Ukraine Report

The International Monetary Fund published its Ukraine country report on October 3, 2016. The following is an excerpt from the report. The full report can be viewed here: www.imf.org/en/Publications/CR/Issues/2016/12/31/Ukrai ne-Second-Review-Under-the-Extended-Fund-Facility-and-Requests-for-Waivers-of-Non-44318

The authorities have continued to make progress in implementing the program. Notwithstanding the delay in completing this review, mainly related to a difficult approval process of the 2016 budget and political tensions culminating in a change in government in April 2016, important policy measures have been taken since the last review. This includes a sizable fiscal adjustment; a successful completion of the debt operation with private bondholders; the increase in gas and heating tariffs to full cost recovery; and decisive steps to rehabilitate the banking system. However, progress in tackling corruption, privatizing state-owned enterprises (SOEs), and advancing pension reform has been slower than envisaged against significant political resistance.

The economy has stabilized and is showing signs of a gradual recovery. Following a severe economic crisis, activity is picking up, inflation has receded quickly, and confidence is improving. International reserves have doubled to over US\$14 billion.

Continued determined policy implementation is needed to achieve program objectives, given the still significant challenges lying ahead. The new government has affirmed its commitment to the program's reform agenda. Policies in the period ahead aim to: (i) further strengthen public finances via expenditure consolidation— including pension reform—and improvements in tax administration; (ii) continue to improve banks' financial health; (iii) maintain prudent monetary policy and exchange rate flexibility; and (iv) speed up structural reforms to overhaul the SOE sector, improve the business climate, and, importantly, tackle corruption, without which the program cannot be successful. The policy agenda is ambitious, and its timely implementation remains critical.

Staff supports the completion of the second review, and the authorities' requests for waivers of the missed performance criteria, rephasing of access, and financing assurances review. All prior actions have been met, demonstrating the authorities' commitment to the program and offering assurances of their ability to achieve program objectives. The purchase available upon completion of this review would be equivalent to SDR 716.110 million, bringing total purchases under the EFF to SDR 5,444.21 million.

The same day as the IMF report, October 3, 2016, the BBC reported slave labor is being used in prisons in Russian-occupied territories of Donetsk, Luhansk. The following is borrowed from the BBC article, which can be read here: www.bbc.com/news/magazine-37512356

Human rights activists in eastern Ukraine say they have evidence that slave labour camps reminiscent of Soviet gulags are operating in rebel-controlled areas. A newly published report alleges that 5,000 people in the self-declared Luhansk People's Republic are held in solitary confinement, beaten, starved or tortured if they refuse to carry out unpaid work. [...]

"About 5,000 people work without payment every day to preserve their life and health, to receive visits from relatives and not to die of hunger," [the report] goes on. "All this takes place for enriching a certain group of people in the so-called LPR." [...]

The director of the Eastern Human Rights Group, Pavel Lisyansky, says he has evidence that a similar forced labour system is employed in prisons in the neighbouring Donetsk People's Republic (DPR), another rebel-held region, affecting a further 5,000 prisoners. A report on conditions in the DPR will be published next month.

"It's hard to believe that we are witnessing slave labour in the middle of Europe in the 21st Century. But this is happening, and something needs to be done," Lisyansky says.

The following is taken from an October 3, 2016 blog post by Alexei Sobchenko on the website of the Atlantic Council called "Kremlin Panics after Dutch Report, and it Should" The full article can be viewed here: www.atlanticcouncil.org/blogs/ukrainealert/kremlin-panics-after-dutch-report-and-it-should

The report of the Dutch-led investigation team on the shoot down of Malaysian Airlines Flight 17 over eastern Ukraine offered a momentary glimpse into the true nature of the proverbial riddle wrapped in a mystery inside an enigma. Instead of denying any Russian involvement in the death of 298 people in July 2014, many official spokespersons, journalists, and bloggers known for their close ties to the Kremlin reacted nervously and with contradictory responses. [...]

This unusual variety of perspectives on such a crucial issue betrays fear in Moscow's official circles. Before the report, Kremlin propaganda denied not only Russian or separatist involvement in the tragedy, but even refused to admit that the Boeing was shot down by a Russian-made missile. [...]

Putin and his cohorts have been caught red-handed in willful mendacity on many previous occasions and the Russian regime has invariably maintained its collective poker face. [...]

The international investigative team indicated that about a

hundred individuals were "linked to the crash or to the transport of the Buk" missile, though the investigators have yet to determine who could be held criminally responsible. There is a chance that some of them belong to Russia's top leadership, perhaps all the way up to Putin himself. We know what happened to the Libyan leader Muammar Gaddafi after he was implicated in the 1988 bombing of Pan Am Flight 103, which blew up over Lockerbie, Scotland. Gaddafi became an international pariah, banned from visiting all Western capitals other than New York during UN General Assembly sessions.

A similar ban might be considered for the perpetrators of the MH17 shootdown. A quick detour through recent Soviet history can help clarify what such a ban would mean for contemporary Russian elites. [...]

Being cut off from enjoying their wealth in the West would render Russian elites' existence drab and even senseless. Nothing would scare them more than an extension of the 2012 Magnitsky Act, which banned a handful of Russian nationals from entering the US due to their complicity in the death of a Russian lawyer investigating corruption.

The people responsible for downing MH17 could be subject to a similar travel ban. [...]

Russian history has several examples of Russian elites turning against their national leader. Putin has every reason to fear the fate of Tsars Peter III and Pavel I, or even General Secretary Joseph Stalin, who died under mysterious circumstances.

APPENDIX 9

Olena (Yarema) Kuz, 1915 Heroine, Ukrainian Sich Riflemen.

Following are several accounts of Olena (Yarema) Kuz. She volunteered with the Sich Riflemen, about which Wikipedia has this to say:

> *The unit was formed in August 1914 on the initiative of the Supreme Ukrainian Council. It was composed of members of different Ukrainian paramilitary organizations in Galicia, led by Frank Schott, and participated in hostilities on the Russian front.*

In 1915, the Russian Tsar's forces pressed further west and battled for strategic Mount Makivka in Galicia, northwest of Banyliv. The control of the hill oscillated between the Tsar and Austrian forces.

Account #1: A Woman Who Fought Better than Men
The accounts below are from European and American newspapers:

Twenty-year-old Olena (Yarema) Kuz was a graduate of Chernivtsi teachers' seminary higher trade school and volunteered with the Sich Riflemen. She underwent training on par with men, and later fought in the cavalry, demonstrating unprecedented courage. Olena was twice wounded, the second time very seriously. Her treatment took her to Vienna. The Emperor's personal physician treated her. Olena Kuz, at the beginning of war, was with the Red Cross, then in the cavalry YCC. She was one of thirty women in the Austro-Hungarian army's independent Ukraine cavalry.

In archives in the United States, Austria and Germany,

one can find a lot of information about the wild Bukovina of the past and now. Her story is an example of heroism. A work of Ukrainian historians identifies the name as "A. Kuz" in the descriptions of the struggle of Sich Riflemen. Olena (Yarema) Kuz, 1885 — unknown date of death), cadet at the equestrian academy in USS. She was awarded silver and bronze medals of bravery. Born in the village Banyliv, she graduated as a teacher, became a heroine and now her actions are revealed to us, after being concealed by the Soviet Union.

Chairman of the association of the "Ukrainian National Home" in Chernivtsi, Vladimir Starik, translated and published an article about her from the 1915 Viennese newspaper *Neue Post Freie Press*. Later, a mosaic of information about her from various sources (newspapers of that time, European and American current publications, research papers) emerged. Some facts have recently become known. For example, Yarema Kuz (Кузъ) experienced serious personal drama, which led her to enrolling with the Sich Shooters).

The Austrian authorities sent her father Tanase Kuz (Кузъ) (my great grandmother's brother) to the Talerhof concentration camp in Austria at the beginning of the war on a false charge of him betraying the Emperor by siding with the Tsar. He was found innocent, released and died of typhus before returning home. She lived a life of almost Shakespearean drama: daughter and father were accused of betraying the Emperor, a story recorded by the Legion Sich Riflemen (Ukrainian military unit in the Austrian army, which operated on the Russian front in 1914-1918).

Olena's father, Tanase Kuz, was a native of the village

of Ruska Banyliv, a fact recorded in the village census book. George Menzak, a well-respected man, states Tanase was an educated, intelligent man. When married, he moved to Chernivtsi, where he bought a house on Berezhansky Street. He was a railway officer with six children, Olena (Yarema) being the fourth. The arrival of Russian troops had tragic consequences for Tanase. After the Austrian troops returned to Bukovina, someone made an accusation against him that he collaborated with the Russians. The Austrians arrested and deported him to the camp in Talerhof, an internment camp created by the Austro-Hungarian authorities during World War I, in a valley in the foothills of the Alps, near Graz, the main city of the province of Styria. Styria is a state or Bundesland, in southeast Austria. A judge found him not guilty and released him. He did not return home and died of typhoid in 1915.

Account #2:

I wanted to study in Vienna. A reporter for the Regional news weekly, "Union of Liberation of Ukraine" wrote in 1915, about a badly wounded Olena (Yarema) Kuz at the Queen Elizabeth Hospital in Vienna, Austria.

Olena, a graduate of teaching from the University of Chernivtsi went to Vienna to obtain a higher degree in teaching from the merchant IT Academy, but instead enrolled in rifle sharpshooting classes in Vienna. She then signed up with the Sich Riflemen, cavalry division, led by Hoffmann (Ukrainian Sich Riflemen [USS Riflemen]): the only independent Ukrainian national military force, as part of the Austro-Hungarian army formed of volunteers, who responded to the orders of the Ukrainian Supreme Council of 6 August 1914, and were led by the Ukrainian Battle Board (UBU) in the first battalion division, Korsika, at the village of Upper Vyhnanka, now Chortkivsk district of Ternopil region.

The reporter states that Tanase Kuz, Olena's father, was wrongly accused, and that Tanase died. One brother died at the front; the other was captured. Olena, a petit 20-year-old, with slender masculine features was attractive to males. She was a good soldier and wore standard male army boots and field uniforms. Her chest is decorated with two medals, silver and bronze, for courage.

The reporter states that Olena (Yarema) participated in many battles of the early war. She was first wounded in the leg in the Carpathians, and then returned to become famous in the battle at Mount Makivka, Ukraine, for which she received the title of senior officer and medals of bravery.

At the top of Mount Makivka, guarding a strategic pass, the Russian Tsar's forces had several types of weapons (rifled and smoothbore guns, flintlock muskets, cannon and the rotating- cylinder machine guns, call "Chris" (a name used more frequently in Western Ukraine, especially in the Carpathians). The Muscovites were well-entrenched at the mountain top, with many troops, located directly over the strategic pass. On a patrol with eight soldiers led by Olena Kuz, at night, the group threw hand grenades, destroying the machine guns of the hated enemy.

On my last visit to Ukraine I walked the 4.5-kilometer new Makivka trail to a newly erected memorial at the strategic top. I estimate Olena's ascent by the shortest route in the dark, without making noise to alert sentries, would have taken at least two nights to climb.

The "Union of Liberation of Ukraine" reporter continues

that on another occasion Olena led thirty Bukovina Hutzul Sharpshooters, who carried on their backs (dripping with sweat and blood) ammunition for the fighters in the Mountain Division. She advanced under the bullets, hiding in the pits created from bombs. With the ammunition, her compatriots dispersed the enemy.

After Mount Makivka they went, to the Russian front moving east with the Allied forces, which were led by the riflemen. The Muscovites were scattered. Olena learned from three residents the hiding location of some Muscovites. On horseback, she reached Hebetic (a village in Ukraine's Skole district, Lviv region) and a peasant woman informed Olena that the neighboring house had Cossacks. Olena, with a revolver, came up to the house, captured three Cossacks and took important documents. From the captives, she learnt that nearby were senior Russian officers. She then proceeded to capture one Russian lieutenant, who said, "I am sorry and ashamed that I am captured by a young girl."

The following is the inscription on a plaque on the Angel sculpture at the top of Mount Makivka. It is written in Ukrainian and English:

Пам'яті Олени (Яреми) Кузь уродженки с. Банилів стрільця з лав Українських Січових Стрільців, гора Маківка

29 квітня 1915 року разом з 8-ма іншими героями Олена гранатами знищила російське кулеметне гніздо, що посприяло припиненню царської влади в Україні.

Скульптура "АНГЕЛ"

Автор: Роман Паранюк, с.Банилів

Встановлено: Іван Ватрич, с.Іспас, 2017

На спільні пожертвування: мешканців с.Банилів, с.Іспас та канадців Doreen & Zen Moisey

BANYLIV HEROINE OLENA (YAREMA) KUZ,

Volunteer "Ukraine Legion Sich Riflemen" at Mount Makivka with 8 men, at morning day-break, on April 29, 1915 grenade the Russian machine gun nests leading to the removal of the last from Ukraine.

ANGEL SCULPTURE by BANYLIV ROMAN PARANIUK, ERECTED by ISPAS, IVAN VATRICH, 2017.

DONATED by the RESIDENTS of BANYLIV, ISPAS and CANADIANS DOREEN & ZEN MOISEY

Account #3

About Olena Kuz, on January 24, 1916 more is written in several American newspapers, says Vladimir Staruk, who obtained a photo of Olena Kuz, which was distributed to the American Press Association.

The photo captioned: Countess Olena Kuz, Austrian woman officer, twice awarded for Honor. Bukovinka, came from a simple family to be called Countess; such a great honor. What was the heroine's fate after she left hospital?

Did she return to fight? The report includes only a short sentence on this question: "Olena demobilized in 1917 and lived with her sister Wasylena in Vienna, where she died." When, is not known.

Account #4

Maria Tanasiyivna (née Kuz) Luchka who lives in Banyliv wrote "The bravest woman from Bukovina, who is famous all over the world" about Olena (Yarema) Kuz. Luchka states that Olena, while recuperating in Vienna, worked as a French language teacher. Maria and family always knew that her cousin was a heroine, but in Soviet times, to say this was impossible. The family knew the daughter of Tanase Kuz was a courageous woman, who went to the Sich Riflemen for her father. Maria's grandmother Wasylena Kuz said that during the war, Olena Kuz came to her house. Maria's grandmother said Olena came riding from across the Cheremosh River, accompanied by her soldiers. She was wounded in the arm. Maria believes this was the first wound from fighting in the Carpathians. Maria said, "She lived with my grandmother for a month, until the wound healed. My grandmother cooked her food. Olena was carrying a map, which she often looked at. This is all I know of her."

I met Maria Luchka, who wrote the above article in September 2016. There was a slight drizzle as we sat and talked in Tanasi's car. Maria was in the back and had her file with maps and newspaper clippings. It was at this moment I learned my great-grandmother was the older sister of the heroine's father, Tanase. This was later confirmed from the Chernivtsi archives.

Our car was in front of Maria's home at the north edge of Banyliv, near the Cheremosh River. She pointed in the direction of the river to a large, two-story, uninhabited building. This building is on the exact location of an old house where heroine Olena (Yarema) Kuz, wounded for the first time, was nursed by her grandmother.

After the pleasant meeting Maria returned with umbrella to her house. Tanasi, translator Ohla and I drove to the vacated building, where we were immediately charged by two German Shepheard dogs from a nearby fish farm. We quickly jumped back in the car, calling it a day and departed for Valentyn's home.

Olena was on a wave of nationalism that saw Ukraine adopt today's Flag, National Anthem and Tryzub symbol.

Account #5

Olena (Yarema) Kuz (Кузъ), wounded for the first time recouped at her grandmother's house in Banyliv. She returned and fought several more battles, earning the Silver and Bronze Metals for bravery. In April of 1915, Olena with eight brave volunteers in the middle of the night lobbed grenades, taking out the strategic located machine guns on Mount Makivka and establishing the turning point against the Tsar, in favor of Austria and Western Ukraine.

Olena, wounded again at Golden River, Ivano-Frankivsk Province with shattered ribs of grenade shrapnel and falling from her horse lay in a coma for eight hours. She received medical care in Budapest and then transfer to the Queen Elizabeth hospital in Vienna where she was attended to by the personal physician of the Emperor. The Emperor took a personal interest in Yarema (Olena) Кузъ, a petite pretty woman, with exceptional bravery. She became a hero in a relatively free Ukraine. She stoked independence.

Olena's sister was at her side during recuperation. The sisters lived together in Vienna, where Olena made a living teaching French. She died young; the date and place of her burial in Vienna are still unknown. Some of us are sleuthing this distant relative. She was brave and loved her beloved family and Ukraine. Olena emotionally stirred millions of Ukrainians to dream of an independent Ukraine. Her actions were printed in the major press of the day; even reaching America.

Wikipedia also has this to say about the Ukrainian Sich Riflemen:

> *After World War I, with Austria's disintegration, the unit became the regular military unit of the West Ukrainian People's Republic. During German and Austrian occupation of Ukraine in 1918 the unit was stationed in southern Ukraine. Former unit soldiers participated in the formation of Sich Riflemen, a military unit of the Ukrainian People's Republic. In 1919 the Ukrainian Sich Riflemen expanded into the Ukrainian Galician Army [...] They participated in the Polish–Ukrainian War around Lviv and suffered heavy losses. On May 2, 1920, the unit was disbanded.*

Account # 6: Wikipedia Entry on the Ukrainian Sich Riflemen
The Wikipedia entry on the Ukrainian Sich Riflemen explains the "Origins and Formation" of the Sich Riflemen. The page can be viewed here:

en.wikipedia.org/wiki/Ukrainian_Sich_Riflemen

> *Many Ukrainian youth organizations formed in Galicia as early as 1894, the result of the growing national consciousness among Ukrainians in Galicia. In 1900, a sports/firefighting organization Sich was founded by a lawyer and social activist Kyrylo Tryliovs'kyi in Sniatyn (today's Ivano-Frankivsk Oblast), which rejuvenated the ideas of Cossack Zaporozhian Sich to foster the national patriotism among the young generation. Alongside these organizations, forming across Galicia, parallel sports/firefighting organizations (Sokil) (Falcon) were also springing up. By 1912, many smaller Sich*

companies appeared in numerous Ukrainian communities. Along with these youth organizations, a Women's Organizational Committee was set up to train nurses. The Ukrainian Sich Union coordinated the activities of all local Sich companies and printed its own newspaper, "The Sich News". By the start of the First World War there were at least 2000 such organizations in Galicia and Bukovyna.

In 1911, a philosophy student from Lviv, Ivan Chmola, organized a secret paramilitary group, composed of young men and women from Lviv University, Academic Gymnasium, and other local schools. These enthusiasts learned how to use firearms, prepared military manuals, translated military terminology and lobbied the Austrian authorities to legalize the Ukrainian paramilitary organizations. They were greatly influenced by the similar Polish paramilitary organizations, such as Związek Strzelecki, that were quite numerous, well-organized and — unlike the Ukrainian organizations — legal. This group later published its own newspaper, "Vidhuk", and continued to organize Lviv's Ukrainian youth. However, several attempts to legalize it were blocked by the local authorities, who were mostly Poles.

Although initially Chmola chose the name "Plast" for this formation, this group represented only one isolated attempt to organize the Ukrainian youth into a legitimate scouting movement under this name. In June 1912, Dr. Oleksandr Tysovs'kyi, a teacher at the Academic Gymnasium in Lviv, administered a ceremony, at which a group of young students under his tutelage took a scout's oath. Thus the official Ukrainian scouting organization Plast was born. Explicitly paramilitary elements were expressly excluded by the organization's constitution, written by Dr. Tysovs'kyi, because he desired to focus the its efforts primarily on fostering the ideological aspect of national patriotism, as well as, of course, on advancing the standard scouting curriculum. Possessing greater authority and commanding respect in the Lviv civil society, Dr. Tysovs'kyi won the upper hand, and Ivan Chmola eventually joined efforts with him. Nevertheless, Chmola continued his efforts to train the youth, started organizing scouting camps and teaching adolescents various survival skills, orienteering in different terrains and similar useful skills based on self-reliance, discipline and, most importantly, fellowship. This initiative attracted several prominent individuals, who would later also play important roles in the creation of the Sich Riflemen — for example, Petro Franko, Ivan Franko's son. And many individuals continued to secretly train militarily, of their own accord.

Finally, Kyrylo Tryliovs'kyi translated a similar statute of a Polish paramilitary sharpshooter organization and submitted it to the Austrian authorities for approval. This time, the officials had no choice but to grant approval, and a society of "Sich Sharpshooters" (Sichovi Stril'tsi) was finally legalized in the Kingdom of Galicia and Lodomeria on 18 March 1913. The first such company was set up in Lviv, soon to be augmented by Ivan Chmola and his group. Legalization of Sich Sharpshooters gave impetus to other Ukrainian youth organizations, and the ranks of Sich, Sokil and Plast subsequently swelled up across Western Ukraine.

In the spring of 1913, the Ukrainian Sich League was formed in Lviv, and a statute of Ukrainian Sich Sharpshooters (USS) was drafted. On 25 January 1914 the second society "Sich Sharpshooters II" was organized in Lviv, numbering over 300 members. Sich Sharpshooters I included mostly students and Sich Sharpshooters II - mostly workers and peasants. By World War I, there were 96 Sich Sharpshooter societies in Galicia alone. Plats was by then transformed into a full-fledged scouting organization with branches in many towns and villages. Many of these young scouts would continue to voluntarily join Ukrainian Sich Sharpshooter movement even well after the war was over, and future generations would also participate in the liberation struggles between the wars and in

World War II. After many trials and tribulations, having survived in the Ukrainian Diaspora, Plast was reorganized in Ukraine shortly before Ukraine's independence in 1991 and continues to be the largest scouting organization in Ukraine, fostering the values of national patriotism among Ukrainian youth.

Initially there was no unanimity among the founders of the Ukrainian Sich League as to its goals: some wanted complete independence of the Ukrainian people from the Austro-Hungarian empire, and some wanted limited autonomy within the empire. The pro-Austrian faction prevailed, and only units loyal to the Habsburg monarchy could exist. From its inception, Ukrainian Sich Sharpshooters saw Russia as their main enemy and were preparing to liberate Ukrainian lands from under the yoke of Russian Empire. In Galicia and Bukovyna, Sich Sharpshooters were also circulating a magazine called "Vidhuk" ("Response"). In 1914, a statute of USS was published, which established the order of service and the uniforms, provided military terminology and commands in the Ukrainian language. That same year ammunition and rifles were procured for a 10,000-strong Legion of Ukrainian Sich Sharpshooters, which participated in Lviv parade on 28 June 1914, along with all the youth organizations - Sich, Sokil and Plast. That same day, Archduke Franz Ferdinand was assassinated in Sarajevo by a Serbian nationalist, precipitating the chain of events that led to World War I.

One month later, World War I broke out and the newly established General Ukrainian Council published in a Lviv newspaper "Dilo" the call for Galician Ukrainians to form volunteer units to fight the Russian Empire. The Ukrainian leaders in Austria-Hungary hoped that the formation of these units would advance the cause of national liberation. They also sought to dispel the suspicions of some Galician Russophiles that the Ukrainians in that area were sympathetic to Russia. The Austrian war ministry was not prepared for this

275

initiative of the General Ukrainian Council and allowed creation of a unit with only 2,500 men. The first volunteers were mainly members of Ukrainian nationalist organizations such as Sich, Sokil and past.

Account #7

The Internet Encyclopedia of Ukraine has an entry on the Ukrainian Sich Riflemen written by Petro Sogol that the following has been copied from. The original can be viewed at:

www.encyclopediaofukraine.com/display.asp?linkpath=pages%5CU%5CK%5CUkrainianSichRiflemen.htm

Ukrainian Sich Riflemen (Ukrainski sichovi striltsi [USS], Legion USS). The only Ukrainian unit in the Austrian army. Organized in Galicia in August 1914 at the initiative of the Supreme Ukrainian Council, it was supervised by the Ukrainian Combat Board. The first volunteers were members of Ukrainian paramilitary organizations, such as the Sich societies, Sokil, and the Plast Ukrainian Youth Association. In September 1914 only 2,500 of them were accepted into the army and sent to Transcarpathia for brief training. After two weeks, individual USS companies were moved to the Russian front in the Carpathian Mountains. [Of the 2500, 30 were women.]

The USS were divided into ten companies, grouped initially into two and one-half battalions and then into three independent groups (commanded by Captain Mykhailo Voloshyn, Captain Hryhorii Kossak, and Maj Stefan Shukhevych). Placed under the operational control of the Austrian 55th Infantry Division, they were employed tactically as battalions or companies of the 129th and 130th Austrian brigades. The legion's commander was Teodor Rozhankovsky, then Mykhailo Halushchynsky. In March 1915 the post of legion commander was abolished, and the USS were divided into two independent battalions (commanded by Kossak and Semen Goruk and, later, V. Didushok), a reserve company, and a training unit. The legion distinguished itself in battle at Makivka (29 April–3 May 1915), Bolekhiv, Halych, Zavadiv, and Semykivtsi. Despite casualties, the force remained at eight infantry companies (in two battalions). In 1916 the battalions were merged into the First Regiment of the USS, under the command of Maj Kossak and then Lt Col Antin Varyvoda. In August–September 1916 the regiment lost over 1,000 men at Lysonia and was reduced to a battalion (commanded by Col F. Kikal). The USS suffered another severe loss at Koniukhy in July 1917. The survivors of the USS Hutsul Company and the USS Kish were re-formed into a new battalion (commanded by D. Krenzhalovsky). In February 1918, under Maj Myron Tarnavsky, it marched with the Austrian army to the Kherson region. In October it was transferred to Bukovyna. On 3 November, the USS arrived in Lviv, too late to hold the city against the Poles. [...]

The Legion USS was the first and most durable (5.5 years) Ukrainian military formation during and after the First World War. Its former officers became the organizers and leaders of the Sich Riflemen in Kyiv. Its officers also played an important role in the November Uprising in Lviv, 1918. It had the best-trained troops of the UHA, and its officers were the army's top commanders.

BIBLIOGRAPHY: Ukraïns'ki sichovi stril'tsi, 1914–1920 (Lviv 1935; 3rd edn, Montreal 1955) Ripets'kyi, S. Ukraïns'ke sichove striletstvo (New York 1956)

Account # 8

Fighting for mountain Makivka — heated positional battles on Mount Makivka in the Carpathians that there were from April 29 to May 4, 1915, during the First World War on the Eastern Front between units of the Austro-Hungarian 55th Infantry Division background Flyayshnera (consisting of seven hundred 1st and 2nd hovel Ukrainian Sich Riflemen) and Russian Imperial troops of the 78th Infantry Division of General Alftana for acquisition of the dominant height of Mount Makivka to control over the village Kozyova.

Because of the heroic defense of domes completely broke down strategic plans of the Russian command. Gaining the top, which was planned on April 29, came true using all available reserves. Due to huge losses, Russian troops were unable to continue the offensive, and a week later had to hastily retreat before the Austrian divisions that came. There was a special courage during the battle for the distinguished head of the Ukrainian Sich Riflemen, which further reflected in people's memory.

Mount Makivka in February 1915 laid the front line, consisting of three peaks — the north-western, central and eastern. The highest peak, was marked on maps of the time as the "height 958." In early 1915, retreating in the German-Austrian winter Carpathian offensive Russian Imperial forces kept the eastern summit dome; the other two were occupied by Austro-German troops. The mountain is located between the highway (in the valley Oriava) and railways (in the valley of the resistance), connecting Mukachevo from Lviv and Stry engaged Russian Imperial troops, and it was dominant over them, as was the strategic importance.

Account # 9:

On January 6, 2010, President of Ukraine Viktor Yushchenko signed a decree № 5 "On Measures for celebration, a comprehensive study and objective coverage of the Ukrainian Sich Riflemen." It marked a key role in reviving the Legion USS national military traditions and the active participation of these groups in the Ukrainian revolution. An ordinance was proposed to organize, particularly in parts of the armed forces of Ukraine in April 2010 the 95th year anniversary of the victory of the Riflemen on Makivka. Research and educational activities at the top of Mount Makivka resulted in a TV series and radio programs about the event. A postage stamp envelope was issued as well as a documentary to commemorate about the Ukrainian Sich Riflemen legion. Government and local authorities Ukraine were asked to consider renaming units and schools, streets and squares in honor of USS.

According to the resolution of the Verkhovna Rada of Ukraine № 184-VIII on 11 February 2015, one hundred years after the battle celebrated at the state level on April 21, the President of Ukraine Petro Poroshenko issued a decree "On Measures to celebrate the Ukrainian Sich Riflemen on the 100th anniversary of victory on Mount Makivka".

In 1998 – 1999, a cemetery was rebuilt with 50 crosses at the mountain top and a monument was erected to honor the fallen Sich.

On the Pantheon are buried:

1. Onufry Fedorchak.
2. Dmitry Formusyak - 22 years.
3. Julian Shevchuk - 19 years.
4. Nicholas Yuzvyak - 18 years.
5. Dmitry Tsvilyniuk - 19 years.
6. Fed Tkachuk - 21 years.
7. Boris Tkachuk - 23 years.
8. Philip Tymchyshyn - 26 years.
9. Sumaruk.
10. John Tymchyshyn - 21 years.
11. Omelian Stratiychuk - 17 years.
12. Michael Stratiychuk.
13. Michael Stefano.

14. Grits Stefurak.
15. Dmitry Snitovych - 18 years.
16. Dmitry Savchuk - 19 years.
17. George Pitylyak - 20 years.
18. Bone Popenyuk - 26 years.
19. John Rebenchuk - 20 years.
20. Theodore peak - 20 years.
21. Dmitry Petrov - 20 years.
22. Basil Paliychuk - 20 years
    (My mother's Kosiv relative)
23. Nicholas Mytskanyuk - 21 year.
24. Michael Mytskanyuk - 23 years.
25. Dmitry Mytskanyuk - 22 years.
26. Nicholas Mikhailyuk.
27. Osip Matkovskyi - 22 years.
28. Ilko Matiychuk.
29. Fed Matiychuk.
30. Nicholas Maximyuk - 18 years.
31. John Lavruk - 19 years.
32. Ivan Cat - 19 years.
33. Osip Konyushevskyy - 25 years.
34. Alexa Kurendash - 19 years.
35. Karpyn says Fyodor - 22 years.
36. Basil Ilychuk - 18 years.
37. Michael Dyachuk.
38. Basil Vitenyuk - 20 years.
39. Tanase Dupreychuk - 21 years.
40. Peter Danyschuk.
41. Ilko Hrytsiuk - 20 years.
42. Basil Henyk - 21 years.
43. Ilko Hanushchak - 19 years.
44. John Hiltaychuk.
45. Alexa Grigorchuk - 18 years.

46. Yurko Grigorchuk - 20 years.
47. Stephen Havryliuk - 20 years.
48. Michael Bilyachuk - 18 years.
49. Ilko Bumpety - 22 years.
50. Theodore Belmeha - 17 years.

There on Mount Makivka a distinguished woman archer, Olena (Yarema) Kuz, who with grenades destroyed machine gun nests became known. Ukrainian daily newspaper in America "Freedom" on August 19, 1915 filed news from the front: "During Trebenovom range Bolekhiv was Kuzivna (Kuz) leading the rooting of the Tsar forces from the mountain top. Swiftly followed by our troops. In a village, she captured two Cossacks, a Moscow general, as well as important war documents.

The Austrian journal Neue Freie Presse on July 10, 1915 described in detail the captured Russians, "Miss Kuz on this occasion captured documents and several valuable items as well as some Muscovite leaders. One said; "most gnaws me that a young man (Olena Kuz) caught me". At that an Austrian officer replied: "Do you know who he is? - Ukrainian lyerionistka". The Muscovite pale and was silent, ponuryvsya.

The Ukrainian Sich Riflemen immortalized Mount Makivka in a folk song;

"There on the mountain at Makivka".

There on the mountain on top,

There sichoviyi be beat archers.

Chorus:

Guys, let's go, fight for glory

For Ukraine, the vilniyi law and state.

Guys, go fight well

For Ukraine, the vilniyi law.

Our guys are fighting well,

They come to fight, still laughing.

We have hundreds ready,

Set out to stem.

In Kyiv PLN gate,

At the gate - blue and yellow flag.

There Lviv usususy –

Ukraine should be.

And we have guys like the Pearl,

Sing "we still are alive ..."

APPENDIX #10

Internally Displaced Persons Women IDPs in Ukraine

The following has been copied from a July 29, 2016 article on the website of the Organization for Security and Co-operation in Europe, which can be viewed here: *www.osce.org/ukraine-smm/251946*

- *The number of IDPs in Ukraine is 1.8 million, according to Ukraine's Ministry for Social Policy as of July 2016;*

- *Of this figure, 1.1 million are women (61 per cent);*

- *Women make up 73 per cent of IDPs residing in collective centres, according to Global Shelter Cluster figures as of May 2016. Collective centres are pre-existing buildings and structures intended for the long-term stay of IDPs. They include dormitories and sanatoriums, modular-type centres and rented houses.*

Recent Momentous Events to January 2005 Shaping Ukraine

The following has been copied from the Study Guide for the film Orange Revolution, which can be read here: www.orangerevolutionmovie.com/pdf/orange-revolution-study-guide.pdf

- *1921 Ukraine joins the Soviet Union*

- *1941-45 Ukraine occupied by Nazi Germany*

- *1960s Covert opposition to Soviet rule grows*

- *1986 Nuclear reactor at Chernobyl explodes*

- *1991 Ukraine declares independence*

- *1994 Leonid Kuchma becomes second president of Ukraine*

- *1996 Democratic constitution adopted*

- *1997 Ukraine signs Friendship Treaty with Russia*

- *1999 Leonid Kuchma re-elected president*

- *September 2000 Journalist Georgiy Gongadze murdered*

- *December 2000 Ukraine Without Kuchma movement demands resignation of President Kuchma and investigation of Gongadze murder*

- *March 2001 Violence erupts at protests organized by Ukraine Without Kuchma; the movement dissolves*

- *2002 Viktor Yushchenko becomes leader of the political coalition, Our Ukraine*

- *2004   July 1 Presidential election campaign begins*

- *September 5 Following dinner with director of Ukrainian Security Service, presidential candidate Viktor Yushchenko becomes ill*

- *September 10 Yushchenko seeks medical treatment in Austria. Rumors of poisoning begin to circulate*

- *October 15-16 PORA youth movement offices raided by special police*

- *October 20 Government freezes assets of pro-opposition TV Channel 5. Employees of Channel 5 go on hunger strike*

- *October 31 Presidential election — first round. Telephone records indicate fraud by Yanukovych*

- *November 1 Central Election Commission [CEC] announces no candidate exceeded 50% and a runoff election will be necessary*

- *November 21 Runoff election, marked by fraud and irregularities*

- *November 22 Massive protests begin in Kyiv and other major cities International election observers (OSCE) declare election unfair. Russian President Putin congratulates Yanukovych on victory*

- *November 24 Election results announced: Yanukovych 49%, Yushchenko 46%. Ukrainian opposition calls for general strike*

- *November 25 Supreme Court prohibits publication of election results until Yushchenko's appeal of CEC vote count can be heard*

- *November 26 Negotiations begin, mediated by EU, Russia and Poland*

- *November 27 Parliament expresses "no-confidence" in CEC, orders Kuchma to disband CEC*

- *November 28 (11 pm) Ukraine's Interior Minister orders 10,000 armed troops to disperse protesters in Kyiv. They begin driving toward Maidan, but Ukraine's Security Service successfully intervenes to stop them*

- *November 29 Kuchma proposes a new election. Yushchenko demands that Kuchma dismiss Yanukovych as prime minister.*

- *The Supreme Court begins hearing Yushchenko's case against the CEC*

- *December 2 Kuchma flies to Moscow to consult Russian President Putin. They reject a re-run of Nov. 21 election, favoring entirely new elections instead*

- *December 3 Supreme Court hears final arguments, begins private deliberations. At 6 pm, the Court invalidates the Nov. 21 election results and orders a repeat election not later than Dec. 26*

- *December 5 Opposition demands electoral law reforms, appointment of new CEC members*

- *December 6 Kuchma announces he will accept electoral reforms in exchange for constitutional amendments to limit the power of the president*

- *December 8 Parliament passes constitutional changes and electoral reform*

- *December 26 Second round of presidential election is repeated. Yushchenko receives 52% of votes; Yanukovych, 44%*

- *January 23, 2005 Viktor Yushchenko is sworn in as president Ukraine.*

APPENDIX #12

Orange Revolution

The following has been copied from the Study Guide for the film Orange Revolution. The original can be viewed here: www.orangerevolutionmovie.com/pdf/orange-revolution-study-guide.pdf

An Election Provides the Spark.

Before a single vote was cast, Ukraine's 2004 presidential election had grabbed a worldwide audience. Television and print media reported every dramatic twist beginning in September, when Viktor Yushchenko, a reform- minded presidential candidate, was mysteriously poisoned and flown to Austria for emergency treatment. Yushchenko survived, but before- and- after pictures of the candidate's once-handsome face, now severely scarred, led the news around the world. The drama continued in November when the second round of voting was marred by blatant election fraud. Millions of outraged citizens surged into the streets of Kyiv, Ukraine's capital, and other Ukrainian cities, in a massive protest that paralyzed the country for weeks. It was the greatest upheaval in Eastern European politics in nearly two decades -- the most spectacular of the post- communist rebellions in favor of democracy, which had already spread through Slovakia, Serbia and Georgia.

Named for Viktor Yushchenko's campaign colour, the Orange Revolution of 2004 was the culmination of a crisis begun three years earlier. In 2001, massive protests had briefly convulsed the country when the Ukraine Without Kuchma (UWK) movement demanded the resignation of the deeply unpopular president, Leonid Kuchma. Kuchma's unresponsive and corrupt leadership had already driven his popularity into the single digits by December 2000 when recordings made by

Kuchma's bodyguard were publicized by a member of parliament. Kuchma's voice is heard recommending the abduction of Georgiy Gongadze, an investigative journalist who had accused Kuchma of corruption. The so-called "cassette scandal" sparked the creation of UWK. The movement was unprecedented in modern Ukraine, supported by groups across the political spectrum.

Gongadze had been missing since September 2000. His headless body was discovered near Kyiv two months later. Hearing the tape recordings, which not only tied Kuchma to Gongadze's murder, but revealed Kuchma to be at the center of a criminal regime, the population took to the streets. UWK declared itself to be a strictly nonviolent movement, but was unable to control its radical members, who attacked riot police in March 2001 at a rally in Kyiv. When police responded, dozens of protesters were injured. Middle-class supporters of UWK deserted the movement overnight, fearful of further violent incidents.

Ukrainians remained deeply dissatisfied with the regime, and the UWK movement had provided experience for a new generation of activists who would play key roles in 2004. Yuriy Lutsenko managed street actions in both 2001 and 2004. He recalled that the bloodshed of March 2001 had "repulsed all of Ukraine I was the end of the movement." In 2004, he knew that nonviolent discipline would be necessary for any successful popular uprising.

Ineligible to serve a third term, Kuchma anointed the sitting prime minister, Viktor Yanukovych, to succeed him. Although Yanukovych lacked charisma, he'd been a faithful servant of the country's wealthy business interests, and was expected to maintain or even strengthen Ukraine's ties to Russia. With the entire machinery of the government supporting the Yanukovych candidacy (at taxpayer expense), Kuchma was confident his man could win. But the Kuchma/Yanukovych forces underestimated the opposition. For months, every *stump speech reminded voters of Kuchma's failures. Viktor Yushchenko spoke out repeatedly against corruption, calling Kuchma's government a "criminal regime." Even when opinion polls pointed to a decisive Yushchenko victory, the Orange coalition kept up the pressure. They assumed Kuchma's party would do anything -- including vote fraud -- to maintain power, so they worked with civic groups to organize voter education campaigns and a vast election monitoring system. The Orange forces hoped to prevent voter fraud, but as a backup, they prepared to document, expose, publicize and protest the fraud if it occurred.*

In the initial round of voting on October 31, Yushchenko finished first of the twenty-five candidates, but since no candidate won over 50%, a second round of voting was set for November 21. In this round, the fraud was blatant and pervasive. Yushchenko's Orange coalition was ready; popular outrage gave them the mobilizing tool they needed. At 2 a.m. on November 22, Orange leaders broadcast an appeal to all citizens to gather in the heart of Kyiv at Independence Square (Maidan Nezalezhnosti), known simply as Maidan.

A Planned Spontaneous Revolution

By noon on November 22, 2004, nearly 100,000 angry demonstrators had converged on Maidan and in other cities to protest the previous day's election fraud. As the crowds mushroomed, even the organizers were surprised. Suddenly, Maidan became a symbol of the revolution, resistance, and opposition. The word "maidan" itself took on several meanings; it was not just a place, but a movement, and a medium of communications. This was exactly what the Yushchenko campaign and Orange coalition had intended. They had correctly anticipated a stolen election -- and prepared for it -- with Maidan as the focal point of their mass action.

Knowing they might have to occupy the city for many days or weeks, organizers distributed food, tents, and blankets. They blocked all important government buildings and effectively shut down day- to- day government functions. All their actions were planned to prevent bloodshed. Knowing their supporters would come face- to- face with police and security forces, Yushchenko and his senior staff had established back channel contacts with commanders of security forces to keep them informed of opposition planning and to reassure them the protest would remain nonviolent.

During the first days, as protesters and security forces looked each other in the eye, something remarkable happened. As one protest leader observed, "They got acquainted and they got used to each other. Within a few days, they began sharing food and tea with each other." Meanwhile, at night, Maidan leaders met with officers from the armed services to share information.

Members of Parliament constructed the stage at Maidan with their own hands. Because they enjoyed parliamentary immunity, the police were not allowed to arrest them. The stage was the platform from which Yushchenko and the Orange leaders could speak to the people, explain their plans, and give instructions. Twenty-four-hour television coverage of the stage kept all Ukrainians informed about events of the revolution.

[...]

Additional Resources

Ukraine and the Orange Revolution

Åslund, Anders and Michael McFaul, eds. Revolution in Orange: Origins of Ukraine's Democratic Breakthrough. *Washington: Carnegie Endowment for International Peace, 2006.*

Karatnycky, Adrian. "Ukraine's Orange Revolution." Foreign Affairs, vol 84, no. 2, March/April 2005.

Koshiw, J. V. Beheaded: The Killing of a Journalist. *Reading (UK): Artemia Press, 2003.*

Subtelny, Orest. Ukraine: A History. *Toronto: University of Toronto Press, 2000.*

Wilson, Andrew. Ukraine's Orange Revolution. *New Haven: Yale University Press, 2005.*

Nonviolent Revolution in Serbia and Georgia

Collin, Matthew. The Time of the Rebels: Youth Resistance Movements and 21st century Revolutions. *London: Serpent's Tail/Profile Books, 2007.*

Doder, Dusko and Louise Branson. Milosevic: Portrait of a Tyrant. *New York: The Free Press, 1999.*

Glenny, Misha. The Balkans: Nationalism, War, and the Great Powers, 1804- 1999. *New York: Viking Penguin, 2000.*

Gordy, Eric D. The Culture of Power in Serbia: Nationalism and the Destruction of Alternatives. *University Park: The Pennsylvania State University Press, 1999.*

Judah, Tim. The Serbs: History, Myth and the Destruction of Yugoslavia. *New Haven: Yale University Press, 1997.*

Karumidze, Zurab and James Wetsch, eds. Enough! The Rose Revolution in the Republic of Georgia 2003. *Hauppauge, NY:*

Nova Science Publishers, 2005.

General — Civil Resistance and Social Movements

Ackerman, Peter and Christopher Kruegler. Strategic Nonviolent Conflict: The Dynamics of People Power in the Twentieth Century. *Westport, CT: Praeger, 1994.*

Ackerman, Peter and Jack DuVall. A Force More Powerful: A century of Nonviolent Conflict. *New York: Palgrave Macmillan, 2000.*

Arendt, Hannah. Crises of the Republic. New York: Harcourt Brace Jovanovich, 1972.

Helvey, Robert. On Strategic Nonviolent Conflict: Thinking About the Fundamentals. *Boston: Albert Einstein Institution, 2004. This book may be downloaded at www.aeinstein.org.*

King, Mary. Mahatma Gandhi and Martin Luther King, Jr. The Power of Nonviolent Action. *Paris: UNESCO Publishing, 1999.*

Meyer, David S. and Sidney Tarrow, Eds. The Social Movement Society: Contentious Politics for a New Century. *Lanham, MD: Rowman & Littlefield, 1998.*

Nagler, Michael N. Is There No Other Way? The Search for a Nonviolent Future. *Berkeley: Berkeley Hills Books, 2001.*

Roberts, Adam and Timothy Garton Ash, eds. Civil Resistance and Power Politics. *Oxford (UK): Oxford University Press, 2009.*

Schock, Kurt. Unarmed Insurrections: People Power Movements in Nondemocracies. *Minneapolis: University of Minnesota Press, 2004.*

Sharp, Gene. From Dictatorship to Democracy: A Conceptual Framework for Liberation. *Boston: Albert Einstein Institution, 2002. Downloadable in several languages at www.aeinstein.org.*

Sharp, Gene. Waging Nonviolent Struggle: 20th century Practice and 21st century Potential. *Boston: Porter Sargent Publishers, 2005.*

Tarrow, Sidney. Power in Movement: Social Movements, Collective Action and Politics. *New York: Cambridge University Press, 1994.*

Zunes, Stephen, Lester R. Kurtz and Sarah Beth Asher, eds. Nonviolent Social Movements: A Geographical Perspective *Malden, MA: Blackwell Publishers, 1999.*

Resources on the Internet

Articles, Papers & Study Guides

Beehner, Lionel. "One Year Afer Ukraine's Orange Revolution." Council on Foreign Relations, 22 Nov 2005. www.cfr.org http://www.cfr.org/publication/9259/

Corwin, Julie A. "Fledgling Youth Groups Worry Post- Soviet Authorities." Eurasia.net 11 Apr 2005. http://www.eurasianet.org/departments/civilsociety/articles/p p041105.shtml

Corwin, Julie A. "Rock's Revolutionary Influence," Radio Free Europe Radio Liberty 12 Jun 2005. http://www.rferl.org/content/Article/1059220.html

Meier, Patrick. "Digital Resistance and the Orange Revolution," blog entry at www.irevolution.wordpress.com 18 Feb 2009.

http://irevolution.wordpress.com/2009/02/18/digital-resistance-and-the-orange-revolution

Simpson, John and Marcus Tanner. "Serb Activists Helped Inspire Ukraine Protests," Institute for War and Peace Reporting.

http://www.iwpr.net/index.php?apc_state=hen&s=o&o=p=b cr&l=EN&s=f&o=155269

United States Institute of Peace. "Study Guide Series on Peace and Conflict." Washington, D.C. 2009.

Forty-page study guide, which can be downloaded at http://www.usip.org/files/sg10.pdf.

Weir, Fred. "The Students Who Shook Ukraine -- Peacefully." Christian Science Monitor 9 Dec 2004.

http://www.csmonitor.com/2004/1209/p01s04-woeu.html

Websites

*The **A Force More Powerful.org** site contains extensive information on all the films and games on nonviolent movements produced by York Zimmerman Inc, including descriptions, study guides, lesson plans, and suggested further readings. It also features excerpts from the book, A Force More Powerful: A century of Nonviolent Conflict. www.aForceMorePowerful.org*

*The **Albert Einstein Institution** is a non-profit organization advancing the study and use of strategic nonviolent action in conflicts throughout the world. The website includes downloadable material in forty languages. www.aeinstein.org*

*The **Center for Applied Nonviolent Action and Strategies (CANVAS)** website contains articles about nonviolent movements and strategies of the past decade. www.canvasopedia.org*

*The **International Center on Nonviolent Conflict** is an independent, non-profit, educational foundation that develops and encourages the study and use of civilian-based, non-military strategies to establish and defend human rights, democracy and justice worldwide. Their website contains* *news about nonviolent conflicts around the world, as well as links to articles, podcasts and other resources of relevance. www.nonviolent-conflict.org*

Kyiv Post *is an English- language daily published in Kyiv. Archives dating back to 2004 are available for search at www.kyivpost.com.*

Maidan.org *describes itself as "an internet hub for Citizens Action Network in Ukraine." It was founded in December 2000 to circumvent government suppression of information on opposition activities, and to protest misinformation on the disappearance of the murdered journalist, Georgy Gongadze. The English language version can be found at http://eng.maidanua.org.*

Mirror Weekly (Zerkalo Nedeli) *is among Ukraine's most influential print weeklies, specializing in political analysis, interviews, and opinion, in Russian and Ukrainian. Founded in 1996, the independent, non- partisan publication is funded by Western (nongovernmental) sources. The English language archives can be accessed at www.mw.ua.*

Daughter Olena's account of her father Nikolaij Moisey

On four of our visits to Ukraine, Nikolaij's daughter Olena (née Moisey) Paraniuk would return from Italy to meet us. She was one of approximatley seven hundred women along the Cheremosh River who travelled abroad to provide economically for their families. I asked Olena to pen what she remembered of some of her father's stories concerning his youth and Canada.

She revealed her father Nikolaij Moisey, as a boy, apprenticed as a blacksmith under the guidance of a Polish Jew. In his early 20s, he continued with the trade and had his own business. She wrote that her grandfather Wasyl Moisey (also spelled Moysey and Mojsej under Austrian and Polish occupations) planned to go to work in Canada with another Moisey about the time of her father Nikolaij's birth in 1914. Apparently Wasyl did not go, but the other Moisey went and worked in a coal mine for a railroad company in the Canadian Rocky Mountains. Coincidently, my grandfather Gregory Moisey and his older brother Oleksa worked in the same area in different coal mines. Their paths never crossed.

This Ukrainian Moisey returned to Ukraine after a year with a lot of money and purchased a track of land on the ancient river flat to the north of Forzena's house, where my Canadian great-grandfather Stefan Moisey had been born. I believe this may have been a Michaelo Moisey. No documentation has been found to substantiate this belief.

Olena Paraniuk with history of her Father Nikolaij Мойсей, 2014

Olena described how her father was well liked. "He borrowed money from the church to buy the fourth lot north of the church, where he operated his business and raised the family. Today it is the seventh house north of the church. Nikolaij was a hard worker and always in his shop. Wife Wasylena passed away in 1980. Two years later, I (Olena) had my only child, Roman Paraniuk. We lived about a kilometer away from Dad, and Roman would spend time with his grandfather Nikolaij."

Acknowledgments

Sincere appreciation to family and friends from Ukraine and Canada for making this book possible. Mary Ann (nee Moisey) Tymchuk, Darlene Davidson, my father John Roman and my wife Doreen, a great partner for helping to write this book. Thank you Sonia and John Shalewa for the first draft review and suggestions. Thanks to Jan, owner of Bossonova Communications for the book's design and graphics and neice Kelly Picard of <u>divantidesigns@shaw.ca</u> for the front cover design. Special mention to Eddie Southern (deceased) and Yaroslav (not his real name). Thanks to hundreds of Ukrainians from Canada and Ukraine; good friends and associates, too many to mention, who inspired this book.

Thank you Rotarians from the Clubs of Kyiv, Lviv, Ivano-Frankivsk (especially Natalie Ifonska), as well as Rotary Clubs from Canadian RD5370. Thanks to village and regional government officials, church leaders, Caritas and many Vyzhnytsia Region School teachers and directors. Thanks to the many artisans, sculptor Roman and family, carvers, poets, writers, singers, dancers, students and interpreters (Oxsana Chorney and Ohla Slokivka), that opened warm hearts and homes to Doreen and me.

In 13 visits to Ukraine, I slept in a hotel only three days. Incredible hospitality. Special thanks to trusting Lawyer Valentyn Krasniuk, faithful driver Tanasi Andryuk, Ivan Vatrich and family for taking us, my parents and many friends into your homes. Your stories and love of Ukraine inticed Doreen and me to record a quarter century of experiences and observations of beautiful Ukraine. With you we eased difficult situations to benefit many, including us and together we bridged the family gap since Wasylena and Stefan Moisey, with children departed for Canada in 1898, never to see or communicate with Ukraine again. How sad this was. Hopefully our grandchildren will continue the relationship we developed.

Overwhelming are the hundreds of familiar last names from Banyliv that I remember from my Canadian childhood in Andrew, Alberta, Canada. Many thanks to all of you for opening your hearts and helping me find my family roots. In most of you I saw my loving Baba and because of you I love Ukraine even more.

Special thanks to University of Alberta's Trevor Rockwell, PhD of Russian History for editing this book.

This book... about contemporary, Post-Soviet Ukraine is a must read to better understand Putin and how ordinary Ukrainian folks overcame oppression to achieve freedom. It is a page-turner, with interesting facts and stories.

I (Bill Rankin), with partial Ukrainian roots highly recommend reading this book. I have worked three decades for many Canadian newspapers including the Edmonton Journal, National Post, Globe and Mail and Opera Canada. I am also a writer, editor and lecture at the University of Alberta and continue to teach freshman at MacEwan University. My mother grew up on a farm near Mundare, just a little southwest of the author's original Moisey homestead. An emotional read.

87006702R00179

Made in the USA
Middletown, DE
01 September 2018